ADHYĀTMA RĀMĀYAṆA
(English Version)

अध्यात्म रामायण

ADHYĀTMA RĀMĀYAṆA

(English Version)

अध्यात्म रामायण

Translated by

(Late) Ramjung Bahadur Singh
Ex-Raja of Bajhang, Nepal

Edited with Introduction by

Jawaharlal Gupta

1997

BHARATIYA KALA PRAKASHAN
DELHI INDIA

Published by
C.P. Gautam
For Bharatiya Kala Prakashan
3611/5, Narang Colony,
Tri Nagar, Delhi-110035
Ph.-7192770

●

First Edition-1997

●

ISBN : 81-86050-07-8

Rs. 400.00

●

Laser Typesetting by
Ishan Comprint
G 16/14, Qutab Enclave-I, (DLF)
Gurgaon (H.R.), Ph. 8-352412

●

Printed at
Santosh Offset
40, Anand Nagar, Inder Lok, Delhi-110035

Dedicated
to
his daughter
Shankari

PREFACE

It is but by the extreme grace of the Almighty Shri Rāma and Mother Sītā that I have been able to translate the Adhyātma Rāmāyaṇa, one of the holiest philosophical scriptures of the Hindus. It is included in the *Padma Purāṇa* in the form of a dialogue between Lord Shiva and Pārvatī in Sanskrit language and is considered to be the actual speech of Lord Shiva like that of *Shrimadbhāgawatgītā* of Lord Krishna.

Later on the great Sage Yājñavalkya reproduced it in the form of *Adhyātma Rāmāyaṇa*.

No word can express the beatitude, enlightenment and peace I had in course of writing this book. It is beyond my capabilities to record feelings of gratitude towards my beloved Lord Rāma, Mother Sītā and Lord Hanumān under whose graceful shelter I pass my life in peace. I hope that the readers of this book will similarly be benefitted by their grace.

I thank gratefully Mr. Devi Prasad Rimalji, a retired Professor of Trichandra College, an ardent devotee, my Guru, who immensely helped me by improving upon the contents of the book and making certain important suggestions.

In the end I express my gratitude to Sri C.P. Gautam of M/s Bharatiya Kala Prakashan, Delhi, for kindly agreeing to undertake the publication of this work.

Ramjung Bahadur Singh
Ex-Raja of Bajhang
West Nepal

CONTENTS

PART I
BĀLAKĀṆḌA

Chapter I
RAMA'S EARLY LIFE 3

Chapter II
RĀMA HṚDAYA 5

Chapter III
PRAYER FOR INCARNATION OF VIṢṆU 12

Chapter IV
BIRTH OF RĀMA AND HIS BROTHERS 15

Chapter V
VISHWĀMITRA'S ARRIVAL AT AYODHYĀ 21

Chapter VI
RĀMA IN SAGE GAUTAMA'S HERMITAGE 23

Chapter VII
RĀMA'S MARRIAGE WITH SĪTĀ 29

Chapter VIII
RĀMA MEETS PARASHURĀMA 35

PART II
AYODHYĀ KĀṆḌA

Chapter I
LIFE OF RĀMA IN AYODHYĀ AND HIS EXILE 43

Chapter II
MANTHARĀ POISONS KAIKEYĪ'S YEARS 46

Chapter III
KAIKEYĪ'S ANGER 50

Chapter IV
RĀMA PREPARES FOR THE FOREST 53

Chapter V
RĀMA LEAVES FOR FOREST 56

Chapter VI
RĀMA MEETS VĀLMĪKI 61

Chapter VII
THE PASSING AWAY OF DASHARATHA 66

Chapter VIII
BHARATA'S DEPARTURE TO FOREST
TO BRING RĀMA BACK 72

Chapter IX
MEETING OF BHARAT TO RĀMA IN THE FOREST 75

PART - III
ĀRAṆYA KĀṆḌA

Chapter I
THE FOREST LIFE: THE KILLING OF BIRĀDHA 83

Chapter II
MEETING WITH SUTĪKSHṆA 86

Chapter III
SAGE AGASTYA GREETS RĀMA 89

Chapter IV
THE PHILOSOPHY OF LIFE 92

Chapter V
SŪPARṆAKHĀ EPISODE 95

Chapter VI
THE MĀRĪCH EPISODE 98

Chapter VII
THE KIDNAPPING OF SĪTĀ 100

Chapter VIII
MEETING WITH JAṬĀYU 104

Chapter IX
KABANDHA'S INVOCATION TO RĀMA 107

Chapter X
EMANCIPATION OF SHAVARĪ 110

PART IV
KIṢKINDHĀ KĀṆḌA

Chapter I
RĀMA'S LIFE IN ASSOCIATION WITH MONKEYS : FRIENDSHIP WITH SUGRIVA 113

Chapter II
THE KILLING OF BĀLĪ 117

Chapter III
CONSOLING TĀRĀ AND ENTHRONING SUGRĪVA 120

Chapter IV
RĀMA'S PREACHINGS TO LAXMAṆA 124

Chapter V
LAXMAṆA CAUTIONS SUGRĪVA 127

Chapter VI
MONKEYS SETOUT IN SEARCH OF SĪTĀ 130

Chapter VII
THE EPISODE OF SAMPĀTĪ 133

Chapter VIII
SAGE CHANDRAMĀ'S CONSOLATION TO SAṀPĀTĪ 136

Chapter IX
MEETING OVER CROSSING THE OCEAN 139

PART V
SUNDARA KĀṆḌA

Chapter I
HANUMĀN CROSSES THE OCEAN 143

Chapter II
RĀVAṆĀ'S THREAT TO SĪTĀ AND TRIJAṬĀ'S DREAM 146

Chapter III
HANUMĀN MEETS SĪTĀ 148

Chapter IV
LAṆKĀ ON FIRE 151

Chapter V
HANUMĀN'S RETURN TO RĀMA 154

PART VI
LAṄKĀ KĀṆḌA

Chapter I
RĀMA PREPARE WAR WITH RĀVAṆA
FOR RESTORATION OF SĪTĀ 159

Chapter II
RĀVAṆA EXPELLS VIBHĪSHAṆA 162

Chapter III
SUGRĪVA JOIND RĀMA'S CAMP 164

Chapter IV
ŚUKA'S ADVICE TO RĀVAṆA 169

Chapter V
START OF THE WAR 171

Chapter VI
LAXMAṆA FALLS UNCONSCIOUS 176

Chapter VII
HANUMĀN KILLS KĀLNEMY AND
LAXMAṆA REGAINS CONSCIOUSNESS 179

Chapter VIII
RĀMA KILLS KUMBHAKARṆA 183

Chapter IX
KILLING OF MEGHANĀTH BY LAXMAṆA 188

Chapter X
RĀVAṆA GETS READY TO FIGHT 192

Chapter XI
RĀMA KILLS RĀVAṆA IN FIERCE FIGHT 196

Chapter XII
ENTHROWING VIBHĪSAṆA AND SĪTĀ'S RETURN 200

Chapter XIII
AGNI AND INDRA PRAY RĀMA 205

Chapter XIV
RĀMA REACHES AYODHYĀ 210

Chapter XV
RĀMA'S CORONATION AS KING OF AYODHYĀ 216

Chapter XVI
RĀMA'S FAREWELL TO HIS MONKEY FRIENDS 221

PART VII
UTTARA KĀṆḌA

Chapter I
AGATSYA NARRATES DEMONS, HISTORY 227

Chaper II
RĀVAṆA'S PENANCES FOR BRAVERY 232

Chapter III
BIRTHS OF BĀLI AND SUGRĪVA 237

Chapter IV
SENDING OF SĪTĀ TO FOREST 241

Chapter V
LAXMAṆA PRAYS TO RĀMA 245

Chapter VI
KILLING OF LAVAṆA BY ŚATRUGHNA AND
BIRTH OF LAVA AND KUSHA 254

Chapter VII
RĀMA RETAINS LAVA AND KUSHA 258

Chapter VIII
LAXMAṆA TAKES SAMĀDHI 163

Chapter IX
RĀMA'S DEPARTURE TO HEAVEN 266

INTRODUCTION

य: पृथ्वीभरवारणाय दिविजैः संप्रार्थितश्चिन्मयः
संजातः पृथिवीतले रविकुले मायामनुष्योऽव्ययः ॥
निश्चक्रं हतराक्षसः पुनरगाद् ब्रह्मत्वमाद्यं स्थिरां
कीर्तिं पापहरां विधाय जगतां तं जानकीशं भजे ॥
विश्वोद्भवस्थितिलयादिषु हेतुमेकं
मायाश्रयं विगतमायमचिन्त्यमूर्तिम् ॥
आनन्दसान्द्रममलं निजबोधरूपं
सीतापतिं विदिततत्त्वमहं नमामि ॥
अध्यात्मरामायणमेव नित्यं
पठेद्यदीच्छेद्भवबन्धमुक्तिम् ॥
गवां सहस्रायुतकोटिदानात्
फलं लभेद्यः श्रृणुयात्स नित्यम् ॥[1]

'Rāma' has become a byword with religious and spiritual populace in India. The story of Rāma or the Rāma-Kathā had its appeal not only in India but its magnetism brought immense popularity even in the world. *Rāmāyaṇa*, the first poetic epic, the Ādikāvya of Vālmīki, made substantial contribution to keep a culture alive amongst vast masses of people through ages. Its hero, Rāma, a likeable, pleasing god-man, later came to be looked upon as a human god. What to talk of Rāma-kathā in the modern time when the Rāmāyaṇa serial had become the most popular program ever shown on Indian television. 'Never before had such a large percentage of South Asia's population been united in a single activity, never before

1. *Adhyātma Rāmāyaṇa,* Bālakāṇḍa, I. 1,2,4

had a single message instantly reached to enormous a regional audience.'[1]

The stories of Rāma are so innumerable, so vast and intricate that none can understand them. The great Hindi poet Sant Tulasīdāsa writes :

हरि अनंत हरि कथा अनंता ।[2]

(The Hari (Lord) is infinite and his stories are too infinite).

With the popularity of the Rāma-Kathā and its appeal of the message it carries, there happened to be hundreds of Rāmāyaṇas, the prime work being the Rāmāyaṇa of Vālmīki. The popular Rāmāyaṇas which were written in India are Goswāmi Tulasīdāsa's *Shri Rāmacharitamanas*, and Kampan's *Irāmavatāram*.

The *Adhyātma Rāmāyaṇa* as the name implies is a treatise that delineates the story of Rāma in a highly spiritual and philosophical manner. The work is presented in a dialogue form between Lord Shiva and his consort Pārvatī in the Padma Purāṇa. It is understood that the great sage Yājñavalkya reproduced it in the form of Adhyātma Rāmāyaṇa. However the translator of Adhyātma Rāmāyaṇa (in Hindi) Shri Munilal affirms in his preface that the present kathā occurs in the later part of the Brahmāṇḍa Purāṇa and he attributes its authorship to Vedavyāsa.[3]

The *Adhyātma Rāmāyaṇa* originally in Sanskrit text is grouped into seven Kāṇḍas with sixty-four chapters (sargas). It comprises four thousand two hundred ślokas

1. "Epic Spin-offs", *India Today*, 15th July 1988, 72.
2. Tulasīdāsa, *Shri Rāmacharitamānas.*
3. Munilal (Tns.), *Adhyātma Rāmāyaṇa,* Gitā Press, Edition Samvat 2052, Gorakhpur.

together with hundreds of śrutis with analysis of the tattvas.[1]

It is found that the saint poet Tulasīdāsa was so much moved with the *Adhyātma Rāmāyaṇa.* His masterpiece 'Shri Rāmacharitamānas' is also very much spiritual and written with utmost faith for Lord Rāma. Its Rāma is the sublime being, an incarnation of Lord Viṣṇu. The same goes true with the present rendition of the Adhyātma Rāmāyaṇa.

Though the description of themes remains almost the same here unlike the *Vālmīki Rāmāyaṇa*, yet its contents are quite summarised and briefly dealt. It is a very small book whereas the Rāmayaṇa of Vālmikī is a voluminous work. The descriptions are slightly given in different styles. The Bālakāṇḍa begins with an invocation to Lord Rāma and then starts the dialogue of Pārvatī with Shiva. The latter unfolds the former the very secrets of Rāma-Kathā which liberates the human beings from the bondage of transmigration in this mundane world. Lord Shiva says:

श्रृणु देवि प्रवक्ष्यामि गुह्याद् गुह्यतरं महत् ।
अध्यात्मरामचरितं रामेणोक्तं पुरा मम ॥[2]

The episodes which subsequently occur are the birth of Rāma, his going to forest with sage Vishwāmitra, 'the killing of demons there, Rāma's marriage with Sītā and an encounter with Parashurāma.

The other Kāṇḍas too present the episodes unlike the Rāmacharitamānas.

The *Adhyātma Rāmāyaṇa* carries the story in brief but touches all the themes. Unlike the Rāmāyaṇa of

1. पार्वत्यै परमेश्वरेण गदिते अध्यात्मरामायणे
काण्डैः सप्तभिरन्वितेऽति शुभदे सर्गाश्चतुःषष्टिकाः ।
श्लोकानां तु शतद्वयेन साहितान्युक्तानि चत्वारि वै
साहस्राणि समातितः श्रुतिशतान्युक्तानि तत्वार्थतः ।
Ibit., op.cit., p. 361

2. *Adhyātma Rāmāyaṇa,* Bālakāṇḍa, II.4

Vālmīki, it too has the sixth Kāṇḍa as Yuddha Kāṇḍa whereas Tulsidāsa has given the name of Lankā Kāṇḍa.

So as for the them not only of the Adhyātma Rāmāyaṇa but all the Rāmayaṇas in the South Asian continent, it can be put in the following verse :

आदौ राम तपोवनादि गमनं हत्वा मृगंकाञ्चनं ।
वैदेहीहरणं जटायुमरणं सुग्रीवसम्भाषणम् ॥
वालीनिर्दलनं समुद्रतरणं लंकापुरीदाहनं ।
पश्चाद्रावण कुम्भकर्ण हननमेतद्धि रामायणम् ॥

However, a peculiarity with the Adhyātma Rāmāyaṇa is that it emphasises on the spiritual and philosophical import of the Rāma-Kathā repeatedly. Whether it is the start of the text with Rāmaḥṛdaya, or the meeting of Nārada to Rāma at Ayodhyā, the Adhyātma Rāmāyaṇa does not deviate in his philosophical approach in presentation of the glory of Rāma. The philosophy of Vedānta is very clearly put forth here when Nārada says, "Oh Lord, it is due to your desire that the Brahmā etc. are created by your illusion, the Māyā imbued with the three guṇas of Sattva, Rajas and Tamas shines taking its base on you.

त्वत्सन्निकर्षाज्जायन्ते तस्यां ब्रह्मादयः प्रजाः ।
त्वदाश्रया सदा भाति माया या त्रिगुणात्मिका ॥[1]

The Sāmkhya philosophy also appears truly here :

त्वदाभासोदिताज्ञानमव्याकृतमितीर्यते ।
तस्मान्महांस्तः सूत्रं लिङ्गं सर्वात्मकं ततः ॥
अहङ्कारश्च बुद्धिश्च पञ्चप्राणेन्द्रियाणि च ।
लिङ्गमित्युच्यते प्राज्ञैर्जन्ममृत्युसुखादिमत् ॥[2]

---

1. *Adhyātma Rāmāyaṇa* Ayodhyā Kāṇḍa, I. 11
2. Ibid., I 20-21

The Adhyātma Rāmāyaṇa occupies more significant place in the present circumstances. The narration of Kriyāyoga (Yoga of Action) has been very appropriately done here in the episode of Rāma's preachings to his younger brother Lakshmaṇa. He tells him the ways of Karma-Kāṇḍa :

प्रातःस्नानं प्रकुर्वीत प्रथमं देहशुद्धये ॥
वेदतन्त्रोदितैर्मन्त्रैर्मृल्लेपन विधानतः ।

सन्ध्यादि कर्म यन्नित्यं तत्कुर्याद्विधिना बुधः ॥
सङ्कल्पमादौ कुर्वीत सिद्ध्यर्थं कर्मणां सुधीः ॥

श्वगुरुं पूजयेद्भक्त्या मद्बुद्ध्या पूजको मम ।
" " " " "

ततो न्यायं प्रकुर्वीति मातृकाबहिरान्तरम् ।
केशवादि ततः कुर्यात्तत्त्वन्यासं ततः परम् ॥[1]

Similarly Lord Rāma explains his Māyā form (illusioned form). Māyā is the Ātma Buddhi that dwells in the Anātma substances of the body.

अनात्मनि शरीरादावात्मबुद्धिस्तु या भवेत् ।
सैव माया तयैवासौ संसारः परिकल्प्यते ॥[2]

The concept of Ātman and Brahman that permeats the Indian thinking alludes to the theory of एकोऽहं बाहुस्याम. So it is only one Supreme Ātman (परम सत्ता). Here Lord Rāma is the Supreme Self, Viṣṇu, who embodies himself as a human being on earth to subdue the dark and evil forces disrupting the moral order - परित्राणायंसाधूनां विनाशाय च दुष्कृताम्. The Lord does not come alone but he is accompanied by his consort Sītā. Rāma is the Supreme tattva and he eternally abides in Union with his Shakti (energy). Rāma without Sītā is devoid of power to act.

---

1. *Adhyātma Rāmāyaṇa*, Ayodhyā Kāṇḍa, IV, 14, 15, 16, 22.
2. Ibid., Araṇya Kāṇḍa, IV, 21-22.

While talking with Hanuman Sītā discloses this secret "I am creator, sustainer, and destroyer of the universe. I am busy in my activities in close union with the Supreme Self i.e. Rāma."

In addition to the philosophical leanings of Adhyātma Rāmāyaṇa, the work stands unparallel in several other aspects of human life, duty, love, truthfulness and integrity which is exhibited in the characters of the work. The ideals portrayed have got sublime appeal.

The rendering of the treatise into English has certainly made it very useful for the non-Hindi people in India and particularly in abroad. The most significant thing that occurred me in the editing of the present volume is the devotional attitude of the translator who has done it in the same spirit of Adhyātma (spirituality) as the work was originally composed. It is very sad that Late Shri Ramjung Bahadur Singh is no more to see the work in book form. It is our humble prayer to Lord Rāma that his soul may have solace in heaven.

Lastly I feel great pleasure that Shri C.P. Gautam, the publisher kindly gave me this opportunity to write a few words on this holy work. I owe him my sincere thanks. A person like me has no place in the scholarship but I am fortunate that Lord Shri Rāma inspired me to do this pious cause and I offer my humble obeissance to that Supreme Ātman Shri Rāma.

नान्या स्पृहा रघुपते हृदयेऽस्मदीये
सत्यं वदामि च भवान् अखिलान्तरात्मा ॥
भक्तिं प्रयच्छ रघुपुङ्गव निर्भरां मे
कामादिदोषरहितं कुरु मानसंच ॥

Śrī Rāma Navamī *Jawaharlal Gupta*
16th April 1997
Delhi

PART I

BĀLAKĀṆḌA

Chapter I

RAMA'S EARLY LIFE

Once the divine Sage Nārada requested Lord Brahmā, the Creator, "Lord, the people in Kaliyuga are very much bent upon committing sinful acts. They sell out even the Vedas to make their livelihood, they do not respect their elders, disobey their parents and father in-laws but are enslaved to their wives, deceive their parents, distrust and disregard religions and commit innumerable sins."

"Please tell me if there is some way of atonement for their sins."

Brahmā replied, "The easiest and unfailing method for the atonement of their sins is to study the *Adhyātma Rāmāyaṇa*.

So long as the *Adhyātma Rāmāyaṇa* does not come under the approach of people, all these troubles are bound to remain, and if they take resort to it, all the sins will get destroyed. Even a half of the śloka of the verse of the *Rāmāyaṇa* can sanctify the soul of the readers, and it can destroy sin. One who abides by the great teachings enshrined in the *Rāmāyaṇa*, can obtain his piety. This is the thing which one can hardly get even after the incessant, long and hard penances including the performance of holy yajñas.

If somebody recites "Rāma Hṛdaya" silently in the presence of Hanumān's image, one can definitely get the desired boons.

"The significant result of the hymns of Shri Rāma's study is indescribable. Even I myself do not know it fully but I can understand only half of what the Goddess Pārvatī knows and she has acquired only half of what Shiva knows being the only God who has been able to understand it fully well."

"Parashurāma had obtained the supreme divine culture called "Nārāyaṇa Kalā" when he had heard it from Pārvatī. It can be declared that there can be no such sin which cannot be destroyed by reading the Rāma Kathā.

In other words, *Adhyātma Rāmāyaṇa* itself is God incarnate in speech.

Chapter II

RĀMA HṚDAYA

I adore the Lord of Jānakī, who on the most solemn requests of the gods for the removal of the heavy burden laid on the earth by the evil-spirited beings, incarnated himself as an apparent human being with mysteriously vast capacities known as Māyā and in the Solar dynasty, though he is mere immutable conscious reality. He, having totally rooted out the devilish race went back to his own supernaturally eternal entity or form leaving behind an indelible and purifying stamp of glorious name in all the three worlds.

I also bow down to the very Lord of Sītā, who is the only cause of the creation, maintenance and annihilation of the cosmic universe and who though the ultimate resort of that mysteriously illusive Māyā, remains constant and inconceivable in His real essence. He is spotless and blissful and is the only knower of his own self.

Those who fervently and respectfully read and hear the spiritual and holy *Rāmāyaṇa* which is in full support agreeing with all the Purāṇas, the epical histories of gods, are absolved of all sorts of sins and find their seats with Lord Hari Himself.

The aspirants wishing for their salvation should read it daily and they who fervently listen to it with dedication gain as much piety as they would do so by donating hundreds of thousands of cows daily.

The Rāmāyaṇa is the holy river that springs forth from the mouth of Lord Shiva and merges into Rāma, the divine ocean sanctifying the three worlds.

Once when Lord Shiva, attended by gods and seers, was sitting on a radiant throne with Pārvatī by his left side on the top of the Himālayan mount Kailash inside the mansion illuminating as it did like hundreds of suns,

Devi Pārvatī entreated him most humbly and respectfully.

"Oh God of the gods, always immersed in Samādhi, three-eyed, fearless, and blissful,' Oh Lord, who atones the sinners, the shelter of the Universe, the dweller in the heart of every creature, the constant witness living as the soul in every being, I bow to you and desire to know from you about the eternal supreme Lord Rāma who is the greatest of all the beings, because I know that you too are supreme and eternal God."

"Be kind enough to tell me about that spiritual knowledge in both theoritical and practical aspects together with the necessary method of devotion, detachment and soothing light in such a way as we, women, including all others, may be able to know the way to cross the turbulent sea of this world easily from what you have said. "The method of devotion is well known on all sides as a successful means for crossing the ocean of the world. I too believe that there is no greater weapon than devotion for this purpose. Still there are perplexing doubts which are deeply ingrained in my mind and which I necessarily feel to be dispelled by your mercifully disposed self with pure and instructive words."

"Yogis and saints who have destroyed their ego, and have enriched their knowledge with philosophy know Rāma to be infinite, next to none and the origin of all the creatures, the Supreme Soul and above nature. They also acquire their highest goal by praying to him day and night. But some people argue that Rāma, even though he might be Supreme Brahma Paramātman, as an incarnated person, was enveloped with his illusion and as such as ignorant like an ordinary human being and had to learn the transcendental truth from his preceptor Vaśiṣtha for enlightenment and knowledge. Otherwise why would he bewail of his separation from Sītā.

If he was really ignorant like ordinary human beings, why should we be devoted to him ? What is your opinion, my Lord? Please remove my doubts clearly by your wise words.

Lord Shiva replied, "You deserve commendable thanks as you are really a devotee to the Supreme Being. Nobody has ever asked me to explain the great hidden truth about Lord Rāma which you appear to know so curiously." "Oh Pārvatī, today you have with much dedication, put this great question, which I shall answer with many respectful bows to the great personage, Rāma of the Raghu race." "Rāma is not an ordinary man but God's incarnation, pure, self-enlightened without modification, supreme soul, beyond nature, without beginning and end and "Brahma" itself. He is immanent hidden soul and has created the universe by his illusionary nature. He is in fact omnipresent in the whole universe like ether. The universe is wholly attracted and moved to Rāma in a way similar to that where iron is solely attracted to the magnet, ordinary individuals beset with ignorance cannot know Rāma to be so as they can only find him in the form of a man and, therefore, ascribe all wordly relations to spotless and perfectly true Rāma as the result of which they move indefinitely round the wordly circle of birth and death. Rāma resides in sooth in the heart of every living being but those attached to mundane objects and kindred ties cannot feel His presence just as people forget to know their own necklaces hanging around their necks."

"There can be no ignorance in Rāma who is the god of all the gods, pure, the source of both theoretical and practical knowledge and science and who is the only perpetually abiding existence."

"An individual thinks that the whole of Universe and its objects are created by God but, in fact, they are the creation of "Māyā" just like a man who thinks the earth to be rotating by his defective eyes or mind which he is moving sharply around due to dizziness."

"Ignorance and knowledge cannot exist together at

the same time like the darkness and light. As darkness cannot stand before the light of the sun, so dark ignorance cannot be possible before Rāma, the most brilliant light of spiritual knowledge.

"Rāma, therefore, as the sun has no contradictory stain of day or night or ignorance and its opposite in reality He is above the both. He is the shelter of Māyā but not its victim."

"I am telling you the actual discourse that had once taken place among Shri Rāma, Sītā and Hanumān, and is regarded as a rare, secret means for salvation."

"Once Rāma was seated on a grand throne on the occasion of his coronation after putting an end to the demons like Rāvaṇa and others and on his return to Ayodhyā. It was attended by all his near and dear ones including Sugrīva, Bhibīshaṇa, Laxmaṇa, Vaśiṣṭha and Viśwāmitra. Rāma said to Sītā for Hanumān who was standing there with folded hands, "Please explain the real fact about Īśvara to Hanumān who has performed his duties very honestly. He is a great intellectual aspirant deserving salvation too."

Sītā described the divinely ascertained philosophical truth to Hanumān. "Know Rāma to be Brahma, existence, bliss, next to none in the Universe , the supreme authority and power, stainless, peaceful, all pervading, formless, unchangeable, imperceivable and immutable in the whole universe and with its objects."

"Know myself to be the main nature, the creator, the sustainer and the destroyer of the universe. I am always busy in my activities in close union with Supreme Soul i.e. Rāma.

Ignorant people falsely think Rāma alone to be the actor and creator of the universe which is my creation only."

The birth of Rāma in the sacred race of Raghu in

Ayodhyā, granting help to Vishwāmitra for his performance of yajñas by killing Tāḍaka, subduing and killing Subāhu, Mārīcha and other evil demons, curse absolution of Ahilyā, my marriage with Rāma, then the humbling down of Parashurāma's ego, Shri Rāma's staying at Ayodhyā for twelve years with me, then repairing to the forest Daṇḍakāraṇya, the killing of Birāḍha, putting to death of Mārīcha, the golden deer in disguise, Lord Rāma's worship by Śabarī and friendly meeting of Sugrība, the attainment of absolution by Jaṭāyu and Kabandha, the death punishment inflicted upon Bāli, then active search for Sītā, the construction of the bridge over the sea, and surrounding the city of Lankā, the success of Rāma in putting Rāvaṇa together with his sons to death and consequently enthroning Bibhīshaṇa and his (Rāma's) returning with me by the Pushpak plane to Ayodhyā and all the incidents from his birth to the present day are my actions which are ascribed to have been the deeds of Rāma. "Rāma is immutable, one and all, equal and He is the Universal soul in which I too exist."

"Rama neither acts, nor moves, nor stands, nor goes, nor does he feel pleasure or pain. He is the symbol of perpetual bliss, limitless, full, beyond and above nature and the only reality i.e. Supreme Soul."

Rāma himself said to Hanumān, "Listen to me attentively. I am explaining to you the difference between the Supreme Brahma, the soul and the spirit i.e. Paramātmā—Ātmā and Anātmā. Brahma is omnipresent in the whole universe, like the whole infinite sky, the soul (Ātmā) is also the actual essence illumining or occupying intellect of an individual, similar to the sky which is limited to the surface of a pond. Jīva, Anātmā or the spirit is the reflection of Brahma or Paramātmā, the Supreme soul, appearing upon the intellect which is the creation of nature, similar to the reflection upon the pond. So these are the three main forms to be conceived of the same reality. In fact, the doer or one which feels pleasure and pain due to more egoism is the jīva or Anātmā, the spirit of an individual and is the creation of nature and ignorance only. Ignorant persons think that the doer is the soul (Ātmā) which, in fact, does nothing but illumines the Jīva and stands as a witness only, and is eternally fixed and inactive. Hence all the reflections are outcome of ignorance which are the origins of individual spirits of Jīva (Anātmā) and as such they are manifestations of ignorance.

Know therefore that you are not false Jīva, the creation of irgnorance or the reflection of the soul (Ātmā) appearing in the intellect, but you are the Reality, same Paramātmā or Brahma because your soul is inseparable entity of the same Brahma or Paramātmā. It is wrong to feel yourself separate individual different from God. Your ignorance or individualilty of egoism will naturally be removed and the shackles of worldliness will be broken as soon as you realise yourself to be the same Reality 'tattwam'asi'. You are God, the sum and substance of spiritual knowledge or philosophy.

"You should bear in mind that knowledge or salvation cannot be attained without faith and love in me. Those that are indifferent to me fall into entangling mazes or pits of diversity of knowledge although they may learn and read in many births to come.

Even the horrible sins committed in many births by people such as slaying of saints and sages, shall be undoubtedly destroyed by self realization, because it is the clear assurance in words from Rāma Himself.

"Even the most corrupt and sinful person having been constantly addicted to the stealing of another's wealth and wife or guilty of patricide, matricide or slaying of Brahmins, possessed of spiritual knowledge shall be entitled to that very highest and holiest place revered by all the gods and which is rare even to the highly enlightened hermits if he reads this Rāma Hṛdaya with profound devotion and unalloyed worship."

Rāma further said, "Hanumān, I have divulged the most secret spiritual facts to you as you are my most beloved and favourite devotee. You should disclose this secret to persons who have no love and faith in me though they may be as great as Indra, the king of Gods."

Lord Shiva said to Pārvatī, "Devi, I have told you the most important philosophical theory which Rāma had personally explained to Hanumān. This theory is certainly the heart of Rāma and is called Rāma Hṛdaya i.e. Rāma's heart which is the holiest of all the holy scriptures."

Chapter III

PRAYER FOR INCARNATION OF VIṢṆU

Pārvatī was much impressed and inspired to know the reason behind Rāma's incarnation. She further requested Lord Shiva, "Oh Lord of the Universe, I am grateful to you for having dispelled my doubts. But I am not still satisfied by Rāma's brief nectarlike story and I desire to know about Rāma's life in greater detail."

Lord Shiva said, "Devi Listen, I shall tell you the most secret and holiest life of Lord Rāma which he was kind enough to reveal me much earlier."

"An individual who hears it is certainly saved from three-fold miseries (egoistic, divine and natural).

Once the earth being extremely miserable on account of the burden of sins and atrocities of Rāvaṇa and his innumerable ferocious demons, assumed the form of a cow, and accompanied by saints and gods she approached Brahmā, the creator, who by meditation understood the means of redressing her troubles.

Brahmā went directly to the seashore to the omnipotent, omniscient and omnipresent Lord Viṣṇu, with the cow, the saints and gods and very fervently and joyfully prayed to Him, who looked young and fresh.

His prayer was very sacred, sweet and was supported philosophically and mythologically; propitiated Lord Viṣṇu who is radiant like thousand suns illuminating every direction and completely driving out every trace of gloom emerged out of the eastern side of the ocean. Even Lord Brahmā did not find it quite easy to see the radiant appearance of Lord Viṣṇu who, in fact, could never be seen by the unholy people.

Lord Viṣṇu's face was luminous and soothing like blue gems. His charming smiles were extraordinarily pleasant and the eyes were as beautiful as lotuss.

Adorned with the brilliant crown, ear-rings divine necklaces, jewels, precious gems, 'Shri Batsa' and 'Kaustubha' and attended by saints like Sanaka etc., and celestial retinues singing prayers, He looked glorious with His garland; conch, chakra, mace and lotuss in each of lovely hands, wearing golden sacred thread around the neck, mounted on Garuḍa, clad in yellow cloths Satin and accompanied by Laxmi and the Goddess of Earth.

Lord Brahmā having been exceedingly happy and charmed with the august personality invoked him most fervently.

"Lord, I most respectfully bow to your lotus feet to which all aspirants of salvation constantly bow throughout their whole life with their intellect and senses. You create the universe by your three-fold powers (quiescent, materialistic and predatory) of Māyā (illusion) but you are never attached to the creations because you are self enlightened and self blissful. Lord, an individual whose mind is impure and unholy cannot gain piety by studies and sacrifices or renunciations but only those that love your holy name shall be easily successful.

"My inner mind has been completely sanctified at the sight of your lotus feet which are the main objects of constant contemplation for saints and aspirants. I and other gods too shelter in your holy feet many times in the past for the fulfilment of our selfish ends whereas saints, sages and aspirants love you for the attainment of enlightened knowledge and salvation only."

"Goddess Laxmi dwells in your bosom, yet she envies the flower 'Tulsi' offered to your feet as if it were your co-wife. Your affection for your aspirants is greater than your love for Goddess Laxmi, because your earnest aspirants are unselfish and truthful and they want nothing except their unflinching devotion to your holiest feet."

God, I, therefore, aspire after affection only from yourself because it is the only ramedy to cure the malady of mundance desires.

Lord Viṣṇu said to Brahmā "What can I do for you?"

Brahmā replied, "Lord, Rāvaṇa, the son of Bishravā, is at present the king of demons and has become very vain and cruel by obtaining boons from me. He has tyrannised all the creatures of the three worlds, heaven, earth and netherland and has really become a serious threat to the whole creation of mine."

"Kind Lord, I have destined his death from a man's hand. Therefore, please kill him by incarnating yourself in the form of a man."

Lord Viṣṇu replied, "I had granted a boon to Sage Kashyap who had pleased me by his austere penance. I had promised him that I would accept his request to be born as his son. He has at present been born as Dasharatha, the king of Ayodhyā and I shall, therefore, incarnate myself into four forms. I shall be Kauśalyā's son, and the others will be sons from other queens. My Yoga Māyā Laxmī will appear in the form of Jānakī and live in king Janaka's house. I shall then accomplish your mission by taking her with me."

Lord Viṣṇu disappeared thereafter. Brahmā said to the other gods," Lord Viṣṇu will incarnate Himself in the dynasty of the King Raghu. All of you shall then descend on the earth by assuming forms of monkeys and their race to help Lord Viṣṇu."

Lord Brahmā then went to his abode having been fully satisfied after he had thus instructed the gods, and assured the Earth (happy in the form of a cow). The gods thenceforth began to take birth at different places for the said purpose in the forms of mighty monkeys. They could fight even by means of hillocks and trees waiting patiently to meet Lord Viṣṇu.

Chapter IV

BIRTH OF RĀMA AND HIS BROTHERS

Once Dasharatha, the King of Ayodhyā, the truthful, mighty, brave, and renowned king all over the world, was very much disappointed for having no issue. He asked his preceptor Vashiṣṭha, "Lord, how can I beget sons blessed with all the virtuous qualities ? I feel miserable as I am heirless."

Vashiṣṭha replied "You shall have four illustrious sons as mighty as the saviour of the three worlds if you bring Rishi Shringa, the husband of Shanta, the greatest Yogi and quickly get the son-awarding sacrifice (yajña) duly performed by him together with us.

King Dasharatha did as advised by his preceptor with great enthusiam and faith under the guidance of the holy and pious sages.

The God of fire, shining like heated gold, appeared from the fire, with a gold plate filled with the divine food and asked Dasharatha, "Sir, accept this milk mixed food prepared by Gods, and the Supreme Lord Viṣṇu will incarnate Himself in the form of your son. There is no doubt. The god of fire disappeared handing over the devine food to the king. The king paid obeisance to the two sages with great satisfaction and with the consent of his preceptor Vashiṣṭha and the holy sage Rishi Shringa he gave that food to both queens Kaushalyā and Kaikeyī and completed the yajña paying due ręspects to the sages.

The queens very happily gave half of the divine food, which they had received from the king to their sister Sumitrā too.

Thus all the three queens conceived after taking the food and in their palace, glowed like goddesses.

In due course of time, queen Kaushalyā delivered one extraordinary son, the Supreme, eternal and great

Viṣṇu, on the ninth lunar day when five auspicious stars and planets were in the month of Chaitra (March) high positions and the sun stood in "Mesh Rāshi". The sky was filled with flowers showered by gods on that glorious occasion.

Lord Viṣṇu was dressed in yellow Satin and his august form was as blue as lotus. He had four arms, the inner portions and lids of his eyes sparkled like the red petals of lotuss, the ears glittered with brilliant ear-rings, his face was effulgent like thousands of suns and he had a gorgeous crown on his head with curled hairs hanging on his forehead. He was holding divine chakra, disc, mace and lotus in each hand; his smiles exhibited the beauty and serenity of the moon, expressing blessings from his joyful and moon-like heart. His eyes too were as beautiful as lotuss that expressed affection and favour, and he was adorned with divine ornaments, Shreebatsa, Keyur, Katak, Kaustuva. Queen Kaushalyā was greatly amazed at the sight of Lord Viṣṇu and she began to pray him affectionately with eyes saturated with tears.

Oh God of gods, I pay very consecrated and respectful homage to you, Lord, holding conch, mace, disc and lotus in each hand. You are perpetual, omnipresent, supreme, infinite, imperceivable, inexpressible above mental senses, self-existant and the great reality itself. You have created the universe by your illusion on māyā and the violent and indolent three 'guṇas' which are saintly, materialistic and predatory, but you yourself are always indifferent from and unmixed with them and live in the 'turīya' stage which is above the limits of waking, sleeping and dreaming stages of the mind."

"In fact, neither you are the doer nor do you move, nor hear, nor see, but you only appear to be doing every thing. The Vedas declare that you are holy and also free from mind or organic senses. You dwell in all individual' minds equally but those who are ignorant by your illusion cannot know you; on the other hand the wise and holy persons who are your favourite can find you easily."

Lord, I wonder innumerable universes are contained in the form of atoms in your belly and you stayed in my womb. You have thus set an example of having kept your promise and have favoured your aspirants."

"Lord, I have always been beguiled by illusion so far because I have been wandering at random since I have always been attached to worldliness and fully absolved in the so-called affection and company of my husband with wealth, prosperity and posterity. But today I sincerely and fully surrender myself to your lotus feet. Let your august personality always enshrine my heart and let the illusion which overcomes me be removed for ever."

"You universal soul, now kindly change your apparel into a lovely child so that I may with constant embraces and sweet talks be able to throw away the terrible darkness in the form of ignorance, i.e. I may cross the ocean of hostile ignorance."

Lord Viṣṇu replied, "Mother, your wish shall be fulfilled. I have incarnated myself as a man on Brahmā's request for relieving the earth from the burden of sins and unpiety."

"Holy Lady, you together with King Dasharatha had asked me to become your son and then you had obtained the boon from me. It was after I had been pleased by your penance performed by you in your previous births. You have now the good priviledge of seeing my form of Viṣṇu as a result of your previous holy deeds. Really such an interview which you have today availed yourself of will grant you salvation never obtainable by unholy persons."

"For the present, I declare that whosoever will go through or hear our discourse shall also attain my form and be amalgamated with me and shall not forget me even at the moments of death.

Lord Viṣṇu thereafter changed himself into a baby and began to cry. The appearance of the child was exquisitely charming and lovely.

He looked as blue as sapphire, indra kamal, his eyes were wide and beautiful as the lotus and he was as lustrous as the rising sun. He made all the guards of heaven and earth happy by descending to the Earth thus. King Dasharatha was very happy to know the birth and he hurried to the queen's bed-room with the preceptor and was overhwelmed with joy on seeing the baby. The king called Vashiṣṭha to perform the birth ceremony with great pleasure.

Soon after, the lotus-eyed queen Kaikeyī delivered a child but Sumitrā gave birth to twins. The new born babies were as illustrious and shining as the full moon.

King Daṣharatha whose joy knew no bounds bestowed upon Brahmins thousands villages, a huge quantity of gold, verieties of precious gems and ornaments, robes, dresses, and auspicious cows.

Guru Vashiṣṭha named Kaushalyā's son Rāma in whom avowed sages find inspirations and shelter at their ignorance totally exterpitated by knowledge.

Vishiṣṭha proposed names for them—Bharata to Kaikeyī's son, and Laxmaṇa and Satrughna to queen Sumitra's sons. Bharata means the sustainer of all the beings and Laxman indicates one who is endowed with all virtues and Satrughna means the destroyer of enemies.

Laxman sided with Rāma and Satrughna with Bharata in union with the nectrine food given by Kaushalyā and Kaikeyī to Sumitrā. Therefore they played and lived together and pleased their parents by the charming behaviour and their childish plays and pranks.

King Dasharatha and queen Kaushalyā were very happy when they saw Rāma, as illustrious and blue as sapphire, smilingly frolicking and running after a calf and playing into the royal courtyard. Rāma would look exceedingly lovely wearing a pipal leaf shaped gold ornaments studded with pearls and other brilliant gems upon the forehead and necklaces of gems around the neck, gold ear-rings like the fruit of Arjuna tree and ringing bangles on the feet and golden dress and gold armlets.

King Dasharatha and queen Kaushalyā would ask Rāma to sit by him for partaking of food with him but Rāma did not care to listen to him and went playing. Kaushalyā would go to bring Rāma who would run away laughing and she could not be able to catch hold of him who would not be properly grasped even by austere minds. Sometimes Rāma would get to come to Kaushalyā when she got tired of running after him and would take a morsel of eat and run away again. She would observe his birth anniversaries by preparing the niceties as poowa, laddu etc. She would dress Rāma very fashionably and smartly and would perform every month a ceremony for the baby by distributing sweets and dainties to Brahmins.

She had to give up many household works on account of frivolity and naughtiness of Rāma's childish pranks.

One day Rāma requested her to give food but she did not hear as she was occupied with some work. Rāma broke the earthen utensils and threw away butter from the cup-board. He took milk, curd and other sweets which he ate himself and distributed to his brothers. When Kaushalyā was informed by the cook, she came there but they fled away with laughable mimmiries. She ran after Rāma to catch but slipped at every step. She took Rāma on her lap and said nothing for his naughty pranks. When Rāma sobbed very gently in a child-like way, she would embrace all the sons with great affection.

Rāma, though God- incarnate, supreme saviour, giver of happiness and prosperity was now pleasing his parents also by exhibiting such childish sports.

On growing older all the boys by their investiture ceremony were made to put on sacred-threads by the preceptor Vashiṣṭha.

They, who were the masters of the universe, acted as human beings at the world-theatre, studied all religious scriptures easily and at very early age and became learned in literature and arts and most skilful in the tactics of archery and military.

Laxmaṇa was prone to Rāma and Satrughna would similarly follow Bharata.

Rāma used to go for hunt on horse back fully equipped with the bow and arrows accompanied by Laxmaṇa and would kill tigers and lions and bring them before his father.

He (Rāma) would rise early in the morning and after taking ablutions, he would go to his parents to bow in respects. There he would very humbly attend to his civil duties. He dined with his brothers daily. He on some occasions held discussions with courtiers and officers. On important matters, he would also listen to the religious scriptures from the sages and take active part in discussions as well.

Rāma, Supreme Lord, though in fact inactive, immanent and always unchangeable in himself seemed to have done even such household and mundane chores as an ordinary human being. But if we contemplate deeply we find that he had done nothing as an agent in the world.

Chapter V

VISHWĀMITRA'S ARRIVAL AT AYODHYĀ

Sage Vishwāmitra, effulgent as the rising sun, reached Ayodhyā to see Rāma, knowing that he had been pleased to incarnate himself there with his Māyā. King Dasharatha then accompanied by Vashiṣṭha very warmly greated the sage and respectfully worshipping him with folded palms said, "Lord of the sages, I am today very grateful to you for such visits really bring prosperity. I will certainly carry out what you say to me to do."

Sage Vishwāmitra tenderly replied. On auspicious days, I am performing yajña ceremony to propitiate gods as well as my ancestors, departed souls but Mārīcha and Subāhu with their followers foil always my performance. It will be very beneficial if you kindly send Rāma and Laxmaṇa with me to kill these demons. You may also consult your preceptor sage Vashiṣṭha if necessary."

King Dasharatha requested Vashiṣṭha anxiously and in a low voice. "What shall I do? My Lord, I cannot send these god-like sons whom I have obtained in my old age with so much difficulty. Rāma is the dearest of all my sons and I cannot live without him. Please tell me how I can avoid sending him."

Vashiṣṭha answered, "Listen to my secret advice. Rāma is not a mortal being but God's incarnation. Long long ago, Brahmā, the creator had requested Lord Viṣṇu to unburden the earth from the sinful deeds. Rāma, therefore has born in your home. In the previous birth, you were Kashyapa, Prajapati's son and Kaushalyā was God's mother, Aditi. You had performed penances for a very long time and Lord Viṣṇu, being pleased with you had given the boons to you that he would be born your son as was desired by you. Rāma is therefore for Lord Vishṇu, Laxmaṇa is 'Sesh Nag—The Serpant God, Bharata is the incarnation of his mighty weapon 'disc' and strughna is his divine conch. Goddess Laxmi has incarnated herself in King Janak's house as Sītā. Sage Vishwāmitra has come here to take Rāma for getting him married to Sītā. This is the most hidden truth to be never disclosed. You, therefore send Rāma and Laxmaṇa along with sage Vishwāmitra with due respects and pleasure."

King Dasharatha having thought himself fortunate enough called Rāma and Laxmaṇa immediately, hugged them, touched their heads with smells and blessings and entrusted them to sage Vishwāmitra.

The illustrious sage returned to his hermitage happily with them with their weapons fully equipped. On his way he bestowed upon them the divine knowledge called "Bala" and "Atibala" by which hunger and thirst and exhaustion could be controlled.

They crossed the river Ganges and reached the forests where Tāḍaka, the demoness, lived.

Sage Vishwāmitra asked valiant Rāma to kill her instantly as she was very cruel and she could assume any form she wished.

Rāma sounded his bow and Tāḍaka in dreadful appearance very furiously dashed out of the forest to kill Rāma on hearing the bow's sound which she could not bear as it had resounded the whole forest. Rāma shot at her heart by his sharp shaft and she instantly fell heaving the last sigh. She did vomit blood profusely.

She got changed into a well dressed and beautifully ornamented girl after the death. It was so because she was emancipated by Lord Rāma from here demon-form which she had to assume as the result of a curse.

She paid her homage to Rāma very respectfully and she was welcomed in heaven by Rāma's merciful orders.

Sage Vishwāmitra tenderly embraced Rāma and smelt of his head as a token of blessings with presents of many bows, divine arrows, and other arms divinely enchanted by mantras (secret words).

Chapter VI

RĀMA IN SAGE GAUTAMA'S HERMITAGE

Vishwāmitra, the Lord of sages, along with Rāma and Laxmaṇa halted at Kāma-Āshrama for a night. The hermitage where many sages and aspirants lived and reached his hermitage named Siddha-Āshram inhabited by his innumerable disciples.

On being welcomed and adored by the sages under the instructions of Vishwāmitra in the hermitage, Rāma requested the sage (Vishwāmitra).

"Lord, please perform your settled ritual ceremony and let me see those demons."

On answering the questions of Rāma, Vishwāmitra with the help of sages, set to perform the ceremony and the magically ferocious demons, Mārīch and Subāhu came over there as usual at the mid-day and hovered over the sky showering blood and bones upon the hermitage. Rāma fixed two arrows at his bow which he drew upto his neck and shot them at each of the demon. One of the shafts tossed Mārīch thousands miles away into the ocean and the other shot instantly burnt Subāhu into ashes. Laxmaṇa too killed all the demon followers in a matter of a few moments.

The dieties showered flowers upon Rāma and Laxmaṇa from the sky in admiration and sounded various drums and trumpets in joy. All the sages were also very much delighted.

Vishwāmitra was extremely pleased with Rāma and Laxmaṇa and after placing them in his laps respectfully worshipped them in ecstacy with eyes swelled in tears and offered delicious ripe fruits.

He passed three days with Rāma and Laxmaṇa very happily and amused them telling stories from holy scriptures.

On the fourth day, Vishwāmitra asked Rāma, "Rāma, let us go to see the great yajña ceremony to be performed by the King Janaka. It is called "Dhanush Yajña" as the great bow of Lord Shiva has been placed there. You shall see it and King Janaka will also welcome you very happily."

Vishwāmitra together with Rāma and Laxmaṇa and accompanied by saints set out for Janaka's kingdom. He happened to arrive at the side of the bank of the River Ganges. There was sage Gautam's sacred hermitage situated with holy fruit-trees all around and Ahilyā was absorbed in austere penance there.

Rāma told Vishwāmitra, "Lord, the hermitage is very beautiful and pleasant. I am really fascinated with its beauty to discover that it is utterly free from harmful beasts and quite deserted and lonely. Whose hermitage is it ? Please tell me in detail."

Vishwāmitra replied, "Long ago Sage Gautama renowned for his severe austerities for propitiating Lord Hari used to reside here. Lord Brahmā satisfied with his purely austere life, gave his most beautiful and obedient daughter Ahilyā to him. Gautama was happy and content at this provential favour. He, therefore, accepted her in his hermitage merely as his attendant as he made up his mind to live in celebacy."

"Once Indra, infatuated by her beauty assumed the form of Gautam and cohabited with her. When he was leaving the hermitage in a cockeyed manner, sage Gautam came across him. He got very much infuriated with Indra finding him in his own apparel and he said "Who are you such a vile and wicked fellow coming in my disguise? Tell me the truth otherwise I shall turn you into ashes."

Indra very meekly answered, "Lord, I am Indra and have indeed committed a heinous crime having been overpowered with lust. Please pardon me."

Gautam in rage with eyes as red as heated copper

cursed "Let your face be stained with marks of thousand veginas so that people may know that you are so much addicted to lust!"

Gautam entered into his hermitage where Ahilyā was waiting for him with folded hands. She was trembling with fear.

He said to her, "Wicked lady, be turned into a stone without food and water in the regour of hot and cold weathers in my hermitage and constantly meditate in your heart Lord Rāma till he reaches here after thousands of years. Henceforth this hermitage shall remain free from all kinds of cruel beasts. Revered Rāma will step his holy feet upon the slab and you will then regain your form fully purified by Rāma and return to my residence and serve me as before." Gautam has since left the hermitage and has gone to the Himālayas."

Vishwāmitra said to Rāma "The greatest of the clan of Raghus please emancipate Brahmā's daughter from her curse as she has been earnestly waiting for you for her redemption by the dusts of your holy feet."

Vishwāmitra holding Rāma by his hands led him to the spot where she was lying in the form of a stone. Rāma placed his foot upon it which instantly changed into the form of a girl. He also said to her, "I am Rāma."

She saw Rāma in Viṣṇu's form clad in shining yellow robes with four arms holding conch, disc, mace and lotus. The bow and the quiver were handing over his shoulders and Laxmaṇa was standing by him. Rāma was very sweetly smiling, wearing Shri Batsa gems on the bosom. His eyes were gleaning like shining lotuses, and his face was radiant with blue gem-like lustre illuminating all the directions.

Ahilyā was overwhelmed with joy and was amazed at the divine sight of Rāma. She also remembered sage Gautam's instructions. Knowing him to be God she stood up and worshipped Him with great zeal and aspirations. She offered sweets, and water and also with humble bows and with joyful tears dropping from her eyes. She began to invoke him in ecstacy in a choked voice.

Ahilyā said, "The shelter of the universe, Lord, I am very grateful today by obtaining dust stoms of your holy feet which are earnestly sought even by the Creator Brahmā, Lord Shiva and other gods. Your plays and actions enchant the creatures of the whole universe. You are blissful, very illusionary and move everywhere though in fact you have no mortal body and legs. You are the perfect soul and also a mysterious actor. The same holy feet which had sanctified the Ganges, Brahmā, Shiva, and other dieties have been available to me as well. How can I estimate the pious deeds of my previous birth as a result of which I have been today very fortunate in having an interview with you ? "I wish to pray to none but yourself Rāma, the holder of the grand bow, the most handsome and glorious human incarnation of Lord Viṣṇu."

"I constantly meditate upon Rāma's personality in my grateful heart. Even the Vedas are always in search of holy dust of Rāma's feet. From his naval Brahmā had been born and of this nectarine name with its essence, Lord Shiva is the knower and warm appreciator."

"I take refuge in Rāma whose life story is always sung in the world of Brahmā by divine sage Nārada, the dieties, Brahmā, and even Saraswatī is beside herself with joyful tears and her breast is thoroughly wet with the tears by the holy songs.

Though self enlightened, infinite, it is Rāma Himself who is the source of the universe and its creations. Though He is formless entity, He assumes illusionary human forms that enamour every living being in the world. It is He who is only the perfect and absolute Supreme God. It pleases Him to be reflected in his own self with the forms of Brahmā, Viṣṇu, and Shiva, sustaining, creating and annihilating. He is you, Oh Rāma, your lotus feet are fondled by Laxmi who always places them upon her bosom in love."

"Once your single step had crossed as scaling the three worlds together. All the meek and prideless sages are devoted to your feet to which I make my humble obeissance. Oh, Lord, you are the creator and have created the objects and the universe itself. You are also its sustainer. "You are also the Goal or the attainable reality suggested by Omkāra. But you are above all sound, word and meaning. Still every difference such as suggestor and suggested in the world shall be imagined in yourself as you are one Universal Entity."

"In fact you are quite apart and separate from them because you are mere unique Supreme Existence—Brahmā, the absolute soul".

"Rāma, you are Omnipresent. You are cause as well as effect, the doer, the deed, the creator and the creation which are all the different functions created by your magically illusionary forces only."

"Rāma, you are the divine Lord 'Om', unknowable, inexpressible, Supreme Soul called Paramātmā above and beyond all the souls. You are subject as well as object in the Universe. Only ignorant people overpowered by your illusion think yourself to be a mortal being."

"You are Omnipresent in and outside the universe like the pervading ether or sky stainless, without modification, immutable, unique, immobile, holy, self-conscious. You are the abiding reality, the one without the second."

"Lord, the glory of the Universe! How can I as an ignorant woman know you fully? I, therefore, can only bow to you earnestly in blind faith and unflinching mind thousand times, day and night."

"Lord, please grant such favour so that I may always remember your lotus feet with deep devotion wherever I remain."

May the earnestness of praying to you inspire me for ever. I bow to you again and again. Master of all the souls and senses, the sympathiser of the aspirants, "Rishikesh" and final abode of every living being, I look up with sincere prayers to you. Rāma, you are Supreme God as effulgent as hundreds of thousand of suns. "You remove the miseries of worldliness holding the bows and arrows. You shine like deep clouds with clear and beautiful lotus like eyes. Dressed in golden robes and with the crown studded with precious gems upon the head, you look glorious and always are attended by Laxmaṇa."

Ahilyā bade farewell duly and humbly to Rāma who was standing before her. She took her way to the Himālayas with his consent and permission to meet her husband sage Gautam. Any body earnestly and devotedly reciting this invocation which she offered to Rāma shall be absolved from all sins and also obtain salvation on realising supreme Brahmā.

If a woman with a devoted heart to Rāma recites it with the aim of getting a son even though she may be a sterile woman, she shall give birth to a worthy son within a year's time because any one can accomplish one's desires by Rama's favour.

What to speak of a well educated person, even the most horrible sinner can atone for his sins if his mind is dedicated to Rāma earnestly and he recites this prayer no matter may be he is a killer of Brahmins or a man who has vitiated his preceptors's wife, or a thief or a drunkard, or a murderer of his parents and brothers or a person always addicted to sexual pleasures.

Chapter VII

RĀMA'S MARRIAGE WITH SĪTĀ

Vishwāmitra said to Rāma, "Let us proceed towards Mithilā."

They reached the banks of the Ganges and crossed the river by a boat. The boatman came to Rāma and said, "Lord, please let me wash your feet lest the dust of your feet should change my boat into a girl, like the stone which was instantly changed into Ahilyā by the touch of your feet. I find no difference between stone and wood. So if my wooden boat is converted into a person of beauty by your feet noted for miraculous power in the form of dust atoms. I should wash away it by carefully cleaning them. I would lose my profession and my family members will suffer starvation. So kindly allow me to wash your feet and I shall take you across the river then."

Thereafter the clever boatman washed the feet and conducted them to the other side of the river.

Vishwāmitra along with Rāma and Laxmaṇa reached the city of Mithilā next morning and halted at a hermitage there.

King Janaka knowing this hastened next morning with a highly excited heart to the hermitage to see Vishwāmitra with many articles of gifts for the sage. He was duly accompanied by his priest as well. He earnestly worshipped Vishwāmitra with great respects and bows and also saw Rāma and Laxmaṇa resplendant as the sun and the moon enlightening all the directions.

Janaka requested the sage "Lord, who are these two handsome lads looking like divine beings as mighty as lions. My mind is greatly attached towards them who seem to be incarnations of Nara and Nārāyaṇa."

Vishwāmitra replied, "Janaka, Rāma and Laxmaṇa

are king Dasharatha's sons. I had taken them to my hermitage for guarding the yajña ceremony and the most valiant Rāma killed Tāḍaka by a single shot on the way, burnt Subāhu in a moment of time and tossed Mārīcha to the sea thousands of miles away. Laxmaṇa killed all the other demons who were assembled at my hermitage for interrupting the ceremony. They then betook themselves to the holy hermitage of Gautam and Rāma emancipated Ahilyā, the sage's wife and now he wishes to see the divine bow of Lord Shiva in your palace."

We have heard that the supreme bow is greatly respected by you and many princes also have seen it. Kindly show this great bow to Rāma and Laxmaṇa who will then go back to Ayodhyā."

Janaka entertained and worshipped Rāma and Laxmaṇa as they deserved. He also ordered his wise minister to show the bow quickly. King Janaka said to Vishwāmitra, "If Rāma can raise the bow and fix an arrow I shall offer Sītā to him for marriage."

With a pleasing smile of approval directed towards Rāma, Vishwāmitra replied to Janaka, "Let it be so. Please do well to have the bow shown as soon as possible before glorious and valiant Rāma."

The wonderful bow shining with gems studded upon it and hundreds of bells hanging upon was carried there by five thousand brave soldiers. The chief minister showed it to Rāma who after girding up his loins raised the bow with his left hand so easily and bent it to fix the string amidst all other kings and princes present at the ceremony. He, the common heart of every being, drew the bow with his right hand and broke it in a way befitting his extraordinary valour. The sound of the breaking resounded all over the universe, in the heaven, the earth and the nether world, which seemed to have been the most wonderful act while the Gods were seeing on from above. Gods and fairies showered flowers upon Rāma and danced in joy to mark the marvellous feat.

King Janaka embraced Rāma very joyfully at the sight of the great bow having been broken into two pieces. The queen mothers who were watching the feat from the windows of the palace-wall also became happy and were taken back.

Sītā very richly dressed and decked with various invaluable ornaments immediately appeared with a golden garland in her hands and very happily put it around Rāma's neck.

All the people including the kings and queens present there were delighted to see Sītā offering the sacred garland adorned in the most befitting manner with lustrous ornaments and gilded clothes from head to foot. The maids and ladies with other queens were peeping at from the windows of the interior palace rooms. Erudite king Janaka requested the sage "Please send the messengers to King Dasharatha asking him to attend the marriage ceremony at the earliest hour with his sons, queens and ministers.

King Dasharatha's joy knew no bounds knowing the wonderful deeds performed by Rāma and his marriage to be celebrated with Sītā. He ordered his ministers to arrange every thing necessary for going to Mithilā and he at once set out in a splendid chariot followed by great army horses, elephants together with Bharata and Satrughna, Guru Vashiṣṭha with his wife and with religious fire which was on the front line escorting Rāma's mothers on the humble request of King Dasharatha. On their arrival at Mithilā Janaka with his priest Satānanda joyfully and cordially received King Dasharatha with due formality and honour.

Rāma and Laxmaṇa paid respectful obeissance to King Dasharatha who very happily said, "Fortunately I see you like a shining lotus, and really I have been favoured by the greatest sage Vishwāmitra.

With these sweet words, Dasharatha touched the sons, heads embracing Rāma again and again in the highest beatitude.

King Janaka comfortably lodged Dasharatha, queens and sons in the royal mansion equipped with all sorts of luxuries.

Religious minded Janaka invited Rāma with other brothers for marriage and got them seated on the grand thrones in the pavillion elevated on the marriage-hall which was exquisitely decorated with various colours, flags precious gems and pearls. The pillars of the hall were golden, its roof was made of costly clothes of different designs and brocades and laces were hanging around.

Learned Brahmins and priests dressed gorgeosly and wearing gold ornaments filled the shed from all sides.

The women similarly aborned, were also present there. Various kinds of musical instruments, such as Bheri, Dundubhi, trumpets, horns, flutes, etc. were being played on while dancers danced merrily.

Priest Satānanda invited Vishwāmitra and Vashiṣṭha and offered seats by both of the sides of Rāma's throne.

The sacred fire was lit according to Vedic injunctions when king Janaka and the queen brought Sītā by the side of Rāma's throne and sprinkled upon the head the holy water of the feet which is incessantly retained by Shiva, Brahmā and saints and sages on their heads. Janaka offered Sītā's hand in token of due establishment of marriage with a basket full of rice and a pot of water of Rāma saying 'I hand over the self of Sītā in a proper way. Be pleased at this."

Janaka was as happy as the God of ocean offering Laxmi to Lord Viṣṇu.

King Janaka offered his daughter Urmilā to Laxmaṇa, Māṇḍavī and Śrutikīrti daughters of his brother to Bharata and Shatrughna.

All the four brothers looked very happy and resplendant as if they were the heaven's guards.

King Janaka referring to Nārada's predictions said to Vishwāmitra and Vashiṣṭha. "Once while ploughing a plot of land with gold harrow to take some earth for the purpose of performing the yajña ceremony I found in the earth Sītā an auspicious baby girl with the charming moon-like face. I loved her as if she were my own daughter and I entrusted her to my wife."

Sage Nārada visited me one day playing on his divine Vīṇā named "Mahati" and being respectfully greeted by me said. "King, listen to the cause of great luck and prosperity. Lord Viṣṇu has incarnated His own self in Rāma's form in a four-fold way for the welfare of humanity in the earth, and for killing evil minded Rāvaṇa. Laxmi too has incarnated hereself as Sītā whom you should get married to Rāma. Since then I have been brooding over as to how I should be able to give Sītā in marriage to Rāma. When all of a sudden a thought flashed upon the mind about the great bow which was flung by God Shiva after putting Tripurāshura to death, the mighty demon. The mighty bow was entrusted by Lord Shiva to my forefathers. I, therefore, have put the bow as the trial of strength of human beings because no one other than Viṣṇu's incarnation would have the might for breaking it."

Today my aim has been successful by your grace because you, Rāma, have broken the bow and have thus fulfilled my pledge."

My life has been fruitful because I see you sitting with Sītā on the same throne.

Your feet's dust had granted Great Brahmā energy for creating the universe, had bestowed upon Bāli, Indira's seat, and had freed Ahilyā from her husband's curse. Who is my greater saviour than your Divine Self ?"

"I seek shelter in yours because the sages which are

the appreciators of the divine charm and sweet smells of your lotus feet, have conquered Time and Destiny and have become totally free from worldly fears and even the gods perpetually chanting holy names have got rid of all sorrows and troubles."

King Janaka and his queens with great affection sent Sītā along with Rāma to her father-in-law's place at Ayodhyā, giving her enormous riches, numerous gems, ornaments, dresses, three hundred maids, elephants, horses and chariots in the dowry. He likewise gave the dowry to his other daughters, married to Laxmaṇa, Bharata and Śatrughna.

He also served duly the sages Vishwāmitra and Vashiṣṭha and King Dasharatha as well presenting them valuable gifts.

At this farewell marriage ceremony the queen mothers with eyes filled with affectionate tears embraced Sītā warmly and showered blessings on her that she with her service to her mother-in-law and with the great devotion of a chaste ideal wife to Rāma would be able to lead a happy life.

The occasion was marked by the thousand dances with various musical instruments on the above in the heaven and on the earth and this appeared immensely grand to all the beings around.

Chapter VIII

RĀMA MEETS PARASHURĀMA

King Dasharatha noticed evil omens on his way when he had gone twenty five miles away from Mithilā. He reverently enquired of his preceptor Vaśiṣṭha, "Lord, it seems to me all around that some mishaps may occur."

Vaśiṣṭha replied, "Certainly they will, but will pass off smoothly. Deer are running by your right side which are indications of goods luck."

Soon, rough wind began to blow with the dust from the ground covering the travellers' eyes. An extremely luminous figure was seen before. Parashurāma resplendant as thousand suns, with appearance as blue as shining clouds, with tuft of hair on the head and a bow and a heavy axe in the hands, looking forward like the God of death, was approaching towards Rāma as if he were going to destroy all the people at the spot.

Every body trembled in fear to see him because he had killed inumerabale princes and kings.

King Dasharatha forgot in terror to worship the sage and very meekly fell on his feet with a solemn request for the safety of his son's life.

Parashurāma, wild in rage, did not pay any heed to the king's words but dashed towards Rāma and harshly said, "Vile Kshatriya Rāma, you take pride for breaking the old and rotten bow in vain. If you are really mighty born in Raghu's dynasty fix the string of my Vaishṇava bow, otherwise I shall fight and kill all of you and fulfil my mission of putting an end to the Kshatriya race.

The earth shook as Parashurāma spoke. Everybody saw darkness all around.

Valiant Rāma snatching the bow from Parashurāma's hand easily fixed an arrow upon the bow and said to Parashurāma "Brahmin, forget all the Lokas (Worlds) conquered by you and I shall strike your feet by my infallible arrow which will destroy your energy for racing from one world to the other. Tell me further what shall I have to do for you ?

Bhrigu's son Parashurāma turned pale and remembered his previous birth's history and humbly bowing to Rāma prayed, "Rāma, I know that you are eternal Supreme and Omnific God Viṣṇu, the creator, sustainer and destroyer of the universe. In my youth I had performed severe penances in holy "Chakra" pilgrimage and had pleased Lord Viṣṇu who with His merciful look and with his favourite weapons in his hand had said to me, "Stand up. Enough of your penances. They are now fruitful and you shall be endowed with my own powers necessary for you and you shall be invincible and conquer the whole earth which you will later on bestow upon Kashyapa by killing Kartabriya guilty of patricide. You will also kill all tyrant kings of the earth roaming for twenty one times. Then I shall withdraw these extraordinary powers and energies of mine from you and I shall incarnate myself as Rāma, the son of Dasharatha and marry Sītā, the permanent and divine source of strength. You shall then live in the earth till its delusion practising wholesome austerities and penances only. With these words Viṣṇu vanished away. Parashurāma further said, "Rāma, you have today withdrawn from me your own power by being born in this Tretā age at the request of Brahmā, the creator. My mission too is complete now as I have known you fully. You with your real self and power are beyond Nature not easily perceivable even to creator Brahmā as well as any other diety."

"You are free from six-fold defects of worldliness and ignorance as you are inactive and immutable. The illusion or "Māyā" depending on you, acts, as it were for the creation in various ways and it intermixed with you like the bubbles in the water and the smoke in the fire.

"How strange the working of your Māyā is ! Ignorant persons, overpowered as long as they are with this illusion cannot probably know you. Illusion is badly opposed to true knowledge. Even the individual's spirit or Jīva is only the reflection of your Supreme Soul upon the intellect only. This is the mere creation of nescience which is the outcome of the lack of knowledge of your pure self."

"The individuality, in fact is nothing but the mind, intellect and senses governed by the ego, that gets life energy from the reflection of God . But the soul immanent in the individual is God himself and has no birth and death and mere intellect is devoid of this knowledge. The soul and the matter mixed together due to lack of right discretion appear as an individual being similar to the hot water which is the combination of heat and water."

"The doer (individual) who feels pleasure, pain, happiness and misery is the ego in combination with the intellect and sense organs but not the soul which is divine and latitude everywhere immanent, conscious, immutable, inscrutable, self existant and immortal."

"An individual cannot know you if he does not associate with a spiritual preceptor. If he or she is devoted to you, he or she finds a preceptor by your grace and is absolved of the wordly bondage, as nescience shall have no hold and consequently disappear."

"Indeed for hundreds of thousands of epochs even, it is not possible for individuals to obtain salvation and beatitude if they are reverse to love and devotion towards you."

"I, therefore, wish that I may always have close association with your devotees and have deep aspiration to your lotus feet perpetually throughout my life and hereafter if there be any such. Your devotees shower the nectar of love upon others and easily sanctify not only their disciples, races and others but also purify the whole world."

"Oh the Master of the Universe, the symbol of love, the graceful and Supreme Soul, I bow to you again and again. Whatever I have done for the sake of the world may be virtually connected with this great bow of your self."

Rāma said, "I am pleased and your wishes shall be fulfilled."

Parashurāma highly delighted requested again, "Rāma, kindly grant your love and association with your aspirants to me for ever if I have been so much favoured. Please grant also that this invocation, by any person though he may not be fully devoted to you, may bring about at last salvation, knowledge and abiding remembrance of your benign self if he earnestly recites it."

Rāma said, "Be it so".

Parashurāma with due repects took leave of Rāma with his regardful approval, and went to Mandarāchal mountain.

King Dasharatha very joyfully and tenderly hugged Rāma as if he were saved from the jaws of death and they reached Ayodhyā safely.

All the brothers lived very happily with their wives to the great satisfaction of their parents. Rāma lived with Sītā as Lord Viṣṇu lived with Laxmi in the paradise.

King Dasharatha sent Bharata and Shatrughna along with their maternal uncle Yuddhajit who had come to take them to his state.

Kaushalyā was also very happy with Rāma and Sītā similar to Aditi who lived with his son Indra and daughter-in-law Sachi, the daughter of Paulamī.

Rāma, well known to the goodness of all the worlds, is really the Supreme God always blissful, immanent, immutable, everywhere perpetual and divinely prosperous. He is the true beatitude, highest bliss of human beings, though he is beyond the sphere of illusion, he used to live with Sītā in Ayodhyā, playing the role of a human being faithfully and ideally. He is Rāma, the Universal and Supreme Lord indeed.

PART II

AYODHYĀ KĀṆḌA

Chapter I

LIFE OF RĀMA IN AYODHYĀ AND HIS EXILE

Once divine sage Nārada unexpectedly visited Rāma and Sītā having descended from the heaven privately. Rāma very gladly received the sage. Nārada looked like a celestial being. Rāma requested him "Kind sage, today I am very lucky to see you. I am very grateful for your kind visit because worldly persons like me rarely find the opportunity of availing the visit of divine sages. Their presence on the earth and instructions benefit the humans richly. Please allow me what I can do for you."

Nārada replied humbly, "Rāma, my lord, the glory of the heaven, why are you beguiling me ? You are, of course, just saying that you are worldly. Your better half is Supreme Māyā, the creative energy itself which gives birth even to Creator Brahmā himself as well as other creatures. She possesses the three principal forms of whiteness, redness and blackness—three Guṇas (attributes called quiscent, materialistic and predatory.) Māyā, or the illusion is inseparable from you and it creates the universe and its creatures. You are the saviour and the sustainer of the three worlds— the heaven, the earth and the nether land.

"Though you appear to be a householder you are the incarnation of Viṣṇu and Sītā is Laxmī. You are the creator Brahmā, you are Indra, the god of the heaven and dieties, the God of fire, the God of death, Yama and Sītā Saraswatī, Paulami, Swāhā and Samyamini. Oh Rāma, all the male gods and male living beings are you only and Sītā the female ones."

"Māyā has overshadowed the soul. It is named as "Abyakrit" which is ignorance by which the soul and illusion cannot be differentiated. The nature and other elements are the creations of Māyā only and the ego, the gross, the subtle and the casual bodies or forms of all individuals are also material as produced by nature god, the reality, immortal and immutable resides in the body of every creature in the form of soul or self. The individual self is with bodily attachments, but the supreme self is without them. In all the three stages of human life, i.e., waking dreaming and sleep the supreme soul exists as the witness."

"Rāma, you are the same soul living as tne witness within every living being invigorating him life or consciousness like that of the lamp that gives light to a room. Birth, growth, decay, change, destruction, misery and happiness of the beings are from you since you are omnipresent and omnipotent and are the first cause of the creation."

"Man gets finally liberated from the bondage of worldliness when he realizes that he is not different from God. It is so because, in fact, the soul in him which is the only reality is none but God Himself. Man assumes wrongly himself to be a different being not knowing that he is the part and percel of the Supreme Soul and that is why he is in delusion and is an ignorant self. He is similar to a man who fears a string when he mistakes it for a snake. But when he is able to discard this division, he is the realised soul."

Every individual should try to attain salvation. Oh Lord, it is available to your devotees to whom I am the humblest slave. Please be kind to me so that I may not be further debused as I am your grandson. It is because my father got his birth from your naval."

Nārada in ecstacy further requested with humble

bows, "King Dasharatha intends coronating you as Yuvarāj (heir apparent) tomorrow. I am afraid you may not go if you accept the throne. So Brahmā has sent me to remind you of your mission."

Rāma smilingly replied "I shall certainly kill Rāvaṇa and keep my words. There is nothing which remains out of my knowledge. I am very truly leaving Ayodhyā tomorrow and going to forests and shall kill Rāvaṇa after he kidnaps Sītā. I will perform my mission in many other ways also as be required."

Nārada happily took leave and flew to the heaven.

The discourse between Rāma and Nārada is considered to be very sacred and it is sure to grant salvation in proper times to those who earnestly read it.

Chapter II

MANTHARĀ POISONS KAIKEYĪ'S YEARS

Once King Dasharatha in a calm and quiet atmosphere said to Vashiṣṭha, "Lord", I desire to coronate Rāma on my throne as my heir apparent tomorrow without fail as he is beloved from all sides. Please inform him and make preparations also for the coronation ceremony.

He also ordered his Prime Minister Sumantra for making preparations for the ceremony according to Vashiṣṭha's instructions.

Vashiṣṭha also ordered Sumantra to bring all necessary articles and invite sages, Brahmins, noblemen, fuedatory chiefs, and princes. Among other articles, chief things were many gold pots filled with holy water, the royal ensign made of gold and precious stones, tiger skins ornamented with gold and gems, numerous garlands, necklaces, etc.

Sixteen beautiful maidens gorgeously decked with gold ornaments, musicians, the infantry, the chavalry, war elephants, sixteen specimens of four tusked elephants of Airāvata elephant's breed, decked with gold ornaments ordered to be present at the royal place compulsorily together with a decorated umbrella and a staff.

Vashiṣṭha also ordered to make managements for worshipping all gods and dieties installed in the temples throughout the city. He soon reached Rāma's great palace in a chariot, crossing the three pathways.

Rāma and Jānakī entertained him very respectfully falling flat on his feet which they also washed in great reverence.

Rāma sprinkled the water of Vashiṣṭha's feet on his head and humbly requested, "Lord, I am really blessed having the water of your holy feet."

Vashiṣṭha happily replied, "Divine Lord Shiva had

been blessed with your feet's water and my father Brahmā too could atone for his sins by touching your holy feet which is like the most sacred pilgrimage. "You are only behaving towards me in this manner for setting a good example for the people to follow. I know that you are Lord Viṣṇu and Sītā goddess Laxmi and have come as incarnations to relieve the earth of the burden laid by the demons and thus to discharge the mission for the welfare of the gods and human beings. I am your preceptor in this earth only whereas in fact you are the preceptor of the preceptors, the father of fathers as you are omniscient, unthinkable, inexpressible, immutable. Your incarnation as a human being on earth is by your own sweet will along with your unfathomable energetic Māyā."

"The priesthood in fact is not a suitable job which I have accepted only because I had known from Brahmā that you would be born in Ikshwāku's family. Today my desire has been fulfilled because I have been related to you as your preceptor.

If you are really kind to me, please remove my ignorance and never allow your illusion to prevail upon me. Please do so if you want to discharge your duties towards me as your priest and preceptor which you have even called me.

"Rāma, king Dasharatha has asked me to inform you that he is going to coronate you on his throne tomorrow. You, therefore, be prepared in proper manner as you will have to obsereve fast and sleep on the ground together with Sītā.

In a matter of my talk with you I have pointed out some thing in connection with your divine birth but I tell you that it should remain undivulged."

After Vaśiṣtha's departure Rāma said to Laxmaṇa, "Brother, you are lucky because you will chiefly enjoy and I shall remain only a passive agent if I am coronated. You are indeed a part of my life. Rama followed the words of Vashiṣṭha who thereafter hastened to Dasharatha and delivered to the king every word which he had said to Rāma.

Somebody very gladly reported the news to Kaushalyā and Sumitrā who very gladly gave some reward to the reporter.

Kaushalyā prayed to and worshipped the Goddess Laxmi for the success of the ceremony. She doubted also that King Dasharatha was truthful. He might not keep his words being under Kaikeyī's influence so she worshipped Goddess Durgā as well.

On the other side Saraswati, the goddess of speech influenced Mantharā's and Kaikeyī's mind on the suggestions of gods and Brahmā by putting hindrance to the performance of the ceremony.

Mantharā, the hunched woman with three knots, at once went to Kaikeyī in a very anxious mood knowing that Rāma would be installed on the throne as heir apparent and said, "Foolish lady, how are you so carelessly lying at ease ? Don't you know that misfortune has knocked at your doors ? Proud lady as you are, you take vanity in your beauty only without caring for anything else. Mind, Rāma is going to be coronated on the throne tomorrow."

Kaikeyī was much pleased to know from Mantharā that Rāma was going to be coronated the next day. She instantly gave her neckless to her (Mantharā) as an award for the auspicious good news. How dare you say that misforthune is befalling me? Rāma really loves me even more than Bharata does, and he is more gentle and good natured and always treats me as his own mother Kaushalyā. Fool, what makes you scared of Rāma ?

Jealous Mantharā replied, "The king only pleases you by sweet words and allures your mind in lust whereas he actually works a beneficiary to Kaushalyā. That is why he has sent Bharata with Shatrughna to his maternal uncle's house and in his absence he is going to bestow the throne on Rāma. Sumitrā will be happy indeed because Rāma loves Laxmaṇa who will enjoy the benefit of Rāma's rule, but I am afraid Bharat may be banished and it will be no wonder if he may even be put to death. It is also certain that you shall have to serve Kaushalyā as her slave. Death is far better than this sort of subjection under a co-wife.

"You, therefore, should get Bharat installed on the throne by banishing Rāma for fourteen years. In this way, you will be the queen mother. I have also thought out a plan for its success. Long ago King Dasharatha had promised to give you two boons when you had saved him during a battle holding the axis of the chariot, the screw of which was broken. The proper opportunity for you to utilise the boons promised to you by the king has arrived."

"You should immediately go to the dark room and lie in an angry mood throwing off your garments and ornaments until the king comes you and complies with your requests.

Kaikeyī was thus instigated by Mantharā's speech which she deemed beneficial and said "Mantharā, well done. You are really my wise well-wisher, and I shall follow your advice and do accordingly. I shall also give you one hundred villages if Bharat succeeds to the throne."

Mantharā returned gladly by poisoning Kaikeyī's ears.

Queen Kaikeyī too instantly entered into the dark room which was meant for one who wanted to express anger. She lay down in wrath on the floor in shabby clothes and muttering to Mantharā that she would risk her life even so long as Rāma would not be exiled to the forests.

An evil company definitely spoils one and it deeply affects even a good natured, dutiful, intelligent, erudite, virtuous, efficient and pious person. One should therefore always avoid evil company otherwise one has to meet the fate like that of queen Kaikeyī.

Chapter III

KAIKEYĪ'S ANGER

King Dasharatha went to Kaikeyī's apartment in happy mood but was disappointed at her absence. He was greatly terrified when he discovered that she was in the dark room giving vent to anger. He said to her very afffectionately, "Dearest queen, why are you lying in the room in such a way ? I am much afflicted on finding you in such mood. Please tell me your intentions and speak to me. I am ready to do anything for your satisfaction. I am even prepared to give up my life, take away or grant life to any person and make beggar a prince and vice versa for your sake. I swear upon Rāma who is dearer to me than my life."

Kaikeyī gradually moving and opening her eyes replied, "You had promised me two boons long ago. Please fulfil them by granting the throne of Ayodhyā to Bharata and banishment to Rāma for fourteen years."

"Rāma shall have to live in dresses of barks and leaves and eat wild fruits for that span of time. You are a truthful king well known everywhere. If you do not comply with my requests, I will commit suicide."

King Dasharatha fell upon the ground senseless when he heard such harsh words, like a tree dashed upon the ground by the stroke of a thunderbolt.

He however gathered some courage and requested the queen in a soothing voice.

"Truly are you so much hostile to Rāma whom you love as you say from the your bottom of your heart and even more than Bharata. Let the throne be granted to Bharat but be kind to Rāma and do not banish him as he never harms any body."

The king fell on her feet and entreated her very humbly, but she was all the more enraged and harshly uttered.

"Why do you boast that you are truthful ? If you cannot keep your promise even swearing upon Rāma, it will certainly fling you to the hell and I shall commit suicide tomorrow."

King Dasharatha again fell in a deep swoon and passed the night miserably. Next morning every thing was punctually ready for the coronation and its celebration. Music and drums were played on but Kaikeyī angrily stopped the musicians.

All the brahmins, priests, the courtiers together with the public had also been already present and had been waiting outside the courtyard of the royal palace. All the boys and the citizens were standing by the sides of streets and parks to see Rāma going with sublime and gorgeously in procession with royal guards and followers as required by the grand ceremony.

Sumantra very anxiously entered the palace when the king was not seen at very late hours.

He saluted the king who was downcast with agony and he asked Kaikeyī humbly about the king's health.

She replied "The king has not slept for the whole night in anxiety. Please bring Rāma very soon."

The king also ordered him to fetch Rāma immediately.

Sumantra hastily reached the mansion of Rāma and requested him to go to king's palace instantly with him.

Rāma though anxious silently went to see his father. He saw the king in great despair lying on the bed. The king tried to embrace Rāma when he came there but he felt too weak to hold him in arms. Rāma raised and took him on his laps embracing him reverently and affectionately.

All the attendants began to shed tears at the deplorable condition of the king and Vashiṣṭha and other officers also reached there.

Rāma enquired the queen about the king's distress. Queen Kaikeyī replied.

"The king had promised me two boons long ago. I have now demanded them by granting the throne of Ayodhyā to Bharata and sending you to exile for fourteen years. He felt hesitant in telling you, and I hope you will prove yourself a worthy son by making good your father's words."

Rāma replied cheerfully "I am happy to do so. I can take poison, renounce the throne, desert Sītā, mother and every other pleasure for king's sake."

Dasharatha very sadly said, "Son, how can I live if I send you to forests ? Please dethrone me. I am unjust and unfit to rule. You will not commit any crime by doing so. How can you roam into forests being so tender and ease-loving ?"

Rāma tried to console his bereaving father and said, "Father, there is no difference between I and Bharata. Moreover I shall accomplish god's mission by going to forests. Please allow me to go without hesitation."

Rāma then went back to his palace and he soon reached Kaushalyā's apartment where she was sitting with eyes closed and immersed in God Viṣṇu's meditation. She was observing worship for his welfare. She did not see even Rāma approaching there as she was holding communion in her internal heart with Viṣṇu, the emblem of effulgent and eternal consciousness and of beatitude.

Chapter IV

RĀMA PREPARES FOR THE FOREST

Kaushalyā was informed of Rāma's arrival by Sumitrā. She opened her eyes and taking Rāma upon her laps very fondly offered him various dainties.

Rāma very humbly requested her, "Mother, I have no time for taking food because I am instantly leaving for forests by the king's order. Mother Kaikeyī has demanded the fulfilment of the boons by granting the throne to Bharat and banishing me for fourteen years. I shall live very peacefully as a hermit in the forests and return safely. Kindly do not worry."

Kaushalyā was hard hit and became senseless for a while. She was overwhelmed with grief and said to Rāma.

"Son, take me also with you for I would not live alone in your absence similar to the cow without her calf. The king could have given his throne and all his wealth for Kaikeyī's boons, but it is sheer injustice on his part to banish you who is innocent."

"Mother is greater than father and the preceptor in respect of relation. I, therefore, prohibit you from going to forests. I shall instantly commit suicide if you disagree."

Laxmaṇa, who was also present there very angrily said to Rāma.

"Dear brother, I may even bind the king who is infatuated by Kaikeyī and shall kill Bharata and his maternal relatives. Be prepared to take the throne by force. I am ready to defend you with my mighty bow against your enemies.

Today the people of the worlds shall notice my valour capable of burning down the whole world."

Rāma embracing Laxmaṇa very peacefully replied, "I know very well that you are my great well-wisher and are valourous too, but it is not worth the occasion."

All the pleasures, prosperity, the kingdom, and even our bodies are short-lived as the lightning appearing in the sky. Our span of life is as shortlived as the drop of water falling on a heated iron. The individuals only hanker after pleasures though they are in the death's clutches for every moment similar to a frog catching a fly to eat though itself is being caught by the snake in its mouth."

"It is in fact surprising to note that men are only engaged in material pleasures and business. The self is quite different and separate from its perishable material body. All the relations such as parents, brothers, wives, and sons are with the body not with the soul, which is the only Reality and Master of the body. Such relations too are so transitory and temporary as the dusts of sands accumulating on the sides of river-water which washes them every moment. Prosperity is like bubbles of water and sexual pleasure is like a dream. The individual takes pride in such a short-lived life which is also always painful and miserable by diseases, fatal coincidences, difficulties and uncertainties. The life becomes shorter and shorter as each day is passing on and it is similar to water stored in a raw earthen vessel which dwindles away drop by drop."

The ignorant person thinks that his material body which is composed of only bones, skins, blood, urine, and such other matters and which are easily turned into dusts and ashes, in his real and everlasting form. He thinks himself to be a king or such and such person, only in ignorance and vanity."

"To think oneself to be a body is only foolishness and is the cause of one's attachment for worldliness. The individual therefore, seeks after knowledge perpetually by knowing his soul, the reality and for the attainment of salvation."

"Laxmaṇa, remember that desires and anger are

great obstacles for the attainment of knowledge. Anger is enough for upsetting the mind because angry persons do not shirk from killing even their parents and other near and dear ones.

It entangles the persons into wordliness by affecting morality and conscience.

"You should, therefore, give up anger, the greatest enemy of man. Desire is also like the infernal Baitarṇī river which cannot be crossed. Contentment is only useful like a celestial fruitful garden and peace is like" Kāmdhenu, a divine cow that fulfil's pious men's wishes." If you are serene and tranquil, you will have no enemies to injure you. The soul is apart from the material intellect, sense organs, and the mind of the body. It is self enlightened, immortal, immutable, stainless and formless. The man suffers from misery because he does not know his soul. If you know the reaility you will be free from wordly bondages and conquer your casual desires which, in fact, bother one. You, therefore, lead your life peacefully being unattached towards happiness or misery which is only the result of your present and past deeds. Always think of your soul which is separate from your material being. Dear Laxmaṇa, spend your life calmly without caring for weal or woe. It is not all worthwhile to display your valour for bodily enjoyments and, therefore, give up the idea of fighting for the kingdom." Rāma then falling flat on the feet of Kaushalyā, very earnestly requested for her favour to allow him to go to forests. He further assured her to bear in mind what he had said and to await for his return with patience, for a period of fourteen years. It would pass away easily. This will also please him leaving devoid of worries for her.

She too at last consented and said, "May all gods—Brahmā, Shiva and Viṣṇu be kind and take care of you in the forests whenever you sleep, wake or go for anywhere!"

She embracing Rāma very affectionately bade him farewell.

Laxmaṇa also said to Rāma, "You have dispelled my ignorance and doubts and now I am prepared to follow you to the forests. I will die if you refuse.

Rama said, "Dear brother, be ready at once if you so wish."

He met Sītā in her room, who hastily brought a pot of water and washed his feet. She also requested him, "Lord how did you reach here alone ? Where are your royal ensign, attendants, the royal robes and the crown? I see no nobles, feudal chiefs and officers attending upon you."

Rāma replied calmly and cheerfully. Blessed lady, father has granted me the kingdom of forests and I am leaving Ayodhyā very shortly. Please stay here to wait upon your mother-in-law.

Sītā anxiously asked, "Lord, why did your generous father send you to forests ?"

Rāma replied, "Father has granted the throne of Ayodhyā to Bharat and has banished me for fourteen years for the fulfilment of two boons which he had long ago promised to bestow upon mother Kaikeyī. I hope you will not put any hindrance on my way."

She happily answered, "It does not look well if you go alone. Let me also accompany you to there. It does not behove you, my lord, to go away without me."

Rāma very much pleased with Sītā said, "How can I take you to the dreary forests, abounding with wild and ferocious animals and demons. Even sour and wild fruits are scarcely available. All paths are thorny and only caves and ditches are found for shelter. I fear you will lose your life if you go to forests undergoing such hardships. So please remain at home."

Sītā replied sorrowfully in anger, "How would you,

being a kind and pious husband, think of leaving a dutiful wife ? I suppose I have committed some guilt for which you intend leaving me. I can live with you very happily and every hardship will be turned into ease by your grace if I accompany you. Even food left by you shall be my nectrine food. I shall not trouble you in any way, but some day I may be helpful to you in your discharging the god's mission according to the prediction of an erudite astrologer. If you really refuse to take me with you I will die instantly."

Rāma at last agreed to take her along with him and said to her.

"Be it so then as you wish. Offer your wealth, ornaments to the preceptor's wife Aurandhatī and other Brahmins and get ready to start today."

Rāma, pleasing all the Brahmins, his own and mothers' servants by presenting the riches, got ready to start and soon went to his father to take leave of him. Sītā and Laxmaṇa also followed him. Laxmaṇa also offered gold dresses to Brahmins as Rāma had done and entrusted his mother Sumitrā into the hands of Kaushalyā.

Rāma as handsome as thousand of gods of beauty, and resplendant as the azure sky enlightening all the directions slowly walked on foot with Sītā and Laxmaṇa towards his father's palace while all the public was curiously and sorrowfully watching him going on the way and purifying the whole earth with his feet.

Chapter V

RĀMA LEAVES FOR FOREST

All the people having heard the news of Rāma's banishment got agitated. They assembled there and when they saw Rāma with Sītā and Laxmaṇa on the way they began to murmur with one another. They got prepared to follow Rāma going to forests as they preferred not to live in Ayodhyā without Rāma. They blamed Dasharatha and Kaikeyī for the cruel deed, uttered harsh words and critical remarks.

Meanwhile sage Bamadeva said to the angry citizens.

"Gentlemen, do not be angry. Rāma is God's incarnation. In very ancient times on many needful occasions Lord Viṣṇu had assumed many forms including the ten renowned incarnations for welfare of humanity in the earth by the power of his Yogamāyā called illusion. Rāma is going to forests now definitely for killing Rāvaṇa and all other evil demons who are tormenting, on all sides, the people, sages and the saints. Yesterday sage Nārada secretly met Rāma who also told him that he was going to forests the next day for accomplishing God's mission."

"Dasharatha and Kaikeyī are also influenced by Yagamāyā and that is why they have in this way banished Rāma. You should not therefore blame them since they are overpowered by illusion."

"Rāma is really Supreme God to whom there can be no trouble in the world. His name sanctifies even the sinners. You will be happy and pious if you chant his name every time and love him knowing him to be the incarnation of God Viṣṇu".

Rāma, followed by Sītā and Laxmaṇa, reached the apartment of Kaikeyī and said.

"Mother, we are ready for forest. Please allow us."

Kaikeyī gave the dresses of barks to them. Rāma

and Laxmaṇa put off their royal dresses and wore the new ones. Sītā was standing by them with the forest dresseṣ when Vashiṣṭha said to Kaikeyī that she should not allow Sītā to wear barks because she had no right to banish her. He added that she was to follow Rāma as a dutiful wife.

The women in the harem shed tears at the rending sight.

King Dasharatha deeply under severe agony ordered Sumantra to take Rāma to the forests on the grand chariot.

Rāma, Laxmaṇa and Sītā soon left the palace and took the way towards the forests.

King Dasharatha some time later desired to visit the apartment of Queen Kaushalyā. When he reached there he fell on the floor senseless. A few times later when he regained senses, he remained silent and could not even move on account of grave afflictions.

Rāma very swiftly left Ayodhyā but all the old and young citizens, and boys ran after the chariot with determination to accompany Rāma wherever he went and they all reached the banks of Tamasā river that day. Virtuous Rāma and Sītā guarded by Laxmaṇa with his bow passed the night under a tree and felt cheerful though they were without food. Early in the morning they in the chariot hastily driven by Sumantra went away towards the forests leaving all the citizens asleep who had been greatly desirous of following Rāma.

Finally Rāma arrived at Śringaberpur, the kingdom of his very intimate friend Guhā who immediately came up to Rāma, his frend and gracious master, with various presents and delicious fruits, which Rāma thankfully accepted and accorded generous embraces to his host friend.

Rāma along with Sītā and Laxmaṇa stayed under a shady Sinshapa tree at the night lying on the ground upon the mattress of Kusha grass.

He did not eat the fruits offered by Guhā because as a hermit he could not take things brought from a village or a city. He twisted his hair making a tuft upon the top of the head with the juice of "Bata" tree.

Guhā very humbly requested "Greatest and most brilliant scion of the Raghu race, my Lord, today I am very fortunate to have the opportunity of greeting you. Kindly live in my kingdom which is but yours, and let us go to the city and sanctify my house too. I am simply your humble and obedient servant and every thing belongs to you."

Rāma very affectionately replied, "I can neither live in a house in any city nor take food offered by any other body. You are my very dear friend. Kindly excuse me for my inability to comply with your requests."

They all spent the night there drinking only the pure water while Laxmaṇa was awake all the night keeping vigil over them and he was fully satisfied at the forest bed which he had already constructed for the complete comfort of his adorable brother Rāma and Sītā.

Chapter VI

RĀMA MEETS VĀLMĪKI

Guhā shedding tears at the sight of Rāma and Sītā asleep on the ground very sadly said to Laxmaṇa.

"Brother, providence is the most powerful in man's life. Just see, Rāma and Sītā, the most prosperous and glorious royal couple now sleeping upon the grass while the gorgeous beds are lying vacant in the palace. Really Kaikeyī has proved herself to be the sinful woman at the instigation of Mantharā."

Laxmaṇa replied, "Friends, nobody else is to be blamed for man's weals and woes. It is his destiny that determines his life because man's life has its own origin from his own deeds of past lives. There is no importance upon his being prosperous or miserable. They are natural and inevitable in course of life. "Nobody can live either happily or miserably for his whole life. Both happiness or misery come in man's life turn by turn. In the same way are seen man's friends, foes or mediation according to the results of his good and evil deeds of the past. So far what should we be elated with pride or be disappointed at woes ?"

"Really speaking there is misery hidden in happiness and happiness in misery. They are always mixed similar to mud. For this reason I remain always unattached by anything whether favourable or unfavourable. In fact it is the best policy for a man to be noncalent towards his condition of life. Whether he be prosperous or miserable, he has got to spend his life. He shall be peaceful only if he does not hanker after happiness and if he is not disheartened during his adversity. These happen just like dawns and sunsets in the pilgrimage of life."

The day broke when Laxmaṇa and Guhā were talking with each other, and Rāma and Sītā got up and said to

Guhā, "Friend, kindly arrange a boat for us."

"Meanwhile Rāma too, performed morning rites and Guhā brought a nice and strong boat and himself rowing it took all of them across the river safely. When they reached the middle of the Ganges Sītā prayed.

"Mother Ganges, I shall worship you very earnestly and ritually if I return with Rāma and Laxmaṇa safely from the forests."

In the meantime the boat reached the other bank, but Guhā was very unwilling to leave Rāma and said.

Lord, take me also with you otherwise I shall die instantly.

Rāma consoled him saying, "Friend, do not worry, I shall certainly return after the lapse of fourteen years. My words are never false."

With repeated embraces, Rāma parted from Guhā who also reluctantly agreed with sinking heart. Rāma together with Sītā and Laxmaṇa reached the Sage Bhāradwāja's hermitage. They conveyed the message of their arrival to the sage through a Brahmin boy.

Saga Bhāradwāj knowing this very gladly and respectfully greeted Rāma with Sītā and Laxmaṇa and worshipped them with due formalities and etiquettes.

He prayed to Rāma "Lord, my penances have been fruitful today. I know that you are Supreme God Viṣṇu incarnated as the human being to fulfil the desire of Brahmā, the Creator by killing evil demons and Rāvaṇa. You are, therefore, going to forests and will certainly accomplish your mission for the good of the people on the earth. By your grace, I can know the events of the present, past and future and I am sure that every thing will go smoothly according to your wishes."

They also reciprocated their homage to the sage and Rāma told him,"Lord, we are but the human beings who need your graceful blessings."

They passed the night in the sage's hermitage. The next morning Rāma, with Sītā and Laxmaṇa arrived at Chitrakūṭa having crossed river Yamunā and went to sage Vālmīki's hermitage. That place was very pleasant with sages, birds and beasts and lasting fruits and flowers all around. They respectfully bowed to the reverent sage. The sage was amazed at seeing Rāma so handsome and resplendant in the garb of a hermit with tufts of heir upon the head.

The sage immediately stood and very tenderly embraced Rāma in ecstacy with eyes full of beaming tears, worshipped him and offered delicious fruits in his entertainment.

Rāma with folded hands said, "Lord, we have arrived here on our way to the forests by father's order and the reason is fully known to your holy self. Kindly direct me to some comfortable place where I may be able to pass sometime with Sītā and Laxmaṇa.

The sage smilingly replied, Rāma, you dwell in all the creatures of the world and they live in you, and there are indeed the common residences of yours and the entire creation. But your special homes and temples with Sītā are within the hearts of those that earnestly love you day and night regardless of good or evil and are non-malignant, peaceful, prideless, devoid of temptation and greed, content with your meditation, amicable, surrendering themselves to you, equal minded with no difference between lumps of gold and dust and happiness and misery knowing the world to be illusionary, detached from worldiness, now have faith in you having realised by constant practices of penances, and contemplated your eternal and supreme reality." Really yours as well Sītā's dwelling places are the hearts of those who know you to be immutable, stainless, omniscient, ominipotent and omnipresent."

"The significance of chanting your name and glory is indescribable and unknowable, for by dint of chanting merely your holy names I have been made a high class sage beyond my imagination."

"In my youth, I was a robber living in association of Kirātas a forest tribe, and had also married a low caste woman though I was born a Brahmin. I used to rob travellers who would pass by. In my base profession of a plunderer, I used to roam about here and there with arms in quest of wealth for the support of my life and many sons at the cost of life and property of others."

"Once I met divine seven sages whom also I wanted to waglay. They knowing my motive told me to ask my wife and sons one by one whether they were also the partners of the sins commited by me for their maintenance. I ran to them and asked them but they told me that they enjoyed upon my labour only and had no concern with what I had done for them. I returned from home dejected and my heart got purified by the association of saints who were waiting for me. I instantly threw away my bows and arrows and fell upon their feet for my redemption."

"Sages were pleased to see that my mind was changed by their humane advice. They unanimously bent to uplift me and told me to chant your name in reverse or opposite way "Marā" thinking me to be a great sinner and unworthy of chanting Rāma."

"I then began to chant Marā very earnestly and soon I was deeply immersed in contemplation. I forgot my bodily existence also. I had been remaining in such a condition for years together as even my body was covered with the clay accummulated by white ants. After lapse of innumerable decades and centuries, seven sages again visited me and got me out of the mould of clay under which I was enveloped deeply immersed in meditation. I was totally changed and was as illustrious as the rising sun appearing out of the clouds."

They said to me, "Sage, your name is Vālmīki since you have emerged out of the sands with the new form of the most exalted sage. Thereafter they went to their celestial abode. So I see you now vis-a-vis and I am perfectly absolved."

Sage Vālmīki followed by his disciples, took Laxmaṇa to a beautiful place by the banks of the Mandākinī and they all built two nice cottages, one stretching from east to west, the other from North to South.

Rāma and Sītā lived very comfortably in one cottage and Laxmaṇa in the other one.

Sage Vālmīki and all other residents were very happy with Rāma's association who also lived with Sītā as merrily as Indra with Sachi.

Chapter VII

THE PASSING AWAY OF DASHARATHA

Sumantra duly returned to Ayodhyā with his vacant chariot by the sunset. He went to see the king with reckless mood.

He bowed down before the King who very anxiously said to Sumantra.

"Where are Rāma, Sītā and Laxmaṇa? What did they say about me, the cruel sinner? He wept crying Rāma, Rāma. Oh ocean of virtues, Sitā, Oh the most truthful lady! Do you not feel for me sinking as I am in the ocean of grief ?"

Then Sumantra reported to the sorrow stricken king.

"Lord, I took them in the chariot upto Śringaberpur by the side of the river Ganges. The king of Nishāda, Guhā met Rāma and he presented various articles and delicious fruits. Rāma did not eat any thing but touched it with thanks. They halted under the shade of a tree and twisted their hair of the head with Bota juice. He said, "Sumantra, please tell the king not to worry. I am as happy and content here as I was in Ayodhyā. Convey my regards and homage to mothers and request them not to be anxious for me, but take special care of old and wearied father."

He further added, "Sitā too shedding tears and humbly looking upto Rāma told to convey her respects to her mother-in-law and went off bending down her head. I watched them crossing the river and also when they were across the river safely."

Kaushalyā weeping said to the king, "You had better given the wealth, and the throne to Kaikeyi's son Bharata for the fulfilment of the boons. Why do you now weep in vain when you have banished the innocent and noble Rāma ?"

The king was greatly hurt by her speech as if he were burnt and he replied in anguish.

"There is no doubt that I am sinking to death. It is needless now to trouble me any more."

"In my early life, a sage had cursed me that I should die of grief of my son's separation."

"I was very fond of hunting wild beasts, and I was roaming in the night in search of some hunt. I heard a sound by the side of a river. I shot an arrow towards that direction instantly in darkness as I thought that some elephant was drinking the water. A sage-boy was filling water in his pot, and the arrow hit him directly. He cried in pain and was about to die when I reached to see him. I begged pardon of him and said that he was Vaisya and asked me to pull away the arrow from his body and to take the waterful pot to his old and blind parents who were languishing by thirst in the cottage at some distance.

"I then approached to pacify them as I was afraid of being burnt off by their curse. The old parents were great saints and they got terribly hurt to learn from me that I had killed their son by mistake. I begged pardon. They had been anticipating their son's return and they were upset to know that I was King Dasharatha. After hearing every detail from me, they told me to take them to the place where their son was. I, who was completely lying on their mercy, took them there. They clasping the corpse of their son, were greatly afflicted and the old and blind sage cursed me saying "King, you will have no other trouble but meet the same lot and die in grief on the separation of your son." I then hastily made a pyre for their dead son, and the old couple burnt themselves along with their dead son in the same funeral pyre."

With these words, King Dasharatha fell dead, crying "Rāma, Sītā, Laxmaṇa. I am to pass away due to the sage's curse connected with the Kaikeyī's boons."

Kaushalyā, Sumitrā and other began to bewail beating

their breasts.

Next morning sage Vashiṣṭha went into the harem where the king lay dead. He consoled the queens and prescribed the king's corpse in a beautiful oil and sent horse riders to Yudhajit's kingdom to deliver his (Sage's) messenger to Bharata· asking him to reach Ayodhyā immediately with Śatrughna.

Bharata and Śatrughna very anxiously returned with the followers to Ayodhyā as swiftly as they could thinking that some calamity had befallen over Ayodhyā.

They found the city gloomy and lonesome and met Kaikeyī alone in the room.

Bharata anxiously requested her, "Mother, where is my dear father who would never leave you alone ?"

Kaikeyī was very glad to see Bharata whom she blessed very affectionately on his arrival and inquired of him about her parent's health. Then she said to him.

"Your father has taken the same course that pious kings who having performed Aśwamedhas had to follow. Oh sinless and dutiful son, do not worry."

Bharata fell on the ground and cried "Dear father, you have left me so suddenly even without entrusting me to Rāma."

Kaikeyī raised weeping Bharata and softly she said. "Dear son, have heart, you are lucky. I have arranged everything for your prosperity."

Bharata asked her, "Mother, has father left any instructions for me?"

Kaikeyī replied fearlessly, "King died only crying Rāma, Sītā, Laxmaṇa."

"Were Sītā, Rāma and Laxmaṇa also not present at his death. Had they gone somewhere else? Bharata asked anxiously."

Kaikeyī answered, "King Dasharatha was preparing to perform celebrations for Rāma's coronation. I created hindrance and demanded the throne for you and the banishment to Rāma in the life of hermit for a period of fourteen years. I did so in fulfilment of two boons which the king had promised me long ago. "The truthful king accorded the throne to you and sent away Rāma to the forest."

Dutiful Rāma immediately went to forests to carry out his father's orders.

Chaste Sītā and Laxmaṇa obedient to Rāma also followed him.

The great king died soon after in extreme tormentation.

Bharata, like a tree struck with a thunderbolt fell senseless on the ground. Some times later he told his mother who was trying to console him.

"I am very sinful having been born of such a sinful and evil woman as you. You shall certainly go to hell as you have killed your husband. Do not blab out such cruel words. I shall die very soon either by burning or by poisoning myself."

With these angry and harsh words he at once went to Kaushalyā's mansion where he found Rāma's illustrious and adorable mother extremely weak by grief and anxieties.

She very sorrowfully said to Bharata, "Dear son, now you have heard of the fatal incidents. Rāma too has left me in the ocean of misery by going to forests as a hermit with Sītā and Laxmaṇa. I know my son Rāma to be Supreme God, but I am still in great agony. The fate is the most powerful decree."

Bharata holding her feet requested, "Mother, I swear upon my preceptor and his wife Arundhatī if I had any hand in sending Rāma to exile."

Kaushalyā embracing him tenderly said. "Son, do not worry. I know fully well that you are innocent."

Sage Vashiṣṭha with other councillors met Bharata

and affectionately said.

"Bharata, you are mourning the king's death for no reason. The king had performed many Aśwamedhas and had become very aged, was renowed all over the world as most truthful and valiant, had begotten God Rāma as his son and at present after the death has attained equal seat with Indra in the heaven. He is now emancipated from worldly troubles and is very happy."

"There is no ground for grief even at the death of any man, because his soul is immortal. He has no birth or death and his material body only perishes. Ignorant persons only cry in grief whereas the wise ones take lesson from the death of their family members, even, because they know that body is subject to destruction with transmigration of life and death according to the merits and demerits of one's past actions. The soul changes the body as we change our garbs."

"The soul has no birth and death and it is always happy, content, enlightened, immutable, infinite, imperishable, without modifications, and is the prototype of Supreme Lord, unique and immanent everywhere. You should know your soul which only is your real existence and pass your life peacefully performing your duties.

"Please take out your father's corpse from the tub of oil and duly perform his funeral rites with us and ministers."

Bharata, thus advised by Vashiṣṭha, performed the funeral ceremony and completed all the rituals according to Vedic rites giving lots of wealth, thousands of cows, numerous villages, clothes, and jewels to Brahmins for the well-being of his father living in the heaven after death.

For sometime Bharata, with his brother Śatrughna remained at Ayodhyā, but he was very much aggrieved and so could not live with family in the absence of Rāma, and he made up his mind to meet Rāma in the forests as early as possible so that he might be able to render his services to Rāma and Sītā with their smiling faces and favourable appearance and to be far away from the presence of his devilish mother Kaikeyī.

Chapter VIII

BHARATA'S DEPARTURE TO FOREST TO BRING RĀMA BACK

Sage Vashiṣṭha together with the ministers, learned persons and saints held a meeting and said to Bharata.

"Dear Prince, we are installing you on the throne today according to the wishes and orders of your late father who had ultimately fulfilled his words for boons to Kaikeyī.

Bharata politely replied.

"Great and honourable sage, what is the use of kingship to me when Rāma, the greatest of all the kings lives in the forests? We are all his slaves only. I have determined to go to forests to see Rāma and bring him back to Ayodhyā. Let all of us accompanied by all the mothers except the devilish woman Kaikeyī in the guise of my mother go to the forest where Rāma is staying. I had a mind to kill Kaikeyī, but cannot do so only because Rāma cannot pardon me for the crime of killing a woman."

"I shall go on foot with Śatrughna and shall live as a hermit wearing barks only and shall lie upon the ground in a hut. I shall lead the cottage-life until he returns."

All the people including Sage Vashiṣṭha were very much pleased at the faithfulness of Bharata towards Rāma and they exclaimed.

"Well, what a grand thought!"

Next day early in the morning, Bharata took the royal army, elephants, horses, chariots, and all the queen-mothers, Sumantra, priests, Brahmins and sage Vashiṣṭha with him to the forests and he and Śatrughna walked on foot wearing barks and binding tufts of hair.

All the citizens thronging all the roads and footpaths followed him in great enthusiasm.

The grand army was led by Śatrughna.

All the followers, thus made their halt at Sringaberpur by the side of the river Ganges.

Guhā on knowing this, suspected if Bharata was going to harm Rāma and he wanted to know the reason of Bharata's arrival to meet Rāma. He thought that he would allow Bharata to proceed further if his intention was fair, otherwise he would even fight with Bharata to force him to stop. He ordered his boatmen to collect all the boats on the middle of the river and ordered his men to ready with bows and arrows.

Guhā went to meet Bharata taping delicious fruits and articles of presents. He saw Bharata in a hermit's dress sitting with his councillors and brother Śatrughna and chanting Rāma Rāma".

Guhā respectfully fell flat upon the ground and paid his homage to Bharata.

Bharata raising him up from the ground warmly in fraternal affection, happily enquired about his well-being and said.

"Brother, you are really blessed by meeting Rāma with Sītā and Laxmaṇa and obtaining the favour by way of his sweet embraces and talks. You are so much fortunate. Please take me to the spot where lotus eyed Rāma had taken rest in the night and had met you."

Then Bharata could see the Kusha grass upon which Rāma had slept, and his eyes were filled with shedding tears in love.

A few particles of the ornaments and of gold embroideries of Sītā's dress were scattered there and Bharata shed tears at the sight and said.

"How could Sītā, beloved daughter of Janaka, sleep upon the grasses as she was habituated to the gorgeously decorated bed, she had to suffer for my sake in this way. I am really a sinner. Lamxaṇa is really lucky and happy with Rāma though in forests. Oh I would certainly have been fortunate had I been even the slave of the slave of Rāma's devotees".

He asked Guhā.

"Brother, I am going to meet Rāma. Do you know where he is these days ?"

Guhā replied.

"Lord, you are indeed blessed because you have no deep affection for Rāma.

Rāma lives in Chitrakūṭa by the bank of the river Mandākinī. He is very cheerfully dwelling with Sītā and Laxmaṇa. Let us go there."

He sent for five hundred boats for taking the army and other persons across the Ganges. He himself rowed a royal boat carrying Bharata, Śatrughna, Kaushalyā and the Sage Vashiṣṭha.

Bharata and Śatrughna went to see the sage Bhāradwāj in his hermitage. The sage as resplendant as the fire was very happy to see king Dasharatha's sons whom he entertained very respectfully.

The sage enquiring after their health said to Bharata.

"Why are you wearing barks and going to reclusories instead of ruling over the country?"

"Bharata shedding tears replied."

"Lord, you are omniscient. What is the use of the kingdom to me while Rāma is living in forests ? I swear upon you holy self that I have no hand in Kaikeyī's evil deeds. Śaturghna with their followers could also see the bark-dresses of Rāma hanging over the walls of the cottage.

Chapter IX

MEETING OF BHARAT TO RĀMA IN THE FOREST

Rāma's cottage looked very pleasant. The dear skins, bows, quivers were hung upon the walls and beautiful lawn with flower plants in front of the hut added to its beauty.

Rāma was sitting with Sītā and Laxmaṇa, and he was engaged in chatting with them cheerfully.

Outside the cottage, he looked very illustrious shining as the sun enlightening all the directions.

Bharata and Śatrughna saw foot-prints of Rāma upon the ground at some distance of the cottage and very respectfully bent their heads upon them which had divine marks such as conch, mace, disc, and lotuses, sought for even by Brahmā and other gods with devotion.

Bharata saw Rāma sitting on the parlour clad in new barks with tufts of hair nicely bound on the head glancing towards Sītā and allowing Laxmaṇa to softly press and rub his feet.

Rāma raised Bharata up who was fallen on his feet to pay respects and placed Bharata on his laps with tender embraces and affectionate tears.

Kaushalyā and other queens too very eagerly met Rāma like the thirsty cows running to drink water.

Rāma paid his respects to his mothers and preceptor Vashiṣṭha saying again and again "I am blessed."

He offered them seats respectfully and very eagerly asked about the welfare of King Dasharatha.

Vashiṣṭha said.

"Dear Raghunandana, your father passed away under severe pangs of separation from you. He remembered you all and uttered every time "Sītā, Rāma and Laxmaṇa."

Rāma fell upon the ground in profound sorrow. Sītā and Laxmaṇa too cried, "We have lost all."

Everybody present there including the queens began to weep. Rāma cried, "Dear father, where have you gone having left me helpless?"

Vashiṣṭha consoled them and they took funeral bath in the Mandākinī and performed "Srāddha" ceremony of the late father and offered water to his soul. Rāma and Laxmaṇa offered Inga fruit mixed with honey for his appeasement. Then all the queens, Bharata and Śatrughna took bath in the river. After observing the morning fast they took rest that day.

The next day Bharata approached Rāma and humbly requested.

"Respected brother, kindly return to Ayodhyā and accept the throne because it is not the time for you to lead the life of recluse in forests. Rule over the kingdom and perform Aśwamedhas and other sacred ceremonies. Be kind to me and forgive me for what mother Kaikeyī has done."

He fell flat upon the grounds earnestly pleading Rāma in such a manner. Rāma raised him from the ground and taking him on his lap calmly replied.

"What you have said is right but we could obey our parents, and, therefore, you should rule over the kingdom and I should go to forests in accordance with the settled order. One is liable to suffering in the hell if one acts against one's father's will.

Bharata replied.

"You should not care for the words of father who had gone mad in lust with his wife."

Rāma answered.

"Father had really kept his promise very truthfully. I shall also follow his example to keep my promise by sojourning for fourteen years only in forests and then go back to Ayodhyā."

Bharata said, "I shall be a recluse in a forest for your sake if you kindly go back to Ayodhyā."

Rāma replied, "We will be false even if we reverse our father's order, because he has given the throne to you and the forest life to me."

Bharata said at last, "I shall at once die if you do not allow me to follow you as you have allowed Laxmaṇa to do."

He sat on Kush grass intending to die if Rāma refused.

Rāma made a silent occular hint to his preceptor Vashiṣṭha for consoling Bharata. Sage Vashiṣṭha took him apart and talked privately.

"Son, do not insist on Rāma's return to Ayodhyā. He is the incarnation of Lord Vishṇu as the son of Dasharatha. Sītā is Laxmī and Laxmaṇa is Śesha. They are going to kill Rāvaṇa and other demons for maintaining the welfare of sages and the people.

"Kaikeyī also is not to be blamed as she had to yield unknowingly to gods' will otherwise how could she come about. Kindly return to Ayodhyā cheerfully and do not harass Rāma any more. He will certainly return after fourteen years having accomplished his mission."

Bharata was much surprised to hear it and he at once returned to Rāma and requested, "Please give me your sandles as the token of yourself. I shall worship and attend upon them as I used to do upon you till you return." He with great devotion put a pair of sandles studded with gems on the feet of Rāma who returned them to Bharata.

He then with repeated bows said in inspiration to Rāma.

"Lord, I shall certainly leap in the burning fire if even a single day expires after the lapse of the scheduled fourteen years."

Rāma consoled and very affectionately bade farewell

to Bharata and all other people. Satrughna made all arrangements of the return journey of Bharata with holy sage Vashiṣṭha, queen mothers, ministers and the army.

Kaikeyī approached Rāma and very meekly said.

"Kindly pardon me for my evil deeds. Good persons are really like oceans. They can forbear mischief done to them. You are no doubt supreme Lord Vishṇu and the whole universe is your illusion."

All the creatures dance upon your sweet will similar to the wooden dolls that dance by the pulling of the strings of the dance-maker.

It is clear that I had acted upon your will because it is you who really wanted to go to forests for fulfilling God's mission. Infinite soul, you are not accessible even to other gods by their speech and mind. Oh Lord of the Universe, I recommend myself to your holy feet. Kindly cut off my worldly ties of false affections for sons, near and dear ones.

At this Rāma with a smiling look replied.

"Mother, it is correct what you have said. Every thing has indeed, happened by my desire alone. You are not to be blamed in any way. Now return to Ayodhyā and if you earnestly remember me, you will be detached from worldly objects and attain salvation."

"I am equal to everybody and have no attachment to any body in particular like that of a magician who has no attachment to his feats of magic. Though I am impartial I am benign to every one. I am answerable to those persons who need me or think of me every time. Ignorant persons do not know my real form and purpose and you are indeed blessed because you have known me now in a right way."

Fully satisified Kaikeyī took leave from Rāma. Bharata came back with all the followers and after pacifying all the subjects he repaired to Nandigram outside Ayodhyā to live there as a hermit remembering Rāma and his mandates. He placed the sandles on the royal throne and used to worship them very earnestly.

Satrughna also loved in the same manner eating fruits and wearing barks and lying on the ground.

Bharata used to perform all the religious and royal duties regularly as if he were a devotedly humble servant of the sandles. He would pass time in chanting Rāma's name waiting his safe return in due time.

Rāma, Sītā and Laxmaṇa lived for some days more at Chitrakūta and went to the forest of Dandakāraṇya since people had begun to throng there day by day. They reached Sage Atri's hermitage and met him. Rāma with polite words said to the sage illuminous as the moon.

"Lord, today I have availed myself of the opportunity of seeing you on my way to Daṇḍaka woods in course of my scheduled period of exile."

The exalted sage knew them to be divine incarnations and greeted them with delicious fruits very happily. He requested Rāma, "Lord (Allow Sītā to see my religious and dutiful old wife, Anusuiyā."

Rāma asked Sītā to go inside and meet the sage's wife with due respects. Anusaiyā very happily embraced and greeted Sītā who had fallen upon her feet for paying respects.

Anusuiyā then presented two earrings, two pairs of silken saris, and divine face powder to Sītā, and said.

"Your beatuy will be preserved by the use of the powder. I bless you that you will return to Ayodhyā safely, and serve your husband.

Very faithfully, Rāma's mission will also be successful in time and you will return home along with him."

She offered food to Rāma and Laxmaṇa and also prayed them.

"Lord, you create the whole universe by your illusion

and you assume the forms of God, man, lower animal and even fish for maintaining peace and welfare of all the creatures of the world. You are not attached to your creations though you live within them. Your Māyā is always under your fear and control though that can delude the whole Universe.

PART - III

ARAṆYA KĀṆḌA

Chapter I

THE FOREST LIFE: THE KILLING OF BIRĀḌHA

Next day Rāma set out for Daṇḍaka forest with the consent of Sage Atri who saw him off. He asked the sage boys to take him with Sītā and Laxmaṇa across the river.

They took their way onwards and entered into very dense and dreary forests which abounded with various ferocious animals. The forest resounded with different melodies of chirping and singing of birds and insects and it was demons' dwelling place as well.

Rāma told Laxmaṇa, "Brother, the forest is very dreary, we should be alert and be very cautious and ready with bows and arrows for use and Sītā should walk in between us. I shall go ahead and you follow Sītā.'

Sītā looked as if Māyā were standing veil in Jiba which is Laxmaṇa from the sight of the God Rāma.

They reached at a beautiful lake which was engulfed with gorgeous aquatic flowers all around. They drank the water that was so cool and clean.

Meanwhile a dreadful giant came over there holding a heavy spike in which many human corpses were pinned. He looked very ferocious with his long jaws and his bulky body was devouring the flesh of wild animals and elephants while he walked towards Rāma who was sitting on a slab of stone along with Sītā and Laxmaṇa.

Rāma told Sītā not to be afraid of him and asked Laxmaṇa to be ready for fight with his weapons.

The giant roared, "Who are you clad in barks like

hermits but holding bows and arrows as well as accompanied by a woman so beautiful? You are just a morsel for my mouth."

Rāma smiled and replied, "I am Rāma. She is my wife Sītā and he is my brother Laxmaṇa. We have come here in due compliance with father's orders so that we may be also able to teach lessons to such persons as you."

The giant again roared angrily.

"Do you not mind myself who is a very dreadful demon devouring all the sages in this area? My name is Birādha, and I am well known to all the residents of this locality. If you want to save yourselves, fly away from here leaving Sītā and bows and and quivers." Birādha ran to catch hold of Sītā, but Rāma severed both his arms by the shot of an arrow. Birādha still leapt towards them, his mouth wide open. Rāma immediately cut both of his legs by another shot and still he crawled forward to swallow up Rāma who severed his head from the body by the third shot.

The giant fell upon the ground streaming in a pool of blood. Sītā was very happy to see it and embraced Rāma. Drums were sounded in the heaven expressing joy and fairies danced while dieties, Gandharvas and Kinnaras sang delightfully. .

A handsome man as luminous as the rising sun dressed in robes adorned with gold appeared out of the corpse of the demon and paid his homage to Rāma very humbly and respectfully falling on the feet with these words.

"Lord, I am Bidyādhara, whom Sage Durbāsā had turned into a demon by his curse. Be kind enough to favour me so that my mind may be always concentrated towards you in love and I may spend my time in worshipping you on hearing your life stories and singing and praying. I know you to be Supreme God and I wish to go to the heaven.

Kindly bless me so that your illusion may not delude me any longer."

Rāma said, "It will be as you wish. You have attained salvation, knowledge and aspiration by my contact with you. Your evil desires will be eliminated by my favour and you are free to go to the heaven."

Any person is entitled to the full attainment of all his or her desires or aspirations if he or she sings in applause of holy Sītā and names of Rāma who killed the most horrible demon (Birādha) and absolved him from sage's curse, favouring him with the graceful boon and restoring once more to his godship of Bidyādhara.

Chapter II

MEETING WITH SUTĪKSHṆA

Rāma together with Sītā and Laxmaṇa arrived at Sarbhangha's hermitage. The renowned sage Sarbhangha was exceedingly happy to meet them and he greeted them warmly.

He prayed to Rāma, "Lord, today my penance has borne me the desired fruits. I have nothing more to do in this world and I desire to leave this mortal form in your presence. I offer the fruits of all my good deeds to your feet. You are just like "Kāmadhenu" the desire yielding divine cow and have come at my mere remembrance."

He then lit fire in a huge pyre of wood and deeply immersed in meditation of Rāma and Sītā, burnt himself in it. His soul assuming the divine form ascended to the abode of Brahmā, the Creator.

Soon after all the aspirants and sages observing penance inhabiting the locality arrived there to pay respects to Rāma. They entertained him in the garb of a human being with Sītā and Laxmaṇa that he should free the hermits from the torture of the demons as he had incarnated for that purpose. Then the sages took him to different reclusions in the forest reminding him that Vishṇu himself had appeared as the four sons of King Dasharatha.

Rāma saw innumerable human skeletons scattered to and fro in the forest and enquired with surprise.

"Good sages! Why are so many skeletons seen in this place?"

The sages replied.

"Lord, these are the skeletons of the sages and saints devoured by demons when they were absorbed in meditation."

Rāma was deeply moved and he solemnly promised

that he would kill in course of time all the evil demons who had eaten up so many saints and sages.

Rāma stayed with Sītā and Laxmaṇa for some years with sages and seers who used to attend upon him with great respect. He later on went to far-famed Sutīkshṇa's hermitage which would be very pleasant in all seasons. It was an ideal dwelling place with all the comforts for sages and recluses. He too received Rāma, Sītā and Laxmaṇa warmly and offered them delicious fruits very happily. He was one of the great aspirants and a favourite disciple of the exalted sage Agastya and he had already attained divinity by chanting Rāma's name continually.

He prayed to Rāma.

"Rama! oh elegant, virtuous, graceful Lord of Sītā, Lord Shiva, Creator Brahmā all other gods devoted to your lotus like feet that take aspirants across the troublesome worldly ocean. You are really formless and imperceivable. But you have been very kind as you have assumed the human form and have personally met me who am but your humble slave entangled into worldly bonds with sons, wife and brothers."

"You bestow favour upon those who chant your name earnestly. But other people cannot find if you even dwell within themselves."

"Lord, you are creator, sustainer and destroyer of the universe assuming forms of Vishṇu, Brahmā and Shiva. Your illusion called Māyā with the attributes (quiscent, material and predatory) always act upon your will. You appear in each and every form of creation such as man, bird, insects and beats like the sun reflected upon different pots of water.

"I am confident that you have been very kind and pleased because I behold you at my own hermitage incarnating yourself in the very charming and handsome human form with your bow and arrow in the company of Sītā and Laxmaṇa. Many aspirants like to know your supreme form of Brahmā, infinite, limitless, formless, beyond space, time and nature, but I like your charming human form only."

Kindly favour me so that I may constantly remember and see your human form alone.

Rāma smiled and said.

'I know that you cannot live in peace without seeing and remembering me. Really your mind has been sanctified by the ceaseless chanting of my names. I have, therefore, personally visited you. There is no other way of realising me. They who practise yoga and chant my names earnestly renouncing worldly pleasures, certainly see me face to face and gain my favour.'

"You have got your worldly ties thoroughly cut off even in your life time owing to my grace. Rest assured that you shall be united with my soul after the death."

"May those who shall hear and read the invocation shall obtain pure knowledge and my love."

Sutīkshṇa requested humbly, "Rāma, you will kindly see the hermitage of my preceptor Agatsya tomorrow and I too shall follow you there as I have not seen him for a pretty long time.

The next morning, Rāma, highly desirous of conversing with Agatsya, accompanied by Sītā and Laxmaṇa and guided by sage Sutīksṇa reached the hermitage of Agatsya's younger brother on their way.

Chapter III

SAGE AGASTYA GREETS RĀMA

They halted that day at Agatsya's brother's hermitage with full hospitality and reached sage Agastya's residence the next day.

Sage Sutīkṣṇa informed the high souled Sage Agatsya about Rāma's arrival and happily paid his respects. Sage Agatsya who was sitting amidst his many disciples and other sages and was earnestly explaining religious matters as well as significance of Rāma's name, happily got up to welcome Rāma. He greeted Rāma, Sītā and Laxmaṇa outside his hermitage. He conducted them inside holding the hand of Rāma and he said to him.

"Lord, kindly get in. You are my beloved guest. I am very fortunate today by receiving you due to the result of my good deeds and penances."

Rāma, Sītā and Laxmaṇa fell upon his feet for paying their respectful homage.

Sage Agatsya embraced Rāma in ecstacy of joy with his eyes filled with beaming tears. He offered very decent seats to them and entertained them with sweet fruits and various nice articles of presents.

After worshipping Rāma very earnestly sage Agatsya prayed.

"Lord, I have been waiting for you at my hermitage because Creator Brahmā had requested you for descending upon the earth. Supreme God, you were the only existence prior to creation. You are inaction and detachable from all your creations and always are accompanied by Māyā or illussion called Avidyā, which veils you. Your Māyā is called nature, ignorance, the worldliness, the bondage or creative energy."

"The sum total of elements i.e. Nature in the shape of primus beginning in your energy which acts upon your will and becomes the generator of Mahat tattva and Ahaṅkāra, the ego. Mahat tattva appears in three-fold natural activities, or attributes which are quiscent, material and predatary (Sāttvic, Rājasik and tāmasik) together with the intellect and five fine elements of matter created by nature i.e. sound, feeling, shape, smell, and liquid, Sabda, Sparsha, Rūpa, Gandha and Rasha."

"The Universal Ego by its quiscent or peaceful nature creates the astral bodies, by material or Rajas nature creates sense organs and by predatary or Tāmasik nature creates matter and its five gross natural substances i.e. Earth, with odour, water, the liquid, fire, the light, ether and air with feeling, touch etc. They all mixed together through your influence constitute the subtle body called Sutratma. The whole universe including all creations, animate or inanimate, with its mystic Master God is called Virāt or Vishwa."

"Lord of the universe, you have manifested your own self into all creatures in the world. You are Lord Vishṇu as the sustainer, Brahmā as the creator, Shiva as the annihilator of the universe. You are inactive and exist as the witness within every creature and you exist beyond the sphere of one's mind whether awake in dream or sleep. When you play as it were the part of worldly drama, Māyā, comes before."

"So it is the mind of a living being that acts according to the activity of the three Guṇas—quiscent, material and predatary forms, but not the soul or God who only grants energy or consciousness to the body."

"Your Māyā or illusion has two functions called Vidyā or Avidyā i.e. knowledge or ignorance. The individuals are attached to worldliness by their ignorance and attain salvation and peace by detachment and knowledge. None can attain knowledge better than those who chant your name and have faith and love in you. It is very difficult to gain knowledge that grants salvation without devotion."

"The best means for attaining salvation is to have associations with saints and aspirants.

Real saints and the most sincere devotees feel no disturbance even in calamity, they have no attachment to worldly objects and its prosperity and remain equal in happiness as well as misery. They have control over mind and sense organs. They are peaceful in all the circumstances of life and are always content and happy with whatever they earn sincerely. They are really dexterious in finding the easy way of salvation."

"Lord, I wish to live always with such saints only. Kindly grant me such a boon by which I may gain such saintly acquaintance for ever and wherever I live."

"Lord, my mission of life and penance have been certainly successful today by meeting and adoring you. Lord, the greatest of the race of Raghu, kindly allow me to enshrine you in my heart, with Sītā so that I may never miss you."

Sage Agastya pleased Rāma with this sincere invocation and presented him a bow, a quiver and a sword with its handle made of gold, left in charge of the sage by Indra for Rāma's sake.

The sage then requested.

"Lord, please accept these weapons and destroy all the evil doers and demons for the welfare of the people in the earth, and stay at the nice place called Pañchabatī by the side of the Gautamī river as long as it is needed for the hidden purpose."

The omniscient Lord Rāma, on hearing the sweet and significant words of Agatsya, duly followed the route hinted out by the great sage. Thus Rāma in very happy mood resumed his onward journey.

Chapter IV

THE PHILOSOPHY OF LIFE

Rāma saw the vulture Jaṭāyu of very awkward body like a hill and took him to be some ferocious demon. He said to Laxmaṇa.

"Let me have my bow and arrow. I am going to shoot down the strange creature standing on the way."

Jaṭāyu hastily requested Rāma, "Kindly do not kill me. I am your father's friend named Jaṭāyu and your well-wisher. I shall guard Sītā during your stay at Pañchabatī."

Rāma embracing him said very affectionately.

"Sir, kindly live in the vicinity of our cottage and help us in the hours of need."

Rāma selected a very healthy, quiet and pleasant spot with excellent fruit trees around by the side of the Gautami river.

Laxmaṇa constructed two cottages skilfully and they lived there in much peace as if they were in the heaven.

Laxmaṇa would serve Sītā and Rāma daily by bringing fruits, water, and flowers from the forests and keep watch over them the whole night with the bow in his hands. They would take baths in the river daily and enjoy the beautiful landscape.

Laxmaṇa was very happy in attending to Sītā and Rāma with obedience. One day he requested Rāma in a quiet mood.

"Lord, I desire to hear from you spiritual preachings so that I may gain real knowledge with deep experiences, devotion and detachment from mundane world to attain salvation. I see no person more learned and competent than you."

Rāma replied.

"Dear Laxmaṇa, I shall explain to you the most secret philosophy by knowing which a person can get over worldly ignorance. First I shall explain what Māyā or ignorance is, then about the unfailing means for the attainment of knowledge, with mature experiences to follow and also about the supreme soul whereby an individual transcends worldly fears and misconceptions for good."

"Ignorance creates a false impression between the body and the soul by which the worldliness appears. For it has two forms—one by building castles in the air and the other by hiding the real knowledge or the Supreme Soul, like that of the appearance of the snake in the rope.

"The individual therefore cannot know the soul, the real self and thinks himself to be material body and is confused in distinguishing the reality from material objects. In reality ignorance has no existence. It is illusion just like dreams and day-dreams, so long an individual is ignorant, he is worldly with birth and deaths continuously occurring to him. All the actions are done by the body but not by the soul. Attachment and relationship to ones family, pleasure and happiness and misery are also with the body only. The body is made of five gross elements of nature i.e. earth, air, fire, water, ether and five subtle phenomena, i.e. sound, feeling, form, liquidness, and odour, and the ego with ten sense-organs and intellect. The soul which is in the body is entirely separate from all these material combinations. In fact Supreme God and the soul are one and the same."

"An individual gains knowledge of his soul if he renounces variety, shows, violence, adopts simplicity, has tolerant nature, performs holy deeds, renders services to his fellowmen, obeys his preceptor and parents, controls his desires, lives in indifference to his self-interest, is not disturbed by worldly talks and calamities, loves me or God and studies philosophy and holy scriptures and practises yoga.

These are the unfailing means for spiritual knowledge and the reverse shall have the opposite result."

The soul is omniscient, omnipotent, immutable, omnipresent, without modification, self-existent, free, perpetual and immortal.

Nothing more is needed for attaining salvation for the soul which is eternally free.

The individual's bodily ties and ignorance are removed if he knows his soul."

"This is salvation by means of self-realisation, the soul is stainless, free and eternal. To know this with faith and devotion is to reach the spiritual goal which is always available to every person. Just as a person cannot see anything in darkness without light, he cannot gain spiritual knowledge and know his soul or God without devotion and love in the same way. So inner light only is necessary for one to realise one's own self."

"To render services to my dear aspirants to worship me, or my image with faith and love, to sing my name and read my life story, to keep fast on holy days as eleventh lunar days, to celebrate holy festivals and to help the poor and the needy assuming them as forms of god, are the general ways for obtaining my love which certainly lead to real salvation.

"Dear brother, keep these facts in your mind and lead your life accordingly. Do not tell these spiritual secrets to them who have no faith in god, but try to advise my aspirants whenever you come in contact with them. Let me assure you once again that he who is always up and doing in search of company with and services to pure hearted and realised souls or my constant devotees, will have their salvation within themselves or at his own fingers end as I am always seen by him face to face but never by him who is not so."

Chapter V

SŪPARṆAKHĀ EPISODE

Rāvaṇa's sister Sūparṇakhā happened to see Rāma in Pañchabatī. After assuming a beautiful girl's form she came to Rāma and said.

"Gentleman, who are you so handsome and young in the garb of a hermit? Why do you live in such a dreary forest leaving your home?

Rāma replied.

"I am Rāma, son of King Dasharatha of Ayodhyā, and have come along with my wife Sītā and brother Laxmaṇa into the forests having been banished for a period of fourteen years. So, we are here to obey our father's order."

Sūparṇakhā said.

"Rāma, I am king Rāvaṇa's sister Sūparṇakhā. I live here with my younger brother Khara and devour saints and sages when I come across them. The forest is left in my sole charge. Please accompany me and appease my lust as I am very much fascinated by your youthful and handsome appearance."

Rāma replied her with a slight gesture towards Sītā.

"Gentle lady, you may persuade my brother Laxmaṇa who has no wife with him. You shall feel miserable to live together with my beloved Sītā from whom I cannot part."

Sūparṇakhā went to Laxmaṇa and said "Dear gentleman, your brother has sent me to you. Please take me to forests and be my husband."

Laxmaṇa replied her.

"Lady, I am Rāma's slave. How shall you be happy in slavery?"

Sūparṇakhā again went to Rāma and said angrily.

"Rāma, why do bore me in vain by sending hither and thither? Look, I shall devour Sītā if you do not agree to follow me."

She ran towards Sītā when Laxmaṇa caught hold of her and chopped her nose and ears on Rāma's hints. She flew away howling and crying awfully and reached her brother Khara, the great leader of the demons.

He asked her anxiously.

"Sister, what is the matter? Who is the unfortunate devil that has invited death by chopping your nose and ears in this way?

Weeping bitterly she replied.

"Rāma, who is living with his wife Sītā, ordered his brother Laxmaṇa to cut my nose and ears off. Please kill him at once and get me his flesh and blood for my food otherwise I shall kill myself instantly."

Khara ordered Dūshaṇa and Trishirā immediately to array fourteen thousands of soldiers for the fight against Rāma and start the march.

The two mighty warriors led the army and attacked Rāma dreadfully hurling upon him big stones, trees and hillocks.

Rāma asked Laxmaṇa to at once enter into the cave and he alone advanced to meet them.

He miraculously killed all of them including Khara, Dūshaṇa and Trishirā, the mighty leaders in a moment by flinging thousands of arrows together in one shot of the bow

Sītā on his return was pleased at the sight of the highly miraculous deed of Rāma and softly dressed the wounds he had received in the fight.

Sūparṇakhā was extremely terrified at Rāma's wonderful feat. She flew to Rāvaṇa's Lankā immediately.

Rāvaṇa was also much terrified and was taken aback to see his sister in wounds and he anxiously enquired her.

"Sister, who has mangled your nose and ears ? He certainly merits death at my hands, however great and valourous he may."

Sūparṇakhā retorted angrily.

"Addicted to drinking bowls, luxurious and foolish, how do you rule over the kingdom when you have no knowledge of such serious happenings in your kingdom?"

I suppose you do no care to appoint state-spies or detectives. Rāma with his wife Sītā and brother Laxmaṇa is fearlessly living at Pañchabatī in Ḍaṇḍaka forest. "I tried to bring Sītā, the most beautiful woman in the world for your wife, but Rāma ordered Laxmaṇa to do away with my nose and ears. When I went to Khara, Dūshaṇa and Trishirā they taking fourteen thousand soldiers had a fight with Rāma. But he killed them all in a very short time. I wonder whether Rāma could destroy the universe even."

Rāvaṇa consoled his sister with sweet and encouraging speech but became very pensive about the matter. He thought within himself that no human being could kill Khara, Dūshaṇa and Trishirā.

Rāma, therefore, must be some God's incarnation having descended on the earth with the intention of killing him (Rāvaṇa) as well as other evil doers at the entreaty of the Creator Brahmā for maintaining peace and welfare on the earth.

He made up his mind to fight with Rāma boldly in the battle. If he succeeded, he would enjoy the pleasure of the demonic king; and if he got killed by Lord Rāma, he would have the heavenly kingdom. So he thought it far better to indulge in enemity with Rāma, because he knew that he could no easily please Rāma by mere devotion or any other peaceful means. Rāvaṇa believed within himself that Rāma is no other than Supreme Hari and that his death at his hands would procure for him the highest place in Elysium.

Chapter VI

THE MĀRĪCH EPISODE

Intelligent Rāvaṇa approached Mārīch who had become a hermit and used to always pass his time in meditation.

Mārīch was alarmed at the unexpected appearance of Rāvaṇa, he however respectfully received him and requested.

Lord, kindly tell me the reason of your visit in such a melancholy mood. I am ready to help you and shall carry out your orders if they are not sinful.

Rāvaṇa replied.

"Rāma, the eldest son of Dasharath, the king of Ayodhyā, with his exceedingly beautiful wife Sītā and his brother Laxmaṇa is at present living at Pañchabatī by the side of Gautamī. He has cut off the nose and ears of Sūparṇakhā and has even killed Khara, Dūshaṇa and Trishirā together with fourteen thousand warriors. I want your help for kidnapping Sītā as I want to abduct her when you, assuming the form of a beautiful gold deer, take Rāma and Laxmaṇa far away from the cottage."

Mārīch was aggrieved and said surprisingly.

"Lord, who is your enemy giving you such a perilous idea? Rāma is certainly invincible. I am extremely terrified at his unthinkable valour. He had flung me thousands miles away by a shot of a blunt arrow when I went to foil Vishwāmitra's yajña ceremony. I had been tossed in the sky once more again when I attacked him by assuming the form a deer, intending to kill him with my sharp and strong horns."

"Since then I have been abiding safely at this hermitage and I am so much horrified by his deeds that I feel his presence every moment whether I am asleep or awake. Even the first letter of his name horrified me.

Lord, please give up the idea of enemity with Rāma and save your dynasty running from ancient times. You should better be devoted to him chanting his names.

Rāma is very kind and he will save you."

"I have known from the sages that Rāma is Lord Vishṇu's incarnation and he has descended upon the earth by Brahmā's request for relieving the earth from the burden of sins by killing you also."

Rāvaṇa got enraged and answered.

"If Rāma is an incarnation of God, so much the better, let him do his mission. I shall be emancipated. If he is a man only, I can easily have Sītā with me. Do as I have told you, if you utter a word more I shall put you to death instantly with this sword."

Mārīch thought, "I shall certainly attain salvation if Rāma kills me, but will go to hell if Rāvaṇa does so."

So he said to Rāvaṇa.

"Lord, forgive me. I shall certainly carry out your wishes."

Then Mārīch went in front of Rāma's cottage in the form of a very beautiful deer with gold body spotted with silver dots with hoofs and horns of precious stones and with eyes of sapphire. Thus he began to frolic about in front of Sītā in various ways.

Chapter VII

THE KIDNAPPING OF SĪTĀ

Rāma also knew that Rāvaṇa would arrive there in a monk's garb to kidnap Sītā. He, therefore, said to her in seclusion.

"Sītā, fabricate an illusionary form of yourself on the earth and remain hidden with your real self in the fire till I kill Rāvaṇa who is reaching here to kidnap you shortly."

Sītā did accordingly. A little later illusionary Sītā saw the gold deer and requested Rāma.

"Lord, look at the strange and pretty deer. Please give its skin to me."

Rāma said to Laxmaṇa.

"Brother, I am going to shoot the deer while you keep watch over Sītā. Be cautious of those ferocious demons lurking in the forests."

Laxmaṇa said.

"It is Mārīch who has assumed deer's form. How can a natural deer be like that?"

Rāma said.

"Be it so, still I shall kill him. You should carefully guard Sītā against any kind of mishap."

Then Rāma followed the deer which ran away alluring him and reached far away in the dense forest.

It seems to be funny that omniscient, omnipresent and omnipotent Rāma, the Supreme God, was following the deer. But he did so as a human being to prove himself true to his promise to his devotees. Rāma then shot at the deer which fell dead and it changed itself into Mārīch and cried in pangs of death pronouncing in Rāma's voice.

"Oh Laxmaṇa, come out immediately for my help. Oh! I am dying."

Mārīcha's soul was amalgamated into Rāma's self. It is God's grace that Mārīch attained highest type of salvation, because he was in the very presence of Rāma. Some one uttering Ram's name at the last moment of death is certainly entitled to eternity.

All the dieties witnessing the death of Mārīch were surprised to find that an evil demon like it with all his atrocities in the past, had turned suddenly into a life of penitence by uttering Rāma's name all the time bringing about his salvation.

Rāma hastily returned to the cottage suspecting some evil actions of demons.

Sītā said to Laxmaṇa.

"Why do you not care for Rāma's call?"

Laxmaṇa humbly replied.

"Goddess, it is not Rāma's words, but some demon has cried at his death. No body can harm Rāma who could destroy the three worlds if he wished."

Sītā shedding tears cried in anger.

"Dishonest Lamxaṇa, you harbour ills of Rāma. Do you dream that you can possess me if Rama dies? I can neither touch you nor Bharat but kill myself instantly."

Lamxaṇa was greatly touched and enraged and shut his ears and said.

"Fie upon you, you shall suffer for your harshness and meanness."

He then left her and went to meet Rāma. Rāvaṇa then appeared at the cottage holding a stick and a bowl in the garb of a brahmin beggar.

She respectfully paid her homage taking him to be a saint and said.

"Your holiness, accept these fruits and rest for a while if you like. My husband and brother in law will soon arrive here and they will entertain you better."

Rāvaṇa said.

"Who are you so beautiful and elegant a woman? Oh you lotus eyed!

Sītā replied.

"I am the daughter of Janaka, the king Mithilā and wife of Rāma who has come here from Ayodhyā to live in exile for fourteen years in compliance of his father King Dasharath's orders."

Rāvaṇa said.

"I am Rāvaṇa, King of Laṅkā and have arrived here to take you away. Please follow me. You will not gain anything better by taking pains in living in forests with Rāma."

Sītā distressfully retorted.

"You really deserve death by Rāma's arrows.

Can a lion's wife be taken by poor rabit?

Rāvaṇa turned red in rage and soon appeared in his real form with ten heads and twenty arms, very black and dreadful and as big as a hillock.

All the dieties fled away in fear. Rāvaṇa then took a lump of earth upon which Sītā was standing and placing it together with Sītā upon his chariot flew away in the sky, while she was crying for help.

"Save me, oh Rāma and Laxmaṇa, where are you? Oh Laxmaṇa, I have really committed a crime for blaming you wrongly."

August Jaṭāyu, the vulture king caught Rāvaṇa's chariot flying in the sky and said.

"Villain, where are you taking Sītā away, like a dog stealing away the oblation from the sacrificed area? Stop. He rocked the chariot and the bow and Rāvaṇa with Sītā fell on the ground.

Rāvaṇa cut the bird's wings by his heavy sword and flew away with Sītā in another chariot leaving the vulture heavily bleeding and gasping for death.

Reckless Sītā was crying all the way "Lord Rāma, save your helpless wife. Oh Laxmaṇa, forgive me. I have rent your heart with cruel words."

She, seeing some monkeys on a hilltop, threw her ornaments bound with a piece of cloth towards them thinking that they would one day meet Rāma.

Rāvaṇa on reaching Laṅkā placed Sītā under the shade of Sinshapa tree in his garden named Ashoka and in the midst of demoness as her guards and thus began to protect her like mother. But Sītā had to live there very miserably and deplorably always crying "Rāma."

Chapter VIII

MEETING WITH JAṬĀYU

When Rāma returned from the forest by killing Mārīch he met Laxmaṇa on the way. He knew that Sītā had been certainly absent from the cottage. He reviewed mentally the diverse purposes to be duly fulfilled by him. So he disparingly told Laxmaṇa.

"Brother, why did you leave Sītā alone? Some mishap must have befallen."

Laxmaṇa replied.

"Lord, Sītā insisted upon my going to see you when she heard a voice calling me which closely resembled yours."

Rāma said.

"You have not done right by doing so."

Rāma hastily went towards the cottage and did not find Sītā. He pretended to be very sad like an ordinary man and began to bewail. He with Laxmaṇa immediately left the cottage in search of Sītā and roamed aimlessly hither and thither. He was seen much afflicted at Sītā's missing and seemed to have lost the balance of mind. So he behaved like a man, sometimes hugging a beautiful flower plant and addressing other beautiful objects of nature around there. He would cry also loudly calling Sītā in vain.

At a distance Rāma and Laxmaṇa saw a broken bow and a shattered chariot scattered upon the ground.

Rāma said.

"Brother, some strange creature has snatched Sītā from one who had kidnapped her from the cottage."

They at length saw vulture king Jaṭāyu bleeding profusely to death at a little distance further.

Rāma said.

"Brother, here is the demon who devoured Sītā. Let

me have my bow. I shall shoot him down. Jaṭāyu slowly spoke.

"Rāma, I am Jaṭāyu approaching death. Rāvaṇa cut my wings and wounded me when I had a fight against him to release Sītā from his clutches." Rāma hastily embraced him and said sorrowfully."

"Sir, I am very sorry to see you in such a condition. Tell me every thing in detail."

"Jaṭāyu answered.

"Rāvaṇa was flying in the air with Sītā in his chariot. I jumped and caught hold of the chariot and smashed it by my beaks and broke his bow also. But Rāvaṇa struck me by his heavy sword and stripped off my wings also. He took another chariot and flew southwards with Sītā who was bitterly weeping. I am just breathing my last. Please touch my body so that I may get relief from your divine touch."

He died while speaking and feeling comfort at Rāma's touch.

Rāma mourned as a relative for Jaṭāyu. He duly arranged funeral rites for Jaṭāyu's liberation. Jaṭāyu appeared in divine form in Rāma's presence and prayed to him.

"I bow to you, Oh Rāma! Most virtuous, illuminous, matchless, creator, sustainer and destroyer of the universe. You are Supreme God. I constantly remember you to be the greatest human incarnation of Lord Vishṇu. Laxmi's beloved Lord, the reliever of Brahmā's and all other dieties' troubles."

"I take refuge in you Supreme God Rama. Most handsome and resplendant like thousands of moons, the fulfiller of aspirants' wishes living within their hearts and being worshipped by all the gods as well as Lord Shiva."

"I fall at the feet, Raghunāth, having blue appearance as the Yamunā river, Supreme, imperceivable, unobtainable by worldly persons, the leader of the Raghu's, dwelling in Shiva's and Pārvatī's heart, the ship that carried aspirants and seers across the ocean of worldliness. Your benign form is adored by gods, the demon kings and sages. You are always happy and ready to make others happy and prosperous by granting them boons. Such an exceedingly handsome divine person with love eyes and sweet smiles, the holder of Govardhana hill, and the creator Brahmā, Vishṇu and Shiva as well in one form, is before me as my saviour."

Rāma said to him.

"Now you go to the paradise, my residence by my grace."

Jaṭāyu's body became illuminous and divine resembling Vishṇu's form holding conch, mace, disc and lotus in four hands and he ascended to the heavenly abode on the air chariot attended by Vishṇu's followers, sages and gods.

This invocation of Rāma by Jaṭāyu is also very sacred and it grants Supreme knowledge to the readers by Rāma's grace.

Chapter IX

KABANDHA'S INVOCATION TO RĀMA

Rāma and Laxmaṇa sadly proceeded in search of Sītā and met a very awkward and strange demon whose mouth was on his own stomach and whose hands were about ten miles long.

He had no eyes and ears and used to entrap creatures within his arms.

Rāma and Laxmaṇa too happened to be within his arms but they cut his arms when they could not find the way to free themselves. The demon named Kabandha then asked.

"Who are you? Who has cut my arms? It seems to me that you are gods."

Rāma laughingly replied.

"We are king Dasharath's sons and have come to live in forests in exile by father's orders. My wife Sītā has been kidnapped by a demon during our absence; and we are going in her search."

Kabandha replied.

I am really blessed to meet you. I was formerly the king of Gandharva and was turned into my present demon form by the curse of sage Aṣṭabakra who was enraged with me at my laughing. I prayed to him to be kind with me and begged his pardon. Then he told me that I would be liberated when Rāma cuts my arms. Once, I chased Indra who dropped his thunderbolt upon me and my head and feet were thrust under my belly by the struck. But I did not die because I am immortal by the Brahmā's boon. Indra took pity on me and made my mouth on the stomach and lengthened my arms ten miles long so that I may live by entrapping creatures."

"Kindly burn my body so that I may regain my original form. I shall also tell you where your beloved wife has been taken away."

Rāma and Laxmaṇa dug a ditch for burning Kabandha in it. Then a very handsome person resembling the God of Cupid appeared out of the ditch and paid respects to Rāma and prayed in words of great joy.

"Lord, you are infinite, imperceivable, inexpressible and extremely difficult to be known, beyond the mind, intellect, nature and also above the gross and subtle bodies. You stand as a witness in every individual and even the spirit or Jīva is simply your reflection falling upon the intellect. All the creatures subtle and undescribable exist in you."

"Lord, how can I describe you fully by my materialistic wisdom? You are called "Hiraṇya Garbha" in your subtle form and "Birāt" in your universal and grand form. Your subtle form is the basic cause of the past, present and future creations and is worth meditating upon and always blissful."

"Elements of nature and phenomena constitute six spheres of "Brahmāṇḍa" or grand universe such as Bhu, Bhuba, Swa, Tapa, Jana, Satyu, Maha, Lokas or worlds which are comprehended in your grand form Birāt." The nether world, Pātāl is you padal base, Mahātul your ankles, Tatālal, the legs, Bhutal, the lower part of thighs, Bital, the upper thighs, Atal and the earth, your waist, Bhūlok, the naval, Swargaloka (heaven), the breasts Mahālok, the neck, Janaloka, the face, Tapalok, the forehead, and Satyalok, the head. Oh Lord Rāma, Indra and other dieties are your arms, directions, the ears, Aswini Kumar, the nostrils, fire, the mouth, the sun, your eyes, the moon, the mind, the time, the eye-brows, movements and Brihaspati, God of wisdom, your intellect, God Shiva, should be known as your egoism, Veda, your speech, Yama, the God of death, your teeth, stars your small teeth, Māyā or illusion, your smiles, the creative energy your looks, religion and piety, your foot side, sin, your back, day and night, your winklings, seven oceans, the belly, rivers, the sinews, trees and medicines the hair, the rains your semen, and the wisdom, your glory."

"Though I am carried way with ecstacy of joy when I meditate upon your grand and universal form, which is easy means for immediate salvation for devotees and seers, yet Oh Lord, for me, I pray to you that I may always see your human form with the bow and arrow in the garb of the hermit followed by Laxmaṇa in search of Sītā."

"Lord Shiva and Pārvatī always contemplate upon this divinely human form of yours. Further Lord Shiva in "Kāshi" is wholly and delightfully occupied in preaching your name "Rāma" by advising especially the dying persons to repeat this holy name for their salvation."

"Lord! ordinary persons deluded by your illusionary deeds do not know you to be Supreme God. I bow to you, the Lord of Ayodhyā, again and again with Laxmaṇa, and implore that you kindly save and never begile me by your illusion."

Rāma said to him.

"Go to the paradise. I am fully satisfied with you. You are sinless. Even those that shall read the invocation shall attain salvation with all their ignorance and sins completely rooted out and shall be one with me eternally."

Chapter X

EMANCIPATION OF SHAVARĪ

Gandharva suggested to Rāma to call upon Shavarī who was a sincere devotee to him and she could tell all about Sītā's whereabouts. Then he ascended to the heaven uttering Rāma's name in an effulgent plane by Rāma's grace.

Rāma and Laxmaṇa then met Shavarī dwelling in a cave in a thick forest abounding with wild beasts.

She entertained Rāma with Laxmaṇa very earnestly as she was very eagerly waiting for his arrival and offered very delicious plums which she had preserved for that purpose.

Rāma and Laxmaṇa were both worshipped with deep devotion and dedication. She said to Rāma.

"Lord, my preceptor sage Matang who had lived here for years, advised me on his departure to Brahmā's abode that I should patiently wait here till your arrival. Then I would have the fortune to cast off this earthly body to secure your divine abode. Lord, I am so lucky that being an ordinary low caste woman, I have today seen you in person. All my preceptor's words have come true. I am not worthy of being even slave of your salves. I am illiterate and do not know how to adore and invoke. Kindly favour me."

Rāma replied.

"Nobody can find me if he has no love for me, because I am attracted to my aspirants, be he a male or female or a high or lows caste. It is only his unflinching love which I value the most." "Association with my aspirants, study of my life stories, singing in praise of my deeds, teaching spiritual matters, services and obedience to ones spiritual guides, worships of God by leading chaste and holy life, controlling mind and sense-organs, chanting my names and sacred words (mantras), respects to my devoted followers more than myself, equanimity with all the living beings, detachment from pleasures and luxuries, living in peace pursuing truth etc. are nine kinds or ways of devotion which never fail to please me.

There is no question of attainment of salvation if one develops in this very life such love for me by knowing my true self."

"Association with sages and saints is the primary unfailing means for the attainment of my love and salvation. You are indeed a true aspirant and you shall certainly attain salvation. Please tell me if you know the present whereabouts of Sītā, my beloved wife, kidnapped by a demon."

Shavarī replied.

"Omniscient Lord! You ask me thus only in worldly way. So I am to say this much. Rāvaṇa has taken Sītā to Laṅkā and she is now living there safely. Please proceed further and meet highly valourous Sugrīva who is most secretly living with his four valiant ministers on Rishyamūka hills for fear of his brother Bāli. Please befriend him and he will help you in finding Sītā and achieving every success in your mission. Kindly wait for a while till I burn my material body and ascend to the heaven by your grace."

Wise Shavarī entered into the fire and burnt herself and thus got rid of worldly troubles; and her soul soon attained celestial form and reached the paradise.

Wise aspirants should make it a point to love Rāma in order to obtain absolution from the worldly bondage. They should take lessons from the saintly life of Shavarī, who even a low cast ignorant and illiterate woman could attain the highest place in the paradise what to speak of pure hearted and high class persons! So people leaving dry leaned talks aside, should fully know that salvation means nothing else but deep and unswerving devotion to Supreme God Rāma who is always resplendant with his bluish and charming form in the great heart of Lord Shiva too.

PART IV

KIṢKINDHĀ KĀṆḌA

Chapter I

RĀMA'S LIFE IN ASSOCIATION WITH MONKEYS : FRIENDSHIP WITH SUGRIVA

Rāma and Laxmaṇa reached the banks of Pampā, the beautiful lake of clean water in which swans and other aquatic birds with various colourful lotuses perfuming the water were seen. They became glad at the sight of the beautiful lake. On quenching their thirst with the clean water, they reached the foot of Rishyamuka hill. Sugrīva saw them approaching towards him and immediately sent Hanumān to know their intention, because he apprehended lest they should be deputed by Bāli to kill him. Hanumān then in the garb of a hermit met Rāma and Laxmaṇa and humbly said, Lord, who are you in disguise of hermits? It seems to me that you are God's incarnations descended upon the earth in the forms of uncommonly brave youths for bestowing favour on aspirants and destroying the sinners and evil demons."

Rāma whispered to Laxmaṇa "Surely the lad seems to be very intelligent and learned as his speech indicates."

He said to Hanumān, "We are King Dasharatha's sons and have come to live in forests in exile for fourteen years by his orders and have arrived here in search of Sītā, my beloved who has been abducted by a demon in our absence. Please tell me who you are."

Hanumān replied "I am the son of the God of Winds and Sugriba's minister, named Hanumān. I request the favour of your kindly visiting Sugriba who lives on the hill-top as he has been driven out of Kiṣhkindhā by his elder brother Bāli who has also forcibly robbed him of his wife."

Rāma replied "I am coming here with the same intention and shall also help in his distress."

Hanumān took them on his shoulders and with a leap on the hill-top in a moment, he informed Sugrība of his attempts at friendly relations between two sides. Sugrība thereafter with all his fears completely gone, hastened to welcome Rāma and Laxmaṇa. When they all were happily seated on the branches broken duly from the trees, Sugriba heard from Laxmaṇa the details about the loss of Sītā. Then Sugrība said to Rāma.

"Lord, do not worry. I shall do my best for finding out Sītā. Once a lady carried away by a certain demon on the flying chariot had dropped a bundle of her ornaments which I have preserved. Please see them and tell me if they belong to Sītā".

Rāma wept bitterly as an ordinary man when he saw Sītā's ornaments. Then both Sugrīva and Laxmaṇa consolded him as they assured him that they would get her back with the help of brave monkeys from Rāvaṇa's possessions. Hanumān blazed the fire and Rāma swore an oath of sacred alliance with Sugrīva and they both embraced each other in token of perpetual friendship, before the fire as their witness.

Sugrīva then related his past history also to Rāma. "One day Māyā's son, the mighty giant, challenged Bāli for fighting at Kiṣkindhā."

"Bāli defeated him and he took to heels wounded as he was hit by Bāli's severe blows. Bāli chased him on; and I also followed Bāli upto a cave into which both the demon Māyābī and Bāli had entered. I waited for Bāli's return at its door for a month and when a stream of blood flowed out of the door. I thought that Bāli was killed. I put a high stone across the mouth of the cave and returned to Kiṣkindhā in great dispair and told the public about his inflexed death. The public and the councillors made me the king in place of Bāli though I was reluctant to accept the throne."

"Bāli arrived Kiṣkindhā unexpectedly after a few days. Finding me as the king very angry he dealt me with severe blows. I had to flee to save my life; but he pursued me wherever I went throughout the whole earth. At last I found my shelter at this hill where Bāli could not come up owing to the curse of a sage. He has confiscated my properties together with my wife.".

"Lord! I am in this deplorable condition as you find me now."

Rāma was moved at Sugrīva's calamities, and he said. Friend, "I shall certainly kill Bali."

Sugrīva said "Friendly Lord, I doubt whether you can do so. Once a very mighty giant named Dundvir fought with Bāli in Kiṣkindhā and Bāli had severed his head and flung it ten miles away. It had fallen at Sage Matanga's hermitage which was polluted by its blood.

Sage Matanga had cursed Bāli that his head would be severed if he would ever go to Matanga's hermitage at Rishyamūka hill. Look at the skeleton of the giant's head as big as a hillock."

Rāma tossed away the head by his toes some hundred miles away to the applause of Sugriva and his ministers.

Sugrīva further said "There are seven tal trees which Bāli used to shake at a time and all the leaves would fall by the shock. I will be assured that you can kill Bāli if you can pierce them away by the single shot of an arrow."

Rāma shot an arrow which instantly pierced them and returned into his quiver.

Sugrīva and all other monkeys were amazed at such feats of marvellous strength and he very happily told Rāma.

"Lord, I have realised now that you are Supreme

God whom I have to day met as a result of my pious deeds of previous births."

"I cannot demand wordly pleasures, luxuries and high prosperity from you whom sages and saints love for their redemption. A big family circle, wealth, kingdom and material objects are your plausible creations and are undesirable to me when I have found you. My shackles of worldliness have now been broken for good. Lord, I have attained the highest thing i.e. beatitude as one while digging the earth suddenly comes across a great treasury. But sacrifices, penances and other pious deeds also may entangle an individual all the more strongly in worldliness. So, even a moment's association or contact with your great touch liberates an individual from ignorance and all the evils. The chanting of your names liberates at ones for one's sins even if he is a murderer of a Brahmin or a vicious drunkard."

"Lord, I desire no worldly prosperities, and even my wife as they are all transitory creations of illusion. It suffices me if I can obtain your love that breaks for ever the shackles of birth and death. My mind was so long overpowered by your illusion and I would not make distinctions between friends, foes and neutrals but now I feel that everything is God only and I have forgotten all the differences."

"I may be permitted, oh benign Rāma, to chant perpetually your names, and to remember the glorious deeds in your various incarnations. Lord, grant me such boons also that I may always be able to live with you and dedicate my mind, heart and all bodily organs to your services day and night with deep conviction that the whole universe is your temple or altar."

Chapter II

THE KILLING OF BĀLĪ

Rāma enchanted pure hearted Sugrīva with his sweet illusionary smiles and he said to him. "Friend, you are right in thinking so. But it will be ridiculous from the worldly standpoint if I do not keep my promise for killing Bāli for your good. Please therefore proceed to Kiṣkindhā and challenge him.

At this Rāma and Sugrīva with all the attendants reached Kiṣkindhā and Sugrīva went to Bāli's palace and roared loudly defying him to a duel fight.

Bāli was exhausperated at Sugrīva's voice and he instantly went out to confront Sugrīva who treated at once with very hard blows. Bāli in his turn also dealt heavier blows to him.

Rāma was much surprised to find Bāli and Sugrīva exactly of same appearance, and could not shoot an arrow lest it should hit at Sugrīva in confusion.

Sugrīva returned to the place where Rāma was waiting as he had been badly belaboured by Bāli who was undoubtedly stronger and then he sorrowfully said to Rāma, "Lord, why have you sent me to Bāli? He would have certainly killed me had I not taken to heels. You could have personally killed me if you had wished in this way."

Rāma replied sadly, "Friend, I did not shoot Bāli as I could not distinctly recognise him as both of you looked alike. Now please go wearing a garland again and challenge him so that I may not make any mistake in distinguishing Bāli and shooting at him.

Rāma ordered Laxmaṇa to arrange a garland for Sugrīva and he again went to fight and roared very dreadfully.

Bāli again was prepared to go to fight but his wife Tārā stopped him and said.

"Lord, do not go now to be confronted with Sugrīva

any further. I fear that some person is certainly backing him for his victory. I have come to know from Angad who heard once in his hunting excursion that Rāma and Laxmaṇa had met Sugrīva at Rishyamūka hills and made friendly alliance duly with him and Rāma had assured Sugrīva that the would make him king by killing Bāli and restore his lost property and wife to him. Therefore give up enemity with Sugrīva and have peace with him.

She cried in fear and requested Bāli to take this suggestion for protecting her Angad and kingdom.

But Bāli replied.

"Dear, you, as a weaker sex, simply fear with out any reason. Rāma is the incarnation of God. I shall please him by dedication if I meet him. He is equal to everybody and grants favour to one who loves him. I cannot remain silent here as I am a world famous warrior and victor. So I shall certainly kill Sugrīva this time if he comes alone for a fight with me."

Bāli went out and began to fight with Sugrīva very dreadfully. In the meantime Rāma hiding himself behind a tree shot a very powerful shaft which directly entered into Bāli's chest.

Bāli sprang up in pain and fell senseless upon the ground. When he regained senses he saw Rāma and Laxmaṇa standing by his side and he began to reproach Rāma.

"Lord, you have indeed done a serious injustice by killing me. I am also your devotee and have committed no crime. I have heard that you have made alliance with Sugrīva for helping you to bring back Sītā from Rāvaṇa. I could have brought her together with Rāvaṇa in a moment had you ordered me to do so. Even my flesh is not acceptable to human beings. I belong to the monkey species. Moreover, you have shot me by hiding yourself like a thief. Had you fought with me, your glory as a Kshatriya race would have been rightly maintained. I wonder why you made such a difference between Sugrīva and me."

Rāma replied.

"You should not boast in this way as you really merit death. You are a guilty sinner as you have deprived your younger brother of his beloved wife. You, as a monkey, do not care to know that we virtuous people roam about to rectify such wrong doers".

Bāli confessed his sin and bowed to Rāma and prayed.

"Lord, you are supreme God. Kindly forgive for what I have said."

Please take out the arrow from my breast and bless me. Benign Lord, I have come to know fully that you are Vishṇu and Sītā is Laxmi and that your incarnations are meant for world peace.

Also be kind to my son Aṅgad."

He breathed his last when Rāma took out his arrow, touched his body and blessed him.

Bāli then in a high celestial form secured the highest abode like that of Indra, the king of Gods. He undoubtedly attained the very exalted position in the paradise unobtainable even by great saints.

Chapter III

CONSOLING TĀRĀ AND ENTHRONING SUGRĪVA

All the attendants of Bāli much terrified at his death approached their queen Tārā and supplicated her to instal Aṅgad on the throne immediately as they were prepared to guard the city with all the main gates firmly shut up. Tārā fell senseless when she heard the news of Bāli's death and replied to them in bitter sorrow.

"Dear monkey, there is no use for me any more of prosperity, kingdom and even Aṅgad as my husband is no more on earth. So I will join my husband by killing myself.

She, with her loose brand hair, immediately reached the spot where the corpse of Bāli was fully saturated with the pool of blood and dust. She began to bewail very pitiously.

She saw Rāma standing by her and with eyes full of tears said to him.

"Lord, kill me also by the same shot by which you have finished my husband who cannot be happy in my absence even in the heaven. You shall certainly obtain much pity if you relieve me of the anguish which I am keenly feeling in my bereavement from my husband."

She said to Sugriva Rāma has favoured you by killing Bāli and it is now your turn to be merry with your wife and prosperity."

Rāma said to Tārā very modestly, "Lady, there is no reason for you being so much afflicted at the separation from your husbands's material body which is perishable and temporary only. His soul is stainless, immortal and always present everywhere. So, there can be no question of separation in any way. Please console yourself because ignorant persons grieve at the death of their near and dear ones."

Tārā replied.

"Rāma, kindly explain to me that if the soul is immortal and always blissful and the body had no sense and is material then why an individual feels happiness and misery in his life in this world?"

Rāma replied.

"The ego alone in the individual, acting in the body through the sense organs, thinks itself to be happy or miserable. The spirit or Jiva of a man in his egoistic form combined with the intellect and mind; alone is the enjoyer or sufferer in life owing to the soul's reflections."

"Worldliness is thus felt by man simply through his egoism and mind whereas his soul wholly stainless and real and has no ignorance and confusion.

"All the creations of the universe are false like dreams. The shackles of births and deaths together with worldly attachments and repulsions have no effect upon the soul; but it is his mind which is entangled with them. Man, therefore, acts by his mind and his soul stands as the witness only in the mind."

"By ignorance, man feels as if his soul were the doer, but in fact it is inactive and is supposed to grant energy to the ego and intellect which work according to three guṇas (Sattva– enlightenment, Rajas– exertion and Tamas ignorance)."

"Worship, meditation and other virtuous deeds are done by man by his mind when it is influenced by Sattva or peaceful guṇas, similarly other worldly activities are done by Rājasic guṇas and predatary works, murder, drinking etc. are done by Tāmasic Guṇas."

"Consequently man has got to undergo births and rebirths and live in worldliness so long as his egoistic connections with deeply rooted worldly impressions prevail. But he attains salvation if he realises his soul and transcends his ego by the permit of knowledge, devotion and god's worships."

Rāma further said to her "You follow my advice with your mind deeply concentrated on me. You will realise your inner soul, and attain, salvation even in your life time though you shall be doing worldly duties."

"You had propitiated me in your previous life, and I have, therefore, seen you and advised you the most secret philosophy which shall bring complete liberation to any aspirant."

Tārā was very happily satisfied at Rāma's advice and her anguish of mind was also removed by his grace.

She, no doubt, gained knowledge of her soul within a few minutes in association with Rāma and could do away with her ignorance for ever.

Sugrīva and Aṅgad together with all attendants and the citizens followed the Royal Corpse procession with the soundings of trumpets and other various musical instruments to the river and burnt the dead body with the due funeral rites in royal pomp and grandeur.

Sugrīva entreated Rāma, "Lord, please accept the throne of Kiṣkindhā and I like to serve you as a slave."

Rāma cheerfully replied.

"There is no difference between you and me. Please go to Kiṣkindhā immediately and declare yourself the king and make Aṅgad your heir apparent, the next successor of the throne. We shall search for Sītā when the rainy season passes. I, with Laxmaṇa, shall stay at the top of the adjacent hill.

Sugrīva with the humblest bow at the feet of Rāma said that he would exactly carry out his order. Then Sugrīva along with Laxmaṇa started for Kiṣkindhā where the ceremony was performed accordingly as Rāma had ordered. Laxmaṇa returned to Rāma. Then Rāma with

Laxmaṇa went to the distant hilltop of Pravarshaṇa. They found there an ideally comfortable cave with abundant water and fruits around. The place was really delighting and cheering as it was shining various kinds of beautiful birds and beasts. With cheerful hearts they began to sojourn there.

Chapter IV

RĀMA'S PREACHINGS TO LAXMAṆA

Rāma with Laxmaṇa passed the rainy day at the hill very peacefully. He enjoyed beautiful varieties of scenary that would often appear in rainy clouds, green mountains, the swelling rivers and the waterfalls that exhibited the grandeur of the season.

Plump deer, happy in the rains used to go near the cottage, sages and also saints would attend Rāma on all sides in deer's disguise.

One day Laxmaṇa in a secluded atmosphere requested Rāma. "Through your grace, I have been able to be free from illusive bondage, now I should like to know the best method of worshipping you in the true sense of the term. I know the learned sages attain salvation by your worship also, and I also think it to be an easy way for pleasing you."

Rāma replied.

"The ways of my worship are countless. But I shall briefly tell the easy way. The person should sanctify himself by chanting Mantras. He should take his bath with the holy water and worship my idols or images according to the instructions of his preceptor whom also he should worship. He may worship me within his heart even or in fire, water or in the sun or in any idol of my form or in Śāligrām (a sacred stone)."

"The aspirant should at first perform his daily ritual or spiritual duties on his seat with mind duly concentrated with exhaling and inhaling (the action of Prāṣāyām). Then he should worship my idol or image very earnestly decorated with holy ingredients, garlands and scents after bathing it in pure and holy water or cleaning it in case of its being a picture. I really get pleased if some body worships my idol wholeheartedly by offering whatever articles of food and nice fruits are available; no matter if he does not have more things to offer. A little water, some flowers offered to me with sincerity and conviction are sufficient to please. But if one worships in fire, he should offer oblations. A sun like chart (picture) is needed if he worships me in the sun. It is necessary that he should arrange light with burning cotton-sticks soaked in ghee at the time of completing the worship. It is called "Nīrājan". He should perform Nyāsa, Dhyāna, concentration, and offer water, Madhuparka, the water mixed with milk, curd, honey and clarified butter and sugar.

Dhyāna is meditation of idol with the unflinching belief of the devotee, that is my own form appearing before him. He should chant Mantras called Japa after meditation and perform havana if he knows the method of performance. Havana is best performed by the method dedicated by Sage Agastya. He should offer rice prepared in milk and sugar, or Till (oilseeds) and barley soaked in ghee in the blazing fire, at every time of chanting my name of Mantra. The ditch or altar in which the fire is to be blazed should be nicely built according to vedic mantras and methods. He should arrange music and sing glorious songs of my names and deeds in course of the worship. He should bow to my image very respectfully and pray for my blessings at the end of my worship. Camphor, agarau, sandal-wood paste, kum-kum, fragrant powder, and other kinds of inscences, betelnuts, coconuts, flowers all kinds of fruits, milk, ghee, honey and many kinds of fine and rich dresses, are chief articles necessary for idol worship."

"But without sincerity, seriousness, faith and love, the worship though performed with huge amount of riches will never please me. Lastly in the form of "prasād" he should take some portion of flowers, paste and fruits and foods offered to the idol. He should be utterly content with the thought entered into his soul through the idol."

Any person who regularly worships me with love and faith in accordance with the way suggested by my own self and even reads or hears my unfailing words shall be blessed by me and shall be happy and prosperous throughout his life. He will attain the heaven after his death by my grace."

Then Lord Rāma began to weep and remained weeping throughout the night like an ordinary man.

In the meantime Hanumān at Kiṣkindhā said to Sugriva.

Lord, you have not paid any heed to the mission of your search for Sītā uptil now. It seems to me that you have forgotten your promise you had made to Rāma, who had been so kind to you and has restored the kingdom and your wife to you by killing the invincible Bāli for your sake. You may also get killed by Rāma if you neglect you duty."

Sugrīva repiied.

"Dear wise Hanumān, please depute all the chief officers to all parts of the earth to bring all the monkeys immediately. Issue strict orders for their reaching Kiṣkindhā within a fortnight without fail and proclaim that any one disobeying my orders will be done to death."

Hanumān did accordingly deputing all the intelligent and mighty monkeys by bestowing on them due rewards and honour for their motive.

Chapter V

LAXMAṆA CAUTIONS SUGRĪVA

One night Rāma became very sad after he remembered Sītā and her moon-like face. In a very angry mood he told Laxmaṇa that he would certainly destroy the demon together with his whole posterities as he had stolen Sītā away. He said that he would find her just as nectar is extracted from the ocean. He added.

"Brother, Sugrīva too seems to have been ungrateful to me. The autumn has started but he has not turned up. He is fully engaged in indulgence with luxuries and pleasures and has really forgotten his promise. He seems to be pecked to his wife and he deserves death at my hands for this ingratitude.

Laxmaṇa replied angrily.

"Lord, I shall instantly go to Kiṣkindhā and kill that ungrateful Sugrīva."

Rāma said. "You may to Kiṣkindhā to meet Sugrīva and only reprimand him as he is really my dear friend. After your return and having heard from him, we shall do the needful."

It is indeed impossible that supreme lord Rāma had been woeful by keeping aloof from Sītā who is goddess Laxmi. But he had virtually pretended to be miserable and woe-stricken in human manners so that people might know him to be a human being. His life story called Rāmāyaṇa might also grant time knowledge to the people for the attainment of salvation, and may thereby set a good example to all the persons on the earth in future.

Laxmaṇa reached Kiṣkindhā and by way of giving vent to his wrath, sounded his bow dreadfully as if he were prepared to kill all the monkeys.

Aṅgad hastened to receive Laxmaṇa immediately and bowed to him respectfully.

Laxmaṇa told Aṅgad that he should immediately inform Sugrīva of his arrival as he had been sent to deliver enraged some message from Rāma.

Sugrīva on the other hand was much afraid and he immediately sent Hanumān with Angad to bring Laxmaṇa to him with due respects, and also asked Tārā for welcoming Laxmaṇa on the way so that his anger might be abated.

They met infuriated Laxmaṇa and very humbly requested him to enter in the palace and see Sugrīva. Sugrīva too left the inner apartment of his wife Ruma and hailed Laxmaṇa with humble bows and sweet words. He said.

"Lord, forgive me. I am your most obedient slave."

Laxmaṇa, replied in anger.

"It seems that you have forgotten Rāma and you are not at all afraid of him. Look, I am going to punish you for your ungratefulness."

Hanumān entreated Laxmaṇa, "Lord, do not think it to be so. Sugrīva is more devoted to Rāma than you. He has managed every thing in the best possible way for the search of Sītā. Millions of mighty and warfaring monkeys have been assembled and are ready for going out in Sītā's search for which you need not doubt even in the least."

Laxmaṇa suppressed his anger and said to Sugrīva.

"Friend, forgive me for my rude speech. I have spoken to you by way of affection only. I have no ill-will against you. Let us go to see Rāma as early as possible."

Sugrīva said.

"Lord, I am indebtedly your obedient servant and always ready for rendering my best services to Rāma. In fact, Rāma in the twinkling of an eye, can defeat countless worlds by force of his inherent lustre. I am only a nominated helper to him. Let us now proceed to

Prabarshaṇa hills to see him there."

He ordered Hanumān to collect all the monkeys meant for the purpose of serving Rāma by way of succeeding in Sītā's search thoroughly.

Sugrīva and Laxmaṇa started in a grand and beautiful chariot attended by numerous followers with mighty bears and monkeys sounding trumpets and other musical instruments for meeting Rāma at Prabarshaṇa hill.

Chapter VI

MONKEYS SETOUT IN SEARCH OF SĪTĀ

Rāma welcomed his friend Sugrīva on his arrival and embraced him very happily.

Sugrīva informed Rāma thus humbly, "Lord, I have collected millions and millions of mighty monkeys. They are ready for departure in Sītā's search."

He introduced to Rāma, the chief leaders, Hanumān, Aṅgad, Nala, Neela, Gabya, Gabaxa, Sushena, Tara, Keshari, the Hanumān's father, Panas, Balmikha, Dashimukha, Sarava, Maindeva, and others and described their valour and merits one by one.

Rāma was exceedingly pleased to see them and said to Sugrīva. "Friend, you are really very sincere to me. Kindly despatch them in Sītā's search."

Sugrīva sent them under the leadership of Aṅgad and Hanumān with strict orders that he would put them to death if they did not find out Sītā within a month. Rāma met Hanumān secretly to hand over his gold ring with his name inscribed on it, so that he might successfully deliver it to Sītā as the token of identity since he knew that Hanumān would surely accomplish the hard task. Rāma, then with blessings, told Hanumān to go ahead.

Then Aṅgad, Hanumān and all the monkeys very enthusiastically went southwards and met a huge demon on their way, whom they killed on surmising that he was Rāvaṇa.

They were on the way extremely perched with thirst and were on the look out of water hither and thither; and at last they saw aquatic birds flying out of a cave's door. They entered into it and found a tank of clean water surrounded by fruits, trees and a small cottage in which a paragon of beauty in the form of a hermit girl was living.

She asked Hanumān as to who they were. Hanumān related the history of Rāma in detail and said they were going in Sītā's search.

The girl replied.

"Gentlemen, please quench your thirst and refresh yourselves with delicious fruits and then I shall talk with you."

She told Hanumān after he had returned taking fruits and drinking water.

Formerly Hemā, Vishwa-karmā's daughter, had propitiated Lord Shiva by her dances, and had got this hermitage in reward. She had lived here thousands of years in performance of penances and I had attended upon her as her mate. My name is Swampravā and I am Gandharvas's daughter. "He had ascended to creator Brahmā's abode and had advised me to live alone in penances till Supreme Lord Vishṇu incarnates himself as Rāma in the human form and some monkeys serve him and he would duly come into the cottage and meet me."

Swampravā further said that she wished to see Rāma at the earliest and would leave the cave.

Hanumān and all the monkeys went out of the cave and took their way southwards.

But Swampravā arrived at the Pravarshaṇa hill and met Rāma and very respectfully said, "Lord, my penances have been fruitful to day by meeting you, the Lord Vishṇu's incarnation, who has descended upon earth for bestowing favour on the right doers and destroying the evil ones. My aspiration is crowned with success. I cannot know God's real form being ignorant and simple folk, but only bow to you again and again."

"Lord, you are the only shelter of the weak and the destitutes. So kindly favour me and let me remember your handsome human form at every moment so that I may get eternal peace and salvation by your grace. I have heard that you fulfilled wishes of Dasharatha and Kaushalyā in their previous birth and for that sake you are now going to kill Rāvaṇa. Most of the people do not know that you are Lord Vishṇu and your illusionary plays cannot be exactly understood by other. I , therefore, pray to you that your illusion may not delude me any further and I may gain your favour so that I may break the shackles of births and deaths and cross the ocean of worldiness once for the ever".

With blessings Rāma said, "Gentle woman, go to forests of Badrikānātha in the northern Himālayas and caṣt off your mortal body you shall attain salvation."

Swampravā did accordingly and ascended to the paradise by the Lord's grace.

Chapter VII

THE EPISODE OF SAMPĀTĪ

The monkeys, on the other side, were greatly depressed on their inability to find out Sītā. They were in deep thought. Then Aṅgad told some of the monkeys.

Nearly a month has passed and we have not been able to trace out Sītā though we have been so perseverely looking for her. Sugrīva will certainly kill us and it will be a good opportunity for him to kill me as he nourishes grudge against me though I am saved by Rāma. He is really sinful, because he did not hesitate to keep his brother's wife even who is like his mother. I shall end my life here and will not go back at any cost.

They replied.

"We will also live with you in the cave and serve you. This cave is very comfortable and beautiful like Indra's palace."

Hanumān overheard these talks and told Aṅgad.

"Why do you worry yourself by such misconception? Please listen to me for your real good. Sugrīva had much affection for you as you are Tārā's affectionate son. Rāma loves you more than Laxmaṇa. His arrows cannot spare even a single being in the three worlds. How can these monkeys live here for your sake as they cannot part from their family members? These monkeys are bluffing you for nothing. I am also your well-wisher and shall assist you whatever calamity surround you. Let me tell you a very great secret.

"Rāma is Supreme God's incarnation and has descended upon the earth to accomplish God's mission. By the devotion of our previous births we have been made for his attendants, now having incarnated in monkey's form for the purpose of Rāma.

Sītā is real Laxmī. We shall return to the paradise

again with Rāma in due time."

Aṅgad was encouraged by Hanumān thus and they resumed their journey in search of Sītā and reached the seashore at the foot of the Mandarāchal hill.

At the sight of vast and unfathomable sea, they were again disappointed; and they began to say.

"We are now helpless to find Sītā. Let us die by fasting as there is no good for us to be killed by Sugrīva when we return there."

They were sitting on Kusha grass determined to die while a huge vulture came out Mandarāchal's cave and said.

"My Good Luck! I have found here so many monkeys for my food."

The monkeys cried in fear and uttered.

"We unfortunate beings are going to be killed without fulfilling our urgent duties even. Jaṭāyu was really fortunate as he could die for Rāma's cause. Sampātī, the grand vulture told them.

"Do not get scared of me. I am happy to bear Jaṭāyu's name as if I had found the nectar. Kindly tell me about him in detail."

Aṅgad replied him.

"Jaṭāyu was wounded to death during his fight with Rāvaṇa who was flying by his chariot abducting Sītā, the beloved wife of Rāma, king Dashratha's son, who had gone to forests in exile for fourteen years by his father's orders."

"Sugrīva had made friendship with Rāma who had killed Bāli and gave the throne of Kishkindhā to Sugrīva. Kindly tell me if you know about her. We are very much anxious and are now prepared to give up our lives by fasting because we could not find out Sītā. If we return with out finding her Sugrīva will certainly do us to death."

Then Sampātī bathed in the sea and offered holy

water to his departed brother Jaṭāyu. He then came back to Aṅgad and said thus.

"I am seeing Sītā from here, seated under the Siṅshapa tree in the city of Laṅkā hundred miles away across the sea. You should not doubt because vultures have very keen and long sights. Anybody can see her if he jumps across the sea. I was also mighty enough to kill Rāvaṇa, the murderer of my brother; but I am unfortunate to be without wings. I know that Rāma will certainly kill Rāvaṇa and get back Sītā in course of time. But find out among yourselves the hero who can reach Laṅkā, converse with Sītā and come back safely.

All the apes in great curiosity asked Sampātī.

"Sir, please tell us your past history of life."

Sampātī said.

"I as well as Jaṭāyu once flew to the sky thousands of miles away from the earth towards the Sun. Jaṭāyu's wings were about to be burnt off by the Sun's rays and I had to save him by covering him under my wings which were also burnt and I fell senseless on Mandarāchal hill. I was hit hard and unable to fly, so I had to crawl on the ground miserably."

"I reached the hermitage of sage Chandrama who was surprised at my deplorable plight and said.

"Sampātī! What is the matter with you? How are you deprived of your wings?

I replied very woefully.

I shall now burn myself to death as I have lost my wings. It is indeed very miserable for me to live in such a condition. I reported to him all what had happened."

Chapter VIII

SAGE CHANDRAMĀ'S CONSOLATION TO SAṀPĀTĪ

Sage Chandramā consoled me and said.

"The material body is obtained by an individual according to the result of his deeds of his previous births. It is his embodied self of Jīva which feels pleasure and pain and he has attachment to and repulsion from the worldly objects. Individual ego is in fact, illusive reflections from God or Supreme Soul only and is, not the real self. So the identity of pure self with the reflection on the body is the cosmic world.

Man's Jīva which has the ego, leaves the material body after the death and with its elemental or causal bodies ascends to the heaven or to other astral abodes such as "Petri Loka" etc. or falls down the hell according to his good and bad deeds of his past lives.

The Jīva lives there until his piety or sin if finished and then it returns alone with fag and mist to the earth in the form of liquid elements and is observed in the saturated soil where it fructifies into foodgrains."

"Anybody who eats the foodgrains assimilates it into his blood. In this scheduled process, it again appears as spermatozoa just to the mixed in natural course with the ova already formed in wombs of the woman. Thus in one day it is formed to acquire slight fixity with the help of uterine covering around. In five days it develops into a piece of thick blood in the womb and in seven days forms a very tender egg like shape. In this way it gradually develops into a babyish form in course of ten months. Generally the complete body with all the organs and parts is formed in eight months; in five months, it gets vague consciousness which goes on ripening till it remembers the happenings of its past lives too. Then it begins to suffer terribly from the heat of the womb and prays to God for its deliverance, and with many repentances for his past deeds and labours, makes promises for loving and adoring God if it is released from the hell-like uterine abode by immediate safe birth."

"But when it is born all such thoughts and remembrances totally vanish from mind and one becomes ingnorant. When born a child, it is always miserable as it has to pass its time in a dirty state of insects or worms. It has to depend on others only.

Similarly in youth and old age, one is always unhappy and miserable by diseases, anxieties, and various other difficulties and troubles, though apparently as a person with big family members, wealth and kiths and kins he or she seems to be cheerful and happy. Sometimes one has to undergo innumerable troubles and hardships in the present life and has to pass from one bodied life to another which I need not relate any more, as you yourself, Oh vulture king, know it from experience. Oh holy bird! consequent shackles of births and deaths are indeed never broken so long as the ego remains there, ignorant he does not know his soul."

"The individual attains peace only if he knows his real perfect self i.e. the immortal soul that resides in his body also. Sampātī, you must pass your time anyhow because you too shall have to reap the fruits of your previous life. It is the natural and settled way of life which no creature in the earth can avoid.

"The only solution of life's serious problem is to attain knowledge and dispel ignorance from the mind by knowing one's real soul. For this reason, the realised soul does not mind even in the least as the how long he should lead the embodied life. Stay with your body as happily as a snake with its slough at Mandarāchal hill till the arrival of some monkeys going abroad in search of Sītā, who will be stolen by Rāvaṇa from the lonely cottage.

You will gain your lost wings by Rāma's grace when you happen to meet them and tell them about Sita in detail.

While Sampātī was talking with the monkeys his wings began to grow by Rāma's grace and by the power of sages' instructions. Then Sampātī flew away after blessing the monkeys and assuring them in this way.

"Rāma's names enable even sinful individuals to cross the ocean of worldliness for the eternal abode easily.

There is no question to arise that being his devoted messengers they can cross even this ordinary sea.

Chapter IX

MEETING OVER CROSSING THE OCEAN

After Sampātī had flown away, the heroic monkeys were highly delighted at the prospect of finding out Sītā. But they were terrified at the vast sea full of dreadful waves and acquatic creatures. Then Aṅgad told all the monkeys.

"Friends! now we should certainly go to Laṅkā to see Sītā and let me select one of us for the accomplishment of this hard task."

The monkeys could not suggest any of them because they were not sure whether one of them was competent for the task. So they kept quiet.

Aṅgad then asked each of them to tell him as to who would be able to jump up the longest distance. Some of them said that they could jump twenty miles or more but nobody was ready to cross the sea as was properly needed for the task.

Jāmbavān said that in his youth he had made twenty one rounds of the early-like foot of Lord Bikram at a stretch but then he could not cross the sea in his feeble health on account of old age. Aṅgad assured them that he could cross the sea, but was not confident whether he could return from Laṅkā safely.

Jāmbavān told him that it was not proper for him to go to Laṅkā even if he would; because after all he was ruler, the heir apparent of Sugrīva.

Aṅgad was disappointed on not finding any body fit for the job.

Jāmbavān said.

"Angad! do not worry.I know the monkey who can succeed in this job very easily."

He said to Hanumān.

"Dear Hanumān, why are you keeping quiet. You are the mightiest of all of us. You could spring five hundred miles nearly above the earth in the sky when you were just born with a childish intention to swallow the sun taking it to be a fruit. Your are the son of God of rains. So you are mighty and valorous as the winds.

Who can describe your exploits? Please be prepared to go to Laṅkā.

Thus encouraged Hanumān enlarged his body as huge as a hill and roared loudly as if he were breaking the sky asunder, and said.

"Sir, just tell me what I have to do?

Am I to bring back Sītā by killing Rāvaṇa with all his racial beings and burning his Laṅkā to ashes or should I bind Rāvaṇa with a rope and lift up the whole island where his Laṅkā is situated so that I may hold every thing on my left hand, place it before august Rāma, or should I return by meeting Sītā only, the illustrious lady.

Then Jāmbavān said.

"Exalted Hanumān, you go to Laṅkā and return after seeing Sītā, only, and you will be required to show valour later when we all go to Laṅkā.

With blessings and cheerings on all sides, Hanumān climbed the top of the hill by the seashore and his arms and enlarged his body. He looked as radiant as the rising sun and as big as a mountain.

PART V

SUNDARA KĀṆḌA

Chapter I

HANUMĀN CROSSES THE OCEAN

Hanumān, highly desirous as he was of crossing the vast sea though it was abounding with crocodiles and other terrible creatures, was fully confident of success in Rāma's mission. He once more addressed the monkeys and let them know that even an ordinary being is authorised to achieve liberation from the worldly mazes, if he utters Rāma's name even once. Hanumān added that he, a true and fortunate devotee of Rāma, with his image within his heart and the finger ring designed to be delivered to Sītā through him, would in no way fail in quest of Sītā.

He adjusted all his limbs as needed and facing the south, undertook at once a marvellous flight in the form of bouncing.

In the meantime the dieties were inquistive to know whether Hanumān would be able to enter into Laṅkā. So, they told Surashā the mother of snakes to create some sort of hindrance, in the way of Hanumān and then to return after testing his skill and capacity.

So, he was detained by Surashā, the serpant's queen-mother on the way and she said.

Hanumān! I am hungry and want to eat you.

He replied.

"Mother! I am going on Rāma's mission to Laṅkā. I promise that I shall offer myself for your food after accomplishing my Lord's mission and seeing him duly."

She said.

"No, I am very hungry and cannot wait. So go in

my mouth otherwise I shall devour you."

He replied.

All right, open your mouth. Hanumān swelled his body ten miles long and broad. Surashā also extended her jaws fifty miles wide. He again increased his figure two hundred miles. They went on broadening their bodies all the more in competition on defeat on another, then Hanumān in the tinniest form entered into her mouth and came out and stood before her and said.

"Mother, I bow down to you. I have just come out of your stomach. I think you have appeased your hunger by swallowing me. Now let me go."

Surashā who did not even know how he had entered into her belly in a moment so she felt ashamed and said. "Dear sir, you can go. I had played the trick with you for knowing your sagacity and might by orders of dieties who wanted to know your capacities. Please excuse me. Your shall see Sītā and return to Rāma." Then he resumed the fight over the sea. The Sea God asked the radiant hill-god Mainkā to meet and welcome Hanumān on his way over the sea. So, Mainkā on the top of his fruitful island could meet Hanumān and said.

"Sir, please have rest for sometime and take refreshments. I am ordered by your Sea God to welcome you as the sea was raised to the rank of an ocean by the kind predecessor of Rāma and you are also Rāma's devotee."

Hanumān replied.

"Thanks for your kindness, but I cannot rest even for a moment while going for Rāma's work."

He proceeded further touching some fruits as mark of reception and proceeded further. As he was nearing Laṅkā's shore, he found that his movements were being hampered by some shadowy object. He then could see easily a demoness lying over the surface of water. She was known as Sinhikā and was drawing him towards her by her magnetic energy. He kicked her to death and safely reached the shore.

He passed the whole day at that place and at night he assumed a very tiny form and quietly entered inside Laṅkā but he was caught hold of by Laṅkinī, the guard of the city. She kicked him saying.

"Villain! who are you to enter into the city?"

Hanumān returned a hard blow upon her mouth and she bleeded profusely and then she requested Hanumān.

"Hanumān, you please enter into Laṅkā freely. I know that the end of Rāvaṇa has come now. Creator Brahmā had said to me that Rāvaṇa would be killed by Rāma when his messenger, a monkey named Hanumān strikes blow on your face while trying to enter Laṅkā.

She told him all about Sītā and thought herself fortunate enough to remember Rāma always in her heart. At the time when Hanumān crossed ocean, the eyes and arms of Sītā, Rāvaṇa, and Rāma began to throb vehemently as good signs for Rāma and Sītā and evil ones for Rāvaṇa.

Chapter II

RĀVAṆĀ'S THREAT TO SĪTĀ AND TRIJAṬĀ'S DREAM

Hanumān in a tiny form entered the city to look for Sītā. He took a round of Rāvaṇa's palace and of all the nooks and corners of the city in vain.

At last he remembered the words of Laṅkinī and could find Sītā strongly guarded by the demonesses and spent up with anxieties, under a Sinshapa tree in the Ashoka garden. She was merely uttering Rāma's names. Hanumān then hid inside the leaves for the purpose of watching her within a keen sense of his being fortunate in his great achievement.

In the meantime, Rāvaṇa being anxious as to why Rāma did not reach Laṅkā for so many days, saw in a dream that a certain monkey had arrived at Laṅkā and met Sītā. So he, together with Mandadorī and other women, came to Sītā's place in a dress of full manner. But in fact he deserved his death at the hands of Rāma. He said to Sītā.

"Why do you hesitate to accept my love? Rāma is worthless for you. In fact, he does not like you. He is only proud and ungrateful, and does not even care for searching you. He thinks himself to be very wise and learned though he is really stupid and absent minded. Sometimes he even disappears and cares for nobody." You shall be my prime queen if you accept me."

Sītā highly exhasperated at his words placed a piece of grass as a curtain between she and Rāvaṇa and harshly replied.

"Villain! how dare you say me such mean words? You shall be torn into pieces by Rāma's arrows at any time. He will very soon arrive here with Laxmaṇa either by drying up the sea or constructing a bridge of arrows.

There is no doubt that you are very mean; so you really deserve punishment; but you still boast in vain of kidnapping me like a dog stealing oblations from the sacrificial area."

Rāvaṇa was much annoyed and rushed forward to strike her by his sword.

Mandodarī checked him saying, "Lord, do not hurt Sītā in this way. You have so many young wives. Why do you hanker after her who is so lean and thin and unfit for you.?"

Rāvaṇa returned to his palace after saying to Sītā.

"Sītā; mind that I shall make you my breakfast if you will not yield to me within two months."

All the demonesses who were keeping vigil and watch over her, were also ordered to bring her to his side any way they could.

So they began to frighten Sītā and tried their worst to pursuade her to accept Rāvaṇa's words.

Trijaṭā one of the guards, prohibited them saying.

"Do not harm Sītā anymore but bow to her respectfully. I have seen a dream that Rāma arrived here to take her back and that Rāvaṇa is naked and smeared with cow dung over his body and has gone away southwards. Bhibīshaṇa is sitting very happily with Rāma. It indicates that Rāvaṇa will be killed and Bhibīshaṇa will get Laṇkā's throne and Sītā will go back with Rāma.

All the guards then kept quiet and went to bed, while Sītā in a helpless mood was weeping and trying to kill herself as she had been very much teased and harassed by them.

Chapter III

HANUMĀN MEETS SĪTĀ

Hanumān was watching Sītā from the tree. He became very much anxious at her definite mood to commit suicide. So he spoke in soft words and began to relate the history of Rāma. Sītā was bewildered when she heard it. She said, "Anybody who is speaking in such an unexpected way, may appear before me so that I may know how far he is sincere." Hanumān in a form as tiny as water bowl got down from the tree and bowed to her. She bent her downwards as she suspected him to the Rāvaṇa coming in monkey's form. Hanumān said.

"Mother! don't suspect me. I am your humble servant." He presented her Rāma's finger-ring. She felt exceedingly happy when she saw the ring as dear as her life. She said, "Great monkey! I am gratified to you for the immense trouble you have taken to come to see me. Please tell Rāma everything about me as you have seen and kindly request him to arrive here as early as possible otherwise Rāvaṇa shall kill me within two months. I am sure that Rāma has great trust in you. May I know who you are?"

"Hanuman replied."

"Mother, my name is Hanumān, the Chief Minister of King Sugrīva of Kishkindhā.

Sugrīva now is the sworn friend of Rāma and has therefore promised to restore you by killing Rāvaṇa with all his race. He has millions and millions of monkeys always prepared to fight for Rāma's sake".

Sītā said.

"Hanumān, I wonder how such tiny monkeys as yourself would be able to fight against such ferocious and mighty demons."

Hanumān enlarged his body as big as a hill and Sītā

was pleased to see him and said.

"Hanumān! I am now confident that you are the mightiest being.

She asked. "How shall you bring Rāma and all the monkeys to Laṅkā ?"

He replied "Either we will construct a bridge or may jump over it as I have done." Sītā said. "Tell Rāma that he should kindly reach here at his earliest convenience. Once he was taking a nap in my lap when Indra's son Jainta in the from of crow peeked and wounded hard my foot. Rāma came to know this and picked up a straw once to release it like an unflinching arrow towards Jainta. The arrow was closely chasing Jainta wherever he flew but not throughout the heaven and the earth could save him from Rāma's arrow.

He has to atleast return to Rāma. He implored him to kindly spare him his life.

Rāma told him that he had to pay the penalty to his infallible arrow by the loss of his left eye. Fully aware as I am of Rāma's extraordinary valour, I am confident that his arrows will certainly kill Rāvaṇa as well as all other mighty demons. But I cannot understand why he is so late in arriving here."

Hanumān replied.

"Mother, Rāma made alliance with Sugrīva who collected millions of monkeys and sent them to every part of the earth in your search as a result of which I have arrived here and found you.

Rāma shall immediately start as soon as I go back and tell him about you. Please now do not worry."

She at his request handed over her brilliant hair-pin in proof of the interview and said.

"Hanumān, take it to Rāma and convey my deep respects to him.

Hanumān thought within himself that he should as

a truly devoted servant, meet also Rāvaṇa and thus perform some other remarkable deeds in Laṅkā before his return to Rāma. He requested Sītā "Mother I am hungry. Please allow me to take some fruits."

She replied.

"You could have taken so many ripe fruits but I fear the guards will trouble you."

Hanumān said.

"I do not care for them."

Hanumān uprooted all the fruit trees of Aśoka garden and ate as many fruits as he liked and killed the guards also. Rāvaṇa sent one million servants and followers. Hanumān killed them in a moment. Rāvaṇa again sent a large number of soldiers and his minister's five sons whom also Hanumān finished in no time. He sent still large numbers of mighty soldiers with his son Akshaya Kumar upon whom also Hanumān pounced to level them to dust by a big iron rod.

Then Ravaṇa himself wanted to take to the field but Indrajit assured his father that he would go out to bind Hanumān and bring him before his father.

There was a dreadful fighting between him and Indrajit who at last could bind Hanumān with divine and unfallible nook "Brahmapāsh" given to Indrajit by Creator Brahmā.

The divine "Brahmapāsh" had effect on Hanumān for a short time only. Since he wanted to be taken before Rāvaṇa, he remained quiet as if he were really bound and was carried to Rāvaṇa by Indrajit.

It is funny indeed to think that Hanumān also was bound up. Even these individuals that chant Lord Rāma's names are freed from worldly bondages. But Hanumān was perpetually devoted to Rāma and was free from illusive shackles. He met Rāvaṇa as a captive because he wanted to hold a talk with him and give him sound and wholesome counsel.

Chapter IV

LAṆKĀ ON FIRE

Indrajit told Rāvaṇa. "I have brought the ape binding him by Brahmapāsh, the divine noose. He is not an ordinary being whom you should treat carefully."

Rāvaṇa said to his minister named Prahasta.

"Ask Hanumān as to why he had come to Laṅkā."

Prahasta said to Hanumān.

Monkey! what brings you here? I hope you shall be freed if you tell the truth.

"Hanumān replied "I am Hanumān, the humble servant of Rāma and the Chief Minister of King Sugrīva of Kishkindhā and I happened to be here in search of Sītā, whom Rāvaṇa has stolen like a wretched dog."

"Rāma, King Dasharath's son with his brother Laxmaṇa and wife Sītā had reached Pañchabatī for his exile for fourteen years in forests to carry out his father's orders. He is at present staying at Prabarshaṇa hill and is attended by millions and millions of monkeys who are fully prepared to attack Laṅkā as early as possible. I am one of them and have seen Sītā here and destroyed the garden as is the natural habit of a monkey. I have also killed the armies of demons to defend myself. Indrajit has brought here by binding me with Brahmapāsha which affected me only for a short time but has completely freed me. I have reached here simply because I have to see Rāvaṇa and give him sound advice for his own good."

He then said to Rāvaṇa.

"You are the descendant of the renowned and pious sage Pulastya and Kubera is also your brother. Your body is therefore not of a demon, and your soul is really pure, immutuable and immortal which you are in real sense. You are not the body and sense organs because you are virtually the soul which is one in the whole universe, without the second. All the material organs and the body are the creations of ignorance only called perpetual, illusion or Māyā of God.

Your soul dwells in your body is immanent everywhere similar to the sky, and it has no contamination with the worldly matters like the sky which is always separate and free though it is immanent in the whole Universe. Your ego which governs the intellect and the mind, feels happiness or misery, pleasure and pain, but your soul is no other than God Himself and the creator of your body, as well as the intellect and mind because these are but perishable matters. "You must be devoted to Rāma, Omnipotent, Omnipresent, Omniscent God. Sītā is Laxmī and Rāma is a Lord Vishṇu's incarnation in the human form. It is your gross folly to incur enemity with Lord Rāma whom you can easily please by love and worship."

So achieve your highest goal in life immediately offering Sītā to Rāma and begging pardon of him for your tremendous mistake, otherwise you cannot remain safe and happy and you will be growing worse and worse day by day."

At this Rāvaṇa angrily and harshly said."

"Proud and stupid monkey, how dare you say such horrible things to me? I can kill Rāma, Laxmaṇ, Sugrīva and all the monkeys easily; and I am just doing away with you for your mischief."

Hanumān very angrily said as if he were burning the demons with wrath.

"Vile demon! I am Rāma's servant; and crores of Rāvaṇa's like yourself can not stand against my unlimited valour."

At this Rāvaṇa became very furious and ordered one of his attendants to strike off Hanumān's head by the sword. Vibhīshaṇa then stood up and advised Ravaṇa politely.

"Brother, it does not look fair to kill one's messenger. Let him go to Rāma and tell the news. You can punish him in another way and send him back.

Rāvaṇa said to his soldiers, "Burn the tail of this mischievous monkey and drive him away."

The soldiers wrapped Hanumān's tail with cloth soaked in oil but Hanumān enlarged his tail to such a great extent as they got finished all cloths, oil and ghee that was available, still the tail was not fully covered. Somehow or other, they bound his tail with ropes and rags and set fire to it. Huge bodied demons carried him round the city in the midst of abuses, threats and blows. Hanumān fully aware of right opportunity, bounced upon the tarraces and roofs of the house with the blazing tail and burnt the whole city to ashes except the mansion of Vibhīshaṇa. He then dipped his tail in the sea to put out the fire and went to see Sītā.

His tail was not hurt at all since Sītā had prayed God for his safety, so how could the natural fire harm him.

Hanumān is the chief messenger of Lord Rāma, so he is always free from binds of fire. Even ordinary persons are fully absolved of burning cares, anxieties and sins by mere remembrance of Rāma's holy name.

Chapter V

HANUMĀN'S RETURN TO RĀMA

Hanumān bowed to Sītā and said.

"Goddess mother, I have completed my work, kindly allow me to go to see Rāma and he will arrive here with Laxmaṇ and Sugrīva as early as possible."

Sītā said.

"I was so happy to see you and again I shall be left alone and miserable. Hanumān requested her.

"Mother, I can take you on my shoulders to Rāma in a moment if you like."

Sītā replied, "Son, go alone, let Rāma come here by any means, relieve me from the clutches of Rāvaṇa and kill him together with all his demons and his armies. He shall have to gain fame and leave behind a glorious and abiding example for the future.

Hanumān leapt over the sea and roared loudly in the sky.

All the monkeys who had been waiting for his return on the shore were very happy to hear his loud voice which indicated joy, victory and success.

He was very cordially received by his fellow monkeys on the sea-shore. Thereafter to their great joy all of them very enthusiastically returned with Hanumān to Prabarshaṇa.

On the way they reached Madhubana, Sugrība's garden, full of fruit trees and honey-hives.

On their request Aṅgad allowed them to refresh themselves by eating honey and fruits. Dadhimukh, Sugrīva's maternal uncle who was the guard of the garden angrily rushed forth to make complaint to Sugrīva. On hearing that the monkeys were taking honey and fruits, Sugrīva knew that they must have seen Sītā. So he gladly ordered Dadhimukh to send them to Rāma as early as possible.

Aṅgad and Hanumān with all the monkeys arrived at Prabarshaṇa hills very happily and Hanumān narrated to Rāma that he had met Sītā in Laṅkā.

Rāma was overwhelmed with joy and said "Hanumān, I thank you for your deeds which you have performed. Even gods would not have been able to do what you have done. Tell me every thing in detail. Is Sītā keeping on well?"

Hanumān requested.

"Lord, I have seen Sītā, the holy mother, in Ashoka Garden under the shade of Sinshapa tree under the strict patrol of demonesses. She has become very lean and thin and looks very shabby. She has sent her respects to your Lordship, with her hairpin for identity.

"I have told her everything about yourself and assured her that you would arrive there. She has requested you to kindly go to Laṅkā immediately."

I have burnt Laṅkā also to ashes. I had a talk with Rāvaṇa who is very obstinate and cruel. He really deserves punishment of death by your august hands."

Hanumān presented the hairpin to Rāma who was very much moved at heart at the miserable state of site.

Then Rāma said.

"Hanumān, I am really grateful to you I cannot give you any reward. I simply embrace you and assure you that my full-self is duly mingled with yours."

Hanumān was exceedingly happy and he was so much fortunate to have Rāma's embrace even not obtainable by gods, sages and aspirants.

PART VI

LAṄKĀ KĀṆḌA

Chapter I

RĀMA PREPARE WAR WITH RĀVAṆA FOR RESTORATION OF SĪTĀ

Rāma said to Sugrīva happily, "Hanumān has saved me as well as Laxmaṇa, yourself and Raghu's dynasty, since he crossed the vast sea and had a talk with Sītā in Laṅkā. He has really accomplished the most difficult task which nobody else in earth could have even dreamt."

"We should now make full preparations. No doubt, for going to Laṅkā but it appears dubious to me whether I shall be ever able to cross the dreadful sea abounding with crocodiles, whales, and ferocious aquatic animals and finally conquer the formidable enemies."

Sugrīva then said humbly.

"Lord, there is no reason for disappointment.

All the valiant monkeys can enter into the fire even for your sake. Anxiety is the cause of failure. Please take heart. We fully assure and say your Lordship! "we will certainly reach Laṅkā and put Rāvaṇa and all other demons to death. I do not see any person in all the three worlds who can stand against you in fighting when you shall hold your grand bow and infallible arrows in your hands. I see auspicious signs all around for our victory."

Rāma enthusiastically said.

"Let us start and cross the sea by any means."

Rāma said to Hanumān.

"Describe the situation of Laṅkā so that we may think out the plan for attacking the fort."

Hanumān replied.

"Lord, Laṅkā is a celestial city constructed on the three tops of a hill. The houses and palaces are grand and beautiful with fine gold and crystal nice pillars, windows and gates.

There are beautiful parks, gardens and tanks of clean water. The city is guarded by a very strong fence. The deep ditches at the foot around are full of blue water difficult to cross."

"Millions and millions of infantries, chivalries and elephants equipped with all sorts of arms and ammunitions and canons also are guarding the city's gates very cautiously. But there is no room for doubt if your Lordship enters into Laṅkā they will in no time be destroyed or reduced to ashes by you."

Rāma said.

"All right. This is the most favourable time, Oh Sugrīva, for the troops to march towards Laṅkā as my right eye is throbbing which indicates victory. I shall ride on Hanumān's shoulders and Laxmaṇa shall do so on Aṅgad's.

Rāma with Laxmaṇ and Sugrīva leading millions of monkeys started and the two brothers looked like the sun and the moon at the head of the armies that followed them.

All the monkeys very swiftly marched ahead day and night in great zeal. They could pass Mandarāchal, Sahādrī hills with splendid and magnificient forests.

They also crossed other hills and dales until they reached the sea-shore.

Rāma seemed to be very much disappointed at the sight of the vast ocean which had to be crossed in order to reach Laṅkā. Besides he found the brave troops about to loose courage. He too seemed to be deeply sad by the remembrance of Sītā as he had to play the part of human being.

No doubt, Rāma was Supreme Lord Vishṇu, Omnipotent, Omniscient and Omnipresent and had no feeling of weal and woe, as ordinary persons have. But people who would not know his essential and real entity might think him to be like themselves.

Chapter II

RĀVAṆA EXPELLS VIBHĪSHAṆA

Rāvaṇa called a meeting with his councillors after Hanumān's departure. He said to them shamefully.

"Hanumān returned after seeing Sītā, killed my son as well as millions of soldiers and burnt the city to ashes. But we could not harm him in any way. Now let me know what we shall have to take further steps for our safety and welfare. So think out unfailing plan among yourselves for the purpose.

The ministers replied.

"There is no reason for any anxiety. Lord, the monkey had escaped only on account of our negligence as we thought him to be an ordinary mischivious ape and we could have killed him easily. You have conquered all the three worlds, Yama, Kuber and gods and it is needless for us to fear men and monkeys whom we can eat very easily. We shall soon go through out the earth and devour all men and monkeys if you order or graciously allow to each of us the work to be duly accomplished."

Rāvaṇa's brother Kumbhakarṇa requested.

"Brother, you have really invited death by abducting Sītā like a man who thoughtlessly swallows poison pills. Sītā is Laxmī and Rāma is Lord Vishṇu's incarnation and he will surely destroy us in due course of time. But we should not be discouraged. I may set the matter right."

Indrajit interrupted.

"Father! I shall soon kill Rāma, Laxmaṇa as well as the monkeys if you allow me."

Vibhīshaṇa said.

"Rāvaṇa, it is a pity that you have stealthily brought Sītā. Neither, Indrajit, Kumbhakarṇa nor any of your warriors shall be able to resist Rāma and the calamity is imminent over the whole race of the demons. If you do not take shelter in Rāma humbly returning Sītā to him at an early date, the mighty monkeys will destroy us as well as the city well in no time. You cannot live safely even if you hide underneath the earth or take help from Gods, Indra, Yama and others, so long you will not return Sītā and beg pardon of Rāma.

Rāvaṇa was very much enraged with Vibhīshaṇa and he harshly began to sag.

"Wretched and dishonest fool! you really deserve death at my hands. Fie on you! You go against the nearest blood relation. Get out at once and do as you like. I am not going to see you any more, as you take my enemies' side."

Vibhīshaṇa smoothly said, "I am sorry that you have misunderstood me. I have always respected you as my father because you are my eldest brother. Sītā is really the cause of our destruction. You cannot escape from the hands of Rāma who is undoubtedly Supreme God whom nobody can defeat. You have turned a deaf ear to my sound counsel because Rāma has incarnated himself in the earth for killing you as well as the evil doers, at the earnest request of Brahmā the creator. Rāma is above nature and is immanent in and outside the whole Universe. He appears in various forms though he is formless like the blazing fire which has no shape and size but seems to be of different sizes when it blazes the trees of different sizes.

"I cannot bear to see the calamity hanging on you and the whole demon race. And, I therefore, leave Laṅkā and go to take shelter under Rāma and thus I hope that you will be content and happy if I go away."

He instantly sprang above in the sky and left Laṅkā with all his establishments. He had a higher aspiration for rendering services devotedly and satisfactorily to Rāma.

Chapter III

SUGRĪVA JOIND RĀMA'S CAMP

Blessed Vibhīshaṇa, with his four councillors, reached Rāma's camp by air and made a solemn request. "Lord Rāma, I am Rāvaṇa's brother named Vibhīshaṇa and have come here for resorting to your kind shelter. Though I am a brother of Rāvaṇa who has stolen your beloved wife and to whom all my counsel for his good proved a total failure."

Then Sugrīva said to Rāma.

"My Lord, demons are generally decietful and I make my humble suggestion that you should order the monkeys to kill him at once."

Rāma with a smile replied. "Friend, I can create and destroy the whole universe in a moment if I wish. But it is my firm vow that I should grant shelter to those who beg for it. We should, therefore, grant shelter to Vibhīshaṇa.

Vibhīshaṇa was excessively delighted to be allowed to stand before Rāma. He then falling flat upon the ground, paid his homage to Rāma and very fervently prayed.

"Lord, the light of Sītā's heart, the holder of the mighty bow, the benefactor of the aspirants, Sugrīva's friend, the leader of Raghu's race; the creator, the sustainer, and destroyer of the Universe, the Supreme Soul immanent in all animate and inanimate objects, I bow to your Supreme Lordships day and night."

"An individual cannot break the shackles of birth and death and cannot give up the temptation, greed, attachment, lust and aversion if he cannot see you through meditation and unswerving love. Ignorant and worldly persons cannot fully know you. They have no discrimination between conscious soul and gross matter just like those persons who cannot distinguish the silver from white Oister. You are all the dieties, Lord Shiva, Vishṇu and smallest of the small and the greatest of the great. You have no beginning nor any interval nor the end, but are perpetual and imperishable. You have no body and limbs but act and move everywhere."

"Lord, you seem to be a human being by your illusory power only and all the devotees and aspirants know you to be 'Nirguṇa', soul without form and attributes. I wish that I may follow the path of salvation by devoting myself entirely to you night and day. Kindly save me from husky misery of worldliness."

Rāma said.

"Vibhīshaṇa, I am very much pleased with you and shall grant the boon you like."

Vibhīshaṇa replied.

"All my desires and ambitions are fulfilled simply by meeting you. Nobody is more lucky than myself. My bondage from worldly attachment has been completely broken today, and I need no further material prosperity. Kindly grant me your abiding favour only so that I may never miss my goal of salvation and forget to serve you."

Rāma said.

Let it be so. I always remain with Sītā within purified hearts of peaceful aspirants who have renounced worldly pleasures for my sake and are also practising yoga with firm and unflinching faith in me. There is no reason why you should not attain salvation as you are sincere aspirant. Even an ordinary aspirant is entitled to salvation he persues or writes down or listens to my hymns."

Rāma therefore said to Laxmaṇa, "Laxmaṇa, I should like to bestow the throne of Laṅkā upon Vibhīshaṇa; at this very moment. Get him coronated ritually with the holy water of the sea."

All the monkeys were very glad to find Vibhīshaṇa

highly favoured by Rāma and they exclaimed. "Blessed be Vibhīshaṇa!"

Sugrīva embraced Vibhīshaṇa and said.

"After all we are Rāma's vassals, and have to assist him in restoring Sītā.

I am confident that you will discharge your duties."

Vibhīshaṇa replied.

Sir, we are but the tolls and Rāma is almighty and we act as he wishes to do."

Sugrīva was glad to hear such humble speech of assurance and devotion from Vibhīshaṇa. In the meantime a spy named Suka sent by Rāvaṇa entered secretly into Rāma's camp and said to Sugrīva.

"Sir, Rāvaṇa respects you as his own brother and has sent a message to you that you should not have any concern with the struggle between Rāma and him, and he has especially requested you to kindly return to Kishkindhā, because it is impossible for you to conquer Laṅkā and every attempt shall prove to be a futile effort."

Some monkeys at once leaped upon him and began to deal out severe blows upon him.

Śuka was much frightened and he cried out. "Lord Rāma, kindly save me."

Rāma prohibited the monkeys from doing so and Śuka again said to Sugrīva.

"Sir, what shall I say to Rāvaṇa?" Sugrīva angrily replied.

"You are my enemy similar to Bāli. You cannot escape death from Rāma's hands, because you have abducted Sītā."

Before this incident, a demon named Śārdūla had communicated every detail about Rāma and his military strength to Rāvaṇa who had since then been overwhelmed with cares and anxieties.

On the other hand, Rāma at the indifference shown by the God of Ocean, very wrathfully said to Laxmaṇ. "Brother! I wish to dry up the ocean by striking an arrow. The sea God has no regard for me."

Rāma raised his bow and fixed a dreadful fiery shaft which glittered like God.

The earth, forests, hills and the sky were shaken by the terrible shock from the blazing anger of Rāma. It seemed to be dark in every direction and aquatic beasts began to rush to and fro in fright under the water.

The seagod then appeared at Rāma's presence carrying with him many precious gems for presentation and respectfully bowed to Rāma and requested.

"Lord of the universe and saviour of three worlds, kindly pardon and save me. I am but ignorant and foolish because my nature itself is gross and materialistic life. I could not know your real supreme form of God who has in fact no form and attributes but is omnipresent, omnipotent and omniscient. You yourself are Lord Vishṇu, Rudra and Creator Brahmā and no body knows your Omnifice power in the form of illusionary actions needed from the prosperity and welfare of all the creatures of the three worlds."

"I shall cede the path to you so that you can easily cross the sea which is my body and I take shelter in you, Oh Lord."

Rāma replied.

"My shaft never goes in vain. Tell me the place where I can fling it."

The sea god said snavily.

"There is a place on the nọrth side named Drumkūlya where sinners harass me constantly."

Rāma dropped the arrow towards that direction and it soon returned into Rāma's quiver having killed the cruel and evil beings of that place.

The Sea God said to Rāma.

"Lord! Please order Vishwakarmā's son Nala for construction of a bridge upon the sea. The sea shall be narrow."

He then returned into the sea and disappeared.

Nala and all the monkeys started with great zeal and agility in the construction of the enormous and long bridge by the orders of Rāma and Laxmaṇa.

Chapter IV

ŚUKA'S ADVICE TO RĀVAṆA

Rāma constructed Lord Shiva's temple and installed Shiva Liṅga which was declared Rāmeshwaram (of Rāma) for the religious benefit of the world on the seashore at the very spot where the bridge was laid.

Rāmeshwaram has become since then a sacred place of pilgrimage, where Rāma himself had worshipped Lord Shiva very ritualistically.

Rāma had also blessed that if any body would bring the Gangā's water, and would offer it to Shiva's idol, he would be absolved of all his sins by Shiva's grace.

Architect Nala with the help of all the monkeys completed the construction of the bridge in five days.

Rāma crossed the sea with millions of monkeys and reached Laṅkā safely and stayed at Subala mountain which overlooked the city. He also saw Rāvaṇa with his ministers on the top of his palace and with anxious look cast towards the armies of the monkeys.

Śuka in hot haste reached there as he had been severely tortured by the monkeys. He very distressfully paid his homage to Rāvaṇa. Rāvaṇa said to him.

"How did you fare and Are you quite well?"

I suppose you are very much harassed by the monkey-troops.

"Lord, I was lucky enough that my life was saved by Rāma. I delivered your message to Sugrīva who replied that you would have to share the same fate as Bāli had. From what I have seen and from what I have gathered, I should suggest you that it is for the betterment of your life to discontinue your enemity with Rāma to whom no animate being can stand against his valour.

"Millions of mighty warriors are coming to destroy

Laṅkā. Even Rāma alone is capable of ruining the city of Laṅkā.

He introduced all the Chief monkeys with their names to Rāvaṇa who was looking from the terrace of his palace.

He further said.

"Lord, I cannot tell the exact number of the monkeys, but I guess that they are at least twenty one multi-billions. Lord, kindly note that Rāma and Sītā are incarnations of Lord Vishṇu and Goddess Laxmī, who is the creator, sustainer and the destroyer of the Universe. There can be no competition with them."

"Your material body is perishable and one day it is sure to turn into dust. Your soul is immortal and is divine and same with God. You have committed innumerable sins for the whole life only to satisfy your casual desires. So long as you do not know your soul, you shall be entangled in worldly ties; and the shackles of births, and death will continue to be stronger at each birth."

Even a dog can feel pleasures and pain in its life. But you are a Brahmin who should not be so reverse as to forget his own soul and always live like a beast enjoying only carnal pleasures."

"I, therefore, request you that you should certainly offer Sītā to Rāma and take his shelter and be devoted to him so that you may attain salvation by his grace. What I speak is solely intended for your welfare. You shall go down to the hell if you do not behave wisely. So endeavour always to please Rāma by love and worship and never forget the brilliant face of Rāma with his bows and arrows, in the company of Goddess Sītā. Place inside your heart the highly and beneficially divine feet of Rāma constantly adored by Sugrīva, Laxmaṇa and Vibhīshaṇa.

Chapter V

START OF THE WAR

Rāvaṇa abhored the wholesome words of Śuka and angrily replied.

"Villain, ungrateful and wretched, do you not feel ashame to instruct me in this manner? You really deserve death punishment, but I pardon you on merits of your previous good services. Get lost at once."

Śuka trembling with fear requested.

"Lord as it pleases you," and he went away.

Śuka was a learned Brahmin who had realised his soul with Brahma. He had led a saintly life by performing many yajñas and sacrifices for the upliftment of gods and the destruction of demons.

A demon named Bajradanstra was seeking opportunity for wreaking revenge upon him. One day sage Agastya reached Śuka's hermitage and Śuka requested the favour of accepting his hospitality that day which the Sage agreed to.

Sage Agastya then went to the river for bath. And in the meantime Bajradanstra went to Śuka's hermitage in disguise of Sage Agastya and said.

"Śuka, I have cherished for many days a relish for meat. So prepare meat for my food today."

Accordingly he was busy in preparation of ring dishes. Bajradanstra on the way enchanted Śuka's wife who fell senseless.

He disguised himself immediately as Śuka's wife and cooked human flesh and served it when the sage returned.

Agastya was very angry to see the human flesh served to him and he began to curse Śuka.

"Be turned into a demon immediately Śuka" he said in appalling tone.

"Lord, you had told to prepare meat. So my wife had cooked it."

Agastya found out the demon's mischief by meditation and said.

"Surely it was demons's atrocity and you are innocent. But my words will not go in vain. You will have to be a demon, but you shall regain Brahmin's form when you will advise Rāvaṇa for giving back Sītā to Rāma, and shall have to serve Rāvaṇa till Rāma goes to Laṅkā for killing him and other demons. You will then regain your previous form of Brahmin through the grace of Rāma and live peacefully in forests as you had done previously."

Meanwhile, father of Rāvaṇa's mother named Mālyavanta, came upto Rāvaṇa and said.

"Lord, many evil omens have been noticed in the city since Sītā's imprisonment here.

Many evil spirits have entered into the city. Dreadful clouds roar with thunder and shower hot blood over Laṅkā. All the idols of dieties weep and sweat and move from seats. Goddess Kālī shower her yellow and hedeous teeth and laughs at the demons. The cows give birth to asses. The rats fight with mangooses and cats and serpents do with the vultures, the Garuda the Lord of birds. A very dreadul god of death with a huge body which is yellow and black appears frequently at the houses of demons and many such evil omens are found to indicate perils and mishaps at hand."

"Please, therefore, offer Sītā together with a vast amount of wealth to Rāma and establish peace for the welfare of dynasty of the demons. Please know Rāma to be real God Nārāyaṇa and give up aversion and enemity for him. All seers and aspirants take shelter in Rāma's feet. And thus they purify their minds by their deep devotion with which they can easily cross the ocean of worldliness. Rāma is not an ordinary human being but is Omnipresent God."

"Though your moral character is not good, you will also be purified by worshipping him with devotion. Oh king of all the kings please accept my advise for the welfare of our dynasty."

Rāvaṇa who was doomed to die did not like Mālyavant's sound counsel and said.

"How do you think Rāma to be so great and mighty? He is only liked by the saints who dwell in forests. He has been banished by his father and has taken shelter with the monkeys. It seems that you have been sent by Rāma. Get away. You simply talk nonsense. You are my old relative and as much I have patiently heard your sharp speech which bites my ear. If you speak any more, it will burn my ears."

Rāvaṇa then went from there ascending to the topmost floor of his palace at the army of the monkeys and began to depute his warriors for fighting.

When Rāma saw him sitting gorgeously on his throne attended by the warriors in the palace, he shot an arrow which cut thousands of royal white ensigns and the crowns of his ten heads into pieces. Rāma also cut the glittering earnings wore by Queen Mandodarī who was sitting by the side of Rāvaṇa on the throne.

Rāvaṇa was taken aback at such wonderful feat of Rāma. He then entered into his room as he was very much ashamed.

He ordered Prahasta and other chief officers for fighting against the monkeys at once.

All the demons equipped with various weapons, such as swords, axes, spikes, bows, nooses and rods, rushed out of the city amidst the sounds of trumpets and together with musical instruments and sprang towards the enemies who waited holding big stones tree and hillocks on their hands. With cheers and applauses of victory for Rāma, Laxmaṇa and Sugrīva, the monkeys who led thousands of millions of monkeys ran with great fury and surrounded the city.

The chief warriors such as Hanumān, Aṅgada, Kumunda, Nīla, Nala, Sharab, Kesary, Maindha, Dwinbidha, Jāmbavān, Dadhimukh, Tara, and all other fighters, sprang towards the gates and surrounded them on all sides.

The monkeys began to maul the demons by hurling stones upon them and biting and tearing them by their nails and teeth.

The demons too ran towards the monkeys and began to retaliate their attack and thus there was a dreadful fight from both the sides. The stream of blood flowed here and there and the battlefield was soon covered with corpses, broken chariots, dead horses, elephants and mules.

The army of demons was soon reduced to one fourth and the monkeys were very furious and they continued to kill the demons very easily. The demons had really become powerless and unnerved because Rāvaṇa had been polluted with sin of kidnapping Sītā. On the other hand, the monkeys grew very much enthusiastic and vigorous as they were constantly guarded and fed as it were with nectorous food by Rāma, Lord Vishṇu.

Meghnāth, on noticing the heavy loss incurred to demons' army, became invisible and hurled, from the air, Brahmāstra and other deadly weapons upon the monkeys who were horribly destroyed by the skillful and ferocious warrior and within a short while a large number of them lay down in the battlefield.

Rāma waited for some time because he had to pay some regard to Brahmāstra, the divine weapon of Indrajit. He very angrily said.

"Laxmaṇa, bring my bow and arrows. I shall certainly kill the cruel demon Indrajit by Brahmāstra. See my valour today.

Meghanāth heard this and he cautiously and mysteriously ran to his home.

Rāma said to Hanumān. Please go to Droṇāchal which is full of divine herbs. Bring them at once to revive the dead monkeys. You will be renowned all over the three worlds if you can do so."

Hanumān swiftly went across the sea, brought the hill containing the herbs, soon revived the monkeys and replaced the hill on the same spot.

Rāvaṇa was much afraid and surprised when he heard that all the dead monkeys were brought to life.

He, then deputed all his best and most valorous soldiers equipped with most deadly weapons for fighting against the monkeys. He said to them.

"Be careful to fight against the monkeys. It is sure that Rāma is destined to be my greatest foe as he has descended upon the earth as human being with the purpose of killing me."

The demons tried their best for defeating the monkeys. They began to kill the monkeys by numerous deadly weapons such as bows, spikes, Tomor, Bhindipal etc.

The monkeys led by Sugrīva, Aṅgad and Hanumān grew very furious and annihilated the demons very easily because nobody could get energy without Lord Rāma's favour as his energy was not available to the demons who fought against god.

Rāma, God of all Gods, Omnipotent, Omniscient and Omnipresent was simply exhibiting human plays by fighting in this way.

Chapter VI

LAXMAṆA FALLS UNCONSCIOUS

Rāvaṇa was very angry when he heard the news of the collosal destruction of his army and the mighty warriors, Atikāya and others. So he himself went out to fight leaving Indrajit in the city for its defence.

He mounted upon a well equipped divine chariot and rushed towards Rāma. He wounded Sugrīva and other brave monkeys by his serpent like sharp shafts and saw Vibhīshaṇa in front of him.

He shot a divinely energic arrow towards Vibhīshaṇa, but Laxmaṇa stood in front of him to shied him so that the arrow might not hit him as he deserved to be protected by Rāma who had given him full assurance of his life. So the greatest infallible arrow entered into the body of Laxmaṇa. But what could it harm him who was an incarnation of Lord Śesha and is therefore the true source of all the energies of the Universe. Still he pretended to fall senseless upon the ground just to play the part of a human being.

Rāvaṇa got down from his chariot and wanted to raise Laxmaṇa for carrying him away with him but was unable to lift him from the ground.

Hanumān saw Rāvaṇa trying to carry Laxmaṇa and so he very strongly struck a blow to Rāvaṇa who fell upon his knees. His powerful bow also fell down from his hands. Rāma threw out Rāvaṇa's royal helmets also by hitting them with the shaft which looked like half the moon in shape and was intensely powerful.

Rāma said to Rāvaṇa, "You are severely wounded today and can go to Laṅkā to take rest, and tomorrow you shall see how I am to behave towards you." Rāvaṇa was ashamed and disheartened to be severely wounded in this manner. So he slowly returned to his palace.

Rāma also was much aggrieved at the condition of

Laxmaṇa who was lying unconscious. So he in a human role began to bewail and said to Hanumān.

"Go and bring the divine drug and revive Laxmaṇa as you had done to the dead monkeys."

Hanumān started immediately for Droṇāchala hill. Rāvaṇa became very anxious when he heard the news from his spies and on that very moment he flew to Kalnemy's house.

When Kalnemy saw Rāvaṇa all of a sudden he very politely with his two hands folded in due respects said.

"The king of the Kings! Why have your majesty arrived at my humble residence? What shall I do for your Imperial self."

Rāvaṇa replied.

"Dear and wise friend, Laxmaṇa is lying senseless with a shot by me and Hanumān has gone to Droṇāchala to bring the divine drug."

Please therefore do something by which he may not be able to find the medicine. You delude Hanumān by your illusion so that he may return in failure."

Kalnemy replied.

"Please listen to me and act accordingly. I shall surely obey your orders and do good to you at the cost of even my life."

"I shall have, no doubt, to share the same fate as Mārīcha had in the form of a gold deer. You have noticed that many of your majesty's relatives, friends, and sons as well as innumerable demons have already been killed. What benefits will you gain even getting Sītā and living with all pleasures after the destruction of all your near and dear ones?"

"Please take resort to some solitary holy place by handing over Sītā to Rāma, and your kingdom to Vibhīshaṇa.

"Renounce all worldly enjoyments and gradually restrain your mind from them and hold communion with your internal soul, condescended to realise in your mind that all the objects that are seen and enjoyed are material and perishable, and your body which is also material will surely perish one day.

Only your soul is immortal, blissful and real. All the objects and embodied creatures of the Universe from Brahmā to insects are perishable because they are the creation of God's illusive power of Māyā. The illusion gives birth to the seeds of worldiness with its three-fold powers, Sāttwik, Rajas and Tamas i.e. Quiscent, material and predatory, which shall produce, sustain, and annihilate all the creatures as well as the universe. Lost anger, greed, injury, slaughter, etc. are the progenies of illusion, and they overpower their master soul, which is stainless, pure and omnipresent. That illusion also ascribes all her actions and doings solely to the individual who becomes egoistic and thus falls a prey to worldiness. In this way, he feels pleasure and pain, mysery and happiness forgetting totally his real self and his soul.

He again regains the birth and realizes his soul and knows God if he meets a real spiritual preceptor to guide him to the right path. He thus breaks the shackles of ignorance and attains salvation even during his life-time.

"Oh Rāvaṇa, you also do the same and fully realise your soul to be quite apart from your material body and meditate deeply in order to know finally the soul or God."

"If you are unable to know your soul, in this way, you can concentrate your mind upon the form of Shree Rāma with pure attributes and realise him to be with a very charming and handsome appearance, with the crown and various ornaments, shining as the rising sun. If you be devoted to Rāma and Sītā in every heart, duly attended by Laxmaṇa, bow in hand, all your sins will be destroyed similar to the cotton burnt by fire. Please give up your enemity with Rāma who is Omnipresent, Omnipotent and Omniscient, pure, eternal and has no name and form in fact and always worship him in fervent devotion."

Chapter VII

HANUMĀN KILLS KĀLNEMY AND LAXMAṆA REGAINS CONSCIOUSNESS

Rāvaṇa was exhausperated at the nectar-like words of Kālnemy as if the fire-heated butter were affected by drops of water. He said.

"Wretched! It seems that you have taken some thing from Rāma and therefore you say as if you were his slave. Mind, I shall certainly kill you if you do not carry out my orders."

Kālnemy replied.

"Lord, why do you get angry for nothing. I shall act as you have ordained me." He instantly went to the Himālayas for obstruction of the way of Hanumān. He constructed a nice illusionary hermitage at the foot of the Himālayas where Hanumān was expected to pass along. He himself sat in the cottage in the garb of a sage.

Hanumān on arriving there in time saw a very beautiful hermitage which he had not seen previously. He thought within himself.

"I wonder that I see a nice hermitage which I had not marked during my previous journey to the Himālayas. Perhaps I have gone by the wrong path or my mind has been upset. I shall, however go to see the sage and drink water too."

He went to see the sage who was the giant Kalnemy in disguise. Hanumān found the place quiet and saintly with uncommon fruit trees. So he said to the sage.

"Lord, I am Hanumān and I am going to cross the mountain on an important mission of Rāma.I am very thirsty. Please tell me where I can find water."

Kālnemy, the disguised sage replied, "Drink the water from my bowl. Do not hurry away. Please take rest and sleep for a while. I know the present, past and future events by my divine knowledge. At present Laxmaṇa has got up and is quite well. Rāma is looking after at him."

Hanumān replied.

"I cannot quench my thirst with the little water contained in the bowl. Please show me if there is any tank or fountain." Kālnemy sent his boy attendant who was also illusionary to lead Hanumān to the tank. Hanumān bent downwards to drink the water when a crocodile rushed forth to devour him. Hanumān caught hold of it and tore it into two pieces. A very beautiful girl came out of the body of the dead crocodile and said to Hanumān.

"Lord, I am a fairy named Dhanyamālā and was turned into the crocodile by the curse of a sage. Today I am sanctified by the touch of your kind hands. The sage whom you have seen is the ferocious demon Kālnemy who has made the illusionary hermitage by his magic to put obstruction on your way. Please kill him and proceed to accomplish your sacred mission. I am going to the heaven by your grace.

Kālnemy said to Hanumān when he returned.

"Now, miss no opportunity. So make haste, but accept my "Mantra" sacred advice, and give me dakshiṇā.

Hanumān angrily dealt a blow and said.

Accept it as your reward. Kālnemy resumed his original form and began to fight very shrewdly with his illusionary tactics. The demon was very powerful and invincible too. But Kālnemy fell flat dead by the hard blow of Hanumān which shattered his head.

Hanumān soon reached Droṇāchala but saw no medicine there. He raised hill with his hands and in a moment reached Laṅkā. He said snairly to Rāma.

"Lord, please make haste and do what is needful to

cure Laxmaṇa."

"Rāma was very glad to see the hill and ordered Sushena to find out the medicine and properly treat Laxmaṇa. Laxmaṇa recovered by taking the drug and cried."

Wait Rāvaṇa. Where are you?" Rāma said to Hanumān.

"I am very thankful to you for your extraordinary valour due to which my brother is alive."

All the monkeys were also very happy and they began to fight with great zeal.

Rāvaṇa was so much tortured by the wounds he had received from Rāma's arrows' as the snakes are afflicted by vulture Garuḍa, and the elephants by lions. He said to his ministers.

Presentation that is given to one preceptor.

"Grandfather Brahmā, the creator had destined that I should be killed by a man. But there can be no man, who on earth can kill me. Rāma, therefore is certainly the incarnation of Lord Vishṇu. The sage Araṇya also has cursed me that I as well as my prosterities would be killed by a man.

It is, therefore definite that I shall have to meet my death from Rāma's hands. But Kumbhakarṇa is sleeping all days. He is simply a fool. You go and rouse him up so that I may send him to fight with Rāma."

Kumbhakarṇa was awakened and brought by Rāvaṇa's soldiers with great efforts. Rāvaṇa said to him. "Brother, Rāma has arrived here and the severe war with him is going on. It is very difficult to defeat him. He is gradually destroying my armies and uprooting the very foundation of demons' dynasty. I, therefore have awakened you so that you may defeat Rāma as I find no other warrior mightier than you."

Kumbhakarṇa laughed loudly and replied.

"Brother, I had already warned you against the inevitable danger. You have certainly welcomed your own death together with that of demon dynasty by continuing fighting with Rāma in this way."

"Once sage Nārada had told me that all the gods had requested Lord Vishṇu for incarnating Himself as a human being for killing both of us. Since Brahmā had destined your death from the hands of a human being only, Nārada had also told me that Rāma was the incarnation of Lord Vishṇu. He would always fulfil His promise in a right way. Therefore it is not wise to incur malicious enemity with Rāma who is Supreme God and who is now born in Raghu race. Your death is unavoidable. Devotion to God is the best means for the attainment of salvation. All the deeds of an individual who has no faith and love in God are of no use. The incarnation of Rāma, with Shiva at the basis, is the greatest and most perfect of all incarnations of Lord Vishṇu. All of them had acted upon the earth in various ways to fulfil the different purposes. But Rāma is very kind too and can be pleased by love and devotion very easily. Those who are devoted to Rāma are very easily able to find him, and can thus cross the worldly ocean. Those who read the life history of Rāma and Sītā are no doubt very much blessed and worthy of attaining salvation with eternal beatitude.

Chapter VIII

RĀMA KILLS KUMBHAKARṆA

Rāvaṇa was very much enraged at Kumbhakarṇa and he harshly answered.

"I know you are very wise, but I have not asked you to advise me. If you do not wish to fight, go to sleep. I think you are overpowered with sleep."

Kumbhakarṇa knew that his brother had lost his temper; and he leapt over the walls of the city instantly and rushed forward to get engaged in the battle against Rāma.

He looked very dreadful and ferocious and as big as a hill. He roared so loudly that all the monkeys were terrified and with noise all land and the sea resounded. He began to catch hold of the monkeys and swallow them.

All the monkeys were frightened beyond measure and they began to run away as all the beings run away at the sight of the death-god.

Wise Vibhīshaṇa approached Kumbhakarṇa, paid his respects and requested.

"Brother Kumbhakarṇa, I am your brother Vibhīshaṇa. Kindly excuse me and be kind to me. I had tried my best to persuade Rāvaṇa to give up the enemity with Rāma. But he did not listen. On the other hand he ordered me to get out. Attended by sinful and foolish courtiers, he denounced and kicked me, and I fled away from his council and have taken refuge with Rāma."

Kumbhakarṇa embraced him and very affectionately replied.

"May you live long and save our dynasty as you have secured Rāma's shelter!"

I had already heard from sage Nārada also that you are a great devotee to Lord Vishṇu.

Now please go away, I am so much bewildered with fury that I am unable to distinguish a friend from a foe.

Vibhīshaṇa very sorrowfully bowed to his elder brother and retreated to his camp.

Kumbhakarṇa began to mangle at many monkeys as he could, and thus he created havoc on all sides.

Rāma got very much exhausperated at such a horror created by Kumbhakarṇa. So he flung Bāyabāshtra—the divine stormy shaft upon Kumbhakarṇa whose right arm was instantly torn out. It fell upon the ground and killed many monkeys by the weight of the heavy arm. All the monkeys watched in scare the dreadful fight which had ensued between Rāma and Kumbhakarṇa. He ran towards Rāma taking a big sāl tree in his left hand. But Rāma chopped his left hand too in the same way. Kumbhakarṇa then rushed towards Rāma to swallow him up but Rāma severed both of his legs which were tossed by the mighty arrow at the gates of Laṅkā. Kumbhakarṇa then began to crawl for overpowering Rāma. He looked so dreadful as if the planet. "Rāhu" was covering the moon. Rāma severed his head from his body in a single shot named "Aindhra" The head thus chopped off fell heavily across the gate of the city but his massive body was flung upon the sea with many aquatic animals crushing instantly. Joyfully all the Gods showered flowers over Rāma from the heaven and began to pray with high applauses.

Meanwhile Nārada, the divine sage, approached Rāma who looked very happy and resplendant like the blooming blue lotuses. He began to applaude Rāma in this manner when he found him mercifully disposed towards the arrow strikened monkeys.

"God of all gods, Supreme Soul, eternal, Nārāyaṇa the support of the Universe, the witness of all the worlds, I bow to you. You are the symbol of pure knowledge and also of worldly knowledge, but you look happy or miserable assuming the human form by your illusionary power which seems to cover you also when you reside in every individual's mind.

Though you are naturally self enlightened, you are visible to pure-hearted devotee of yours. Oh Rāma, all the three worlds are created when you open your eyes and they at once disappear when you close them! You are Brahmā itself from which existence of all other objects follow, and beyond which there can be no substance. "I bow to you again. Learned souls know that you yourself appear in Nature, soul, time, form and objects with no visible forms. You are the manifestation of the Universe itself.

The vedas say that you are the pure knowledge and enlightenment without modification. The Vedas also clearly declare that you act by your illusion only. Again these Vedas confirm that you are pervading in every object in the whole Universe.

So there seems a contradiction where nobody can realize the real truth without your grace. Further, the creation and its objects of the world are seen upon your existence similar to the sun's rays that are seen in the water. Oh lord, you are eternal and perpetual with boundlessly spiritual possessions. So who can see you if you have no form and who can worship or mediate on you if one does not see you? Therefore wisemen attain knowledge and salvation by worshipping your frame of incarnation in the way of the knower as well as the known."

"There are obstructions, no doubt, like lust, anger, greed, illusion etc. during the worship and meditation and they terrify the devotees similar to the cats which terrify the rats.

But those who love you, sing your names, meditate on your form, hear the nectar like stories of your life, and get association with your aspirants, can succeed very easily and cross the worldiness as if they crossed the footprints of a cow."

I always meditate upon your form of Rāma. As a realised soul I roam all over the worlds, and therefore I am respected by all Gods."

"Oh Lord Rama, you have done a great work for the welfare of gods as you have today killed the mighty and cruel demon named Kumbhakarṇa. Laxmaṇa will kill Indrajit tomorrow and you will kill Rāvaṇa the next day and thus will relieve the earth from the burden of sins. I shall witness all the events from the heaven.

"Permit me to go, Oh Lord". Thus by the benign permission of Rāma Narada highly praised by Gods went to the pure Brahmaloka— the abode of the creator.

Rāvaṇa too heard the news of his brother's death to his great grief. In the meantime Meghanāth thereto consoled him and said in a pacifying tone."

"Do not worry wise King. Oh rev'd father, I shall certainly kill all the enemies by obtaining a divine chariot and other infallible weapons by pleasure of God of fire. I shall be victorious. With these words, he at once started worshipping fire in sacrificial altar by going to impenetrable Nikumbhala Cave, taking numerous ingredients of worship wearing red garlands and red dress.

Vibhīshaṇa informed Rāma all about the performance of sacrifices by Meghanāth. He made a request to Rāma.

"Lord, Meghanāth has started his sacrifice to the God of fire. He will be invincible if he pleases the God of Fire. Please allow me to go with Laxmaṇa who is competent to kill Meghanāth."

Rāma replied.

"I shall myself go and certainly kill him by Āgnya shaft—the fire emitting arrow.

Then Vibhīshaṇa said further by way of request.

"Meghanāth cannot be killed by any person other

than that who has not taken food and sleep continuously for twelve years. Since Laxmaṇa has done so for the last twelve years in keeping watch over you and eating no food, it is he alone who can kill him.

Moreover, he is the incarnation of Śeshnāga, the Serpant God, and as such he is the only person on the earth who can kill Meghanāth. I know that both of you have descended upon the earth in human bodies to play the worldly drama for removing the burden of the sins from the earth. You are decidedly Nārāyaṇa and Laxmaṇa is undoubtedly the incarnation of Śesha who has to protect this mundane world.

Chapter IX

KILLING OF MEGHANĀTH BY LAXMAṆA

Then Rāma said to Vibhīshaṇa, "I know everything about the dreadful giant who is very brave, illusory, and skillful in warfare. I also know all about Laxmaṇa as to how he has given up sleep and food for twelve years to be fully occupied with the arduous task in my services.

I have not as yet expressed anything about this as he has also to kill Indrajit."

Rāma said to Laxmaṇa.

"Brother, go to fight against Meghanāth by leading a large army followed by Vibhīshaṇa, Hanumān and other warriors."

Laxmaṇa touching Rāma's feet in reverence and holding the mighty bow said.

"Lord', today my mighty arrows will pierce Indrajit's body and go to the underworld to quench their thirst in the Bhagavati river."

Laxmaṇa reached the Nikumbhila cave, which was guarded by millions of demons who looked like the dense and dark patches of clouds. He was followed by Aṅgad, Hanumān and others with a huge army. In the meantime, Vibhīshaṇa pointed out the smoke coming out of the cave, and requested Laxmaṇa to shoot, his powerful shafts before it would be too late towards Nikumbhila cave. Laxmaṇa then hit Meghanāth who was offering oblations to the God of fire. So Indrajit came out of the cave and took his seat upon a heavy chariot, equipped with all sorts of deadly weapons. He at once began to fight with Laxmaṇa and there was really a dreadful battle from both the sides.

Meghanāth said to Laxmaṇa.

"Laxmaṇa, mind that I am the conqueror of Indra

and master of clouds. You cannot be spared from my hands today.

He also said to Vibhīshaṇa.

Uncle, you are born and bred up with us and I am your cousin. I cannot understand as to why you have accepted slavery of our enemies, and also find no cause as to why you have grown so jealous of your own cousin. It seems to be that you are very sinful, wretched and selfish."

Laxmaṇa fixed an arrow upon his bow and breathing hard like an enraged serpant flung it upon Indrajit who had also grown ferocious. Meghanāth fell unconscious for a while when the shaft which was as mighty as Indra's thunderbolt had hit him.

When he regained sense, he rushed towards Laxmaṇa in fierce temper "Laxmaṇa hold on your position and witness now my valour if you have not marked before."

Then he pierced into Laxmaṇa seven hard shafts and Hanumān by ten shafts. He with redoubled force and fury hit by one hundred arrows and in retaliation too showered numerous shafts which shattered and reduced to powder, the gold armour of Indrajit. Then he released one thousand arrows towards Laxmaṇa furiously. In this way the two emboldened warriors were fighting very fiercely and were heavily wounded by the shots from each other. Nobody could foretell how long the fight would continue and who would have the upper hand.

Meanwhile most valorous Laxmaṇa shot five deadly arrows which killed the driver of the chariot, horses, and cut off Meghanāth's bow as an indication of his manual skill. He also crushed the chariot on which Indrajit was seated.

Meghanāth grasped another excellent bow which also Laxmaṇa broke by shooting three arrows. He wounded Meghanāth by shooting numerous shafts when he was bereft of his bow in his hand.

Highly valorous Meghanāth again grasped another weighty bow and wounded Laxmaṇa together with the army of the monkeys by shooting innumerable bright and sharp arrows at a time.

There was very heavy and fierce fighting between Laxmaṇa and Indrajit for three days and nights incessantly.

At last Laxmaṇa fixed "Aindra" the mightiest arrow upon his bow which he drew upto his ears very vigorously and remembering Rāma's lotus feet shot the arrow saying.

"If Rāma is most pious and second to none in fighting, this shaft shall surely kill Indrajit."

The arrow did severe Meghanāth's head and threw it upon the ground.

All the gods were overjoyed when they saw Indrajit lying dead upon the ground. They sang songs in praise of Laxmaṇa and showered flowers from the heaven upon him.

Indra and all other saints were also very much delighted. The celestial beings sounded also various drums and trumpets. Everywhere in the heaven and on earth, there was applause with a solemn prayers to Rāma. So from the sky to the earth everywhere seemed to be peaceful and bright.

Laxmaṇa, blew his grand conch with zeal in token of his victory when his fatigue was gone. He twanged his bow also by way of proclamation which cheered the monkeys in the battlefield. He then, with all the troops, went to Rāma's camp and bowed to him and said.

"Brother, I have killed Indrajit by your grace."

Rāma felt very happy and embracing Laxmaṇa said.

"Brother, I thank you very much and bless you for your marvellous feat.

You have accomplished the hardest task today. We have really won the war as you have finished Indrajit by your continuous fighting for three days and nights. Rāvaṇa shall be killed very easily by me now, because he will lose his energy on account of his son's death.

Rāvaṇa much aggrieved at his son's death began to bewail of his irreparable lose in many a way. He consulted with his ministers once more. But he lost his temper so much that he ran to kill Sītā. But his wise councillor named Suparshva intervened and made a solemn request to Rāvaṇa.

"Lord, how do you think of killing a woman? You are Kuber's brother and the revered son of Bishrawā and you are very much learned, dutiful and generous. Take heart, you shall certainly gain victory and kill Rāma and Laxmaṇa on your own.

Then Rāvaṇa accepted the wholesome and beneficial words of his well wisher. He held a meeting the next day to discuss over the issue.

Chapter X

RĀVAṆA GETS READY TO FIGHT

Rāvaṇa resumed the fight next day together with the remaining ministers and forces. But he was severely wounded and mortified. All the demons who went out to fight against Rāma never returned alive similar to the locusts that rushed forth towards the burning fire. He was fully aware of the extraordinary valour and powers of Rāma and Hanumān. He was also deeply affected by the heavy loss of his demon troops. So he went to see his preceptor Śukra whom he pathetically said.

"Lord, Rāma has killed my brother, sons and the army and I am not in a position to defeat him. Why has such calamity befallen upon me when I have you as my divine preceptor for my protection?" Śukra replied.

"Take my 'Mantra' (Sacred words) and perform sacrifices; and you shall be invincible when you obtain a very heavy chariot with divine horses and a mighty bow with a quiver filled with divine arrows from the fire of worship. But be careful lest your worship may not be hindered in any way."

Rāvaṇa with necessary materials started his worship hiding himself in a very secret cave underneath the ground.

So he carefully had the doors of the cave locked and all the gates of his palace strongly closed.

Vibhīshaṇa came to know that Rāvaṇa was performing sacrifices and worship when he saw smoke rising in the sky. So he informed Rāma of the motive of Rāvaṇa.

He requested Rāma.

"Lord, Rāvaṇa has perhaps started his sacrifice and he will be invincible if he accomplishes it. Please send monkeys to disturb the worship atonce."

Rāma deputed Hanumān, Aṅgad and other mighty leaders with one hundred million monkeys who sharply leapt up to enter the compound of the palace.

They could easily do so and killed horses, elephants, and millions of soldiers who were put on guard on all sides. There was great uproar and fighting for the whole night. Then Vibhīshaṇa's wife Shurabha next morning beckoned secretly towards the place where Rāvaṇa was worshipping. Mighty Aṅgad then broke at once the gate of the cave by a single blow of his kick and entered into it. All the monkeys also entered into the cave and began to scream loudly and they dispersed all the ingredients of the sacrifice and struck Rāvaṇa with hard blows. They bit Rāvaṇa by their sharp teeth and tried to molest him in his meditation and worship; but he was very firm and remained calm and quiet in his meditation with closed eyes.

Aṅgad swiftly entered the palace and dragged away Mandodarī into the cave in Rāvaṇa's presence, and other monkeys also brought all other Rāvaṇa's wives in the same manner.

Mandodarī's dress and garments were torn and all her ornaments, necklaces and waistlests were broken and thrown hither and thither. She was very much worried when Aṅgad holding the tufts of her hair dragged her.

She most pitiably cried and said.

"Rāvaṇa, you are shameless. Your wives are being ill-treated and beaten by the monkeys in your presence; but you are silent and are still meditating for fulfilling your selfish end. You should have better died than to have allowed your better halves being insulted and tortured by the monkeys in this manner. Oh Indrajit, had you been alive, I would not have borne such calamities. My husband is turning a deaf ear to me and seeking only to save himself."

Rāvaṇa on hearing the most painful and humiliating words of his consort, rose up from his seat and struck a blow upon Aṅgad's waist by his sword and he cried.

"Leave the lady and get out."

Aṅgad and all other monkeys knew that all the hopes and motives of Rāvaṇa fell through and they happily returned to Rāmas' camp.

Rāvaṇa said to Mandodarī.

"Lady do not worry. Happiness and misery come to man subjected as he is to the condition or will of providence." "What is not seen if one lives long? Sorrow is undoubtedly the result of ignorance and can be avoided only by the attainment of knowledge. The egoism of an individual binds him in shackles of birth and deaths. Thus ignorance, egoism, and attachment to sons, relatives and other mundane objects are the root cause of sufferings in life." "The soul is pure and stainless and is the eternal realty which is free and aloof from his material body. It is blissful, self enlightened and has no worldly feelings." "There is no annihilation of the soul. Dear lady, you will feel no misery if you realize your soul. I am again going to fight the last battle with Rāma. In case I shall get killed I shall be united with his Soul. But you will immolate yourself in the fire along with my corpse after you have duly killed Sītā also."

Mandodarī very sorrowfully replied Rāvaṇa.

"Lord, please listen to me and act wisely. Rāma cannot be defeated by you or anybody else. He is the Lord of all Gods and the Universe. He Baivaswat Manu in the eve of creation, had placed the massive Someru Mountain on his back at the time of churning the nectar from the sea on his back in the form of a tortoise as big as hundreds of miles, had idlled the mighty demon Hiraṇyāksha by becoming a grand boar and had saved the earth from plauming into the sea, and had also killed Hiraṇya Kashipu by assuming the form of Nara-Simgha (half man and half lion). He had bestowed all the three worlds upon Indra by taking them away from the possession of Bāli whom he had deceived with a tiny form of a dwarf, when he had assumed the form Trivikram and measured the heaven, the earth and the underworld with his three paces. He had incarnated Himself as Parashurām to root out all the tyrant kings of the earth. Thus he conquered the whole world and had handed it over to Kashyap. This time he has assumed the form of a man, as presented Himself here to kill you."

"You have kidnapped Sītā only to bring such disaster upon us. Now please return Sītā to Rāma and beg his pardon to spare your life. Give over the kingdom to Vibhīshaṇa and let us lead the forest life."

Rāvaṇa replied.

"Dear lady, how can I go to forests to save my life only when so many demons, sons, brothers are already killed by Rāma? I shall be certainly killed by Rāma?"

"I already know that Rāma would kill me. So I shall secure the celetial abode with my followers though I shall have to be killed along with affectionate company. Should I be killed by Rāma I would be really freed from all sorts of miseries, misunderstandings, false attachments to relations and the entanglements of worldly affairs."

Chapter XI

RĀMA KILLS RĀVAṆA IN FIERCE FIGHT

Rāvaṇa thereafter mounting upon a very strong chariot having sixteen wheels and shielded with iron equipments and drawn by devilish and unrelenting mules reached the battle-field. He too was equipped with all sorts of dreadful weapons and was well guarded by innumerable soldiers. The armies of the monkeys were terrified at the dreadful sight of Rāvaṇa. Hanumān struck a bow when he came forward to fight. At this Rāvaṇa bleeding profusely said to Hanumān.

"Hanumān, I admit that you are really very mighty."

Hanumān retorted.

"Fie upon my might as I find you still alive! Let me try once more, and you also test your might by striking me with all your might." The Hanumān stood still allowing Rāvaṇa to strike him. Rāvaṇa hit a blow with all his strength, but Hanumān slightly realed for a second only. When Hanumān wanted to strike, Rāvaṇa went aside to avoid further conflict with Hanumān considering him to be mightier.

When serious fight ensued, Hanumān, Aṅgad, Nīla, Nala and other brave monkeys easily caused death to Agnivāṇa, Saparome, Khadaroma, Brishchika who were very fiery and dangerous, with their hair like-fire, swords, serpants and scorpions. Then with cheerful hearts and victorious roar, the monkeys returned to Rāma. At this Rāvaṇa also very furiously rushed with his chariot towards Rāma and began to shower heavy shafts upon him. Rāma in return shot stronger arrows. In the struggle Rāvaṇa wounded and killed several monkeys.

Indra, the King of gods, noticed from his celestial abode that Rāma on the ground and Rāvaṇa on his exalted chariot were fighting hard. Then he sent his chariot with Mātali, the divine driver who hastened to Rāma and bowed down with these weightly words. "Please mount upon this chariot sent to you by Indra for your complete victory over Rāvaṇa."

Rāma duly and happily took his seat on the fully equipped chariot and showered dreadful shafts as bright as fire upon Rāvaṇa."

Then a very terrible fight ensued between the two great warriors, Rāma and Rāvaṇa. But Rāma miraculously expert in archery smashed Rāvana's Agnivāṇa, Devāśtra and the most dreadful Rakshāstra which glittered like gold by his equally mighty divine shafts. So every strike however great from Rāvaṇa could be easily thwarted by Rāma, the Supreme archer. The broken divine and mighty shafts flung by both of them soon covered the ground.

Rāma would shower Garudāstra which produced vultures to kill furious serpants emitted by the shafts of Rāvaṇa. Then Rāvaṇa mad with extreme rage shot deadly arrows. He broke asunder also the gold banners and flags of the chariot and killed two horses of Rāma.

All the dieties, gandharvas, siddhas, and the spirits in the heaven and sages in earth were very anxious when they found Rāma amidst this difficulty when he was fighting against very fierce and dreadful Rāvaṇa.

Then Rāma too grew equally furious and began to struggle with Rāvaṇa and his shafts like the death-fire and pierced Rāvaṇa seriously. The earth was rocked and all the creatures were scared when Rāma was so angry as if he were going to destroy the universe itself.

Rāvaṇa was really intimidated at Rāma's supernormal valour. Rāma cut several of Rāvaṇa's heads by 'Indrāstra' and they drenched with blood began to fall from his body one by one similar to the fruits that fell from Tāl tree. The heads of Rāvaṇa would grow again and again and soon so many heads were cut by Rāma that they spread all over the battlefield and engulfed the sky also.

Rāma was surprised to find that as the new heads would instantly grow again every time he cut one. More than one hundred heads were cut off simply to be replaced by fresh ones. Rāma's all the dreadful weapons failed to bring an end to Rāvaṇa and he was at a loss to find out a way to serve the intended purpose.

Vibhīshaṇa then requested Rāma, "Lord, Brahmā, the creator has given a boon to Rāvaṇa by which power his heads are growing. The nectar is filled in a square tube under the naval of Rāvaṇa. You should dry it for killing him."

Rāma immediately flung an arrow which emitted fire to burn out Rāvaṇa's naval. So he could severe his heads and arms by the next arrow. Only one head and two arms of Rāvaṇa were left when Rāma burnt the naval, and he became very angry with Vibhīshaṇa who disclosed his secret to Rāma. He shot a terrible arrow towards Vibhīshaṇa to kill him instantly, but Rāma intercepted it by his gold pointed shaft.

Rāvaṇa looked very awkward and dreadful and still he fought with Rāma very courageously shooting numerous deadly arrows. The fight was really very alarming and unique.

Mātali then suggested to Rāma. 'Lord! now the time of Rāvaṇa's death has come. You should now pierce his heart by a powerful shaft because he cannot be killed if his heads only were cut."

Rāma fixed a very heavy shaft which had the power of the winds, the sun, the fire and the gods of directions and was as grand as the mountain Sumeru and Manderāchal and as vast as the sky, upon his bow and dashed towards Rāvaṇa. The blow of the arrow terrified all the creatures of the earth. The earth itself was rocked. The arrow directly entered the bosom of Rāvaṇa who fell dead upon the earth as his heart had been torn into pieces by that shot. All the followers and soldiers of Rāvaṇa took to heels and the victory of Rāma was announced.

Various drums, trumpets and all kinds of musical instruments were loudly played and sounded by the gods in the heaven and they expressed joy by showering flowers upon Rāma. Sages recited prayers and fairies danced in joy.

A light came out of Rāvaṇa's dead body and amalgamated in Rāma's self.

All the gods and saints said, "Rāvaṇa was really very fortunate. We still hanker after worldly objects and are miserable. But Rāvaṇa who had committed innumerable sins and was the most impious demon he was the enemy of the gods and the saints and he attained direct salvation which is even unattainable to saints and sages."

Nārada said to gods.

"Rāvaṇa always remembered Rāma even in enemity and never forgot him in his sleep and dreams. He was already aware of the fact that his death will occur by Rāma's hands and he was always mindful of Rāma's activities. He was no doubt entitled to the highest place in Elysium because Rāma had killed him."

"Every individual though he may have committed sins can certainly attain salvation if he repents and remembers god with love and devotion at the moment of his death.

The name of Rāma definitely sanctifies even the greatest sinners and never fails to secure him the Elysianation. May illustrious Rāma who is standing with the bow and the arrow in his two hands and who is as radiant as thousands of suns together be kind to me!"

Chapter XII

ENTHROWING VIBHĪSAṆA AND SĪTĀ'S RETURN

Rāma joyfully said to Hanumān, Aṅgad, Sugrīva, Jāmbavān and other leaders.

"I have killed Rāvaṇa today by your help and might. The fame shall last so long as the sun and the moon will shine upon his earth. Those who will hear my life-story connected with you all will certainly obtain the highest position in the paradise."

Mandodarī and all the other wives of Rāvaṇa began to bewail when they arrived at the place where Rāvaṇa's corpse was lying. Vibhīshaṇa too was very sad and he too began to bewail very bitterly.

Rāma ordered Laxmaṇa to console Vibhīshaṇa and Rāvaṇa's wives and to ask Vibhīshaṇa to perform the funeral rites of his brother Rāvaṇa without any further delay.

Laxmaṇa told Vibhīshaṇa who was deeply overwhelmed with grief. "Friend, think deeply and know who is he for whom you are so sorry and who are you to him after his death and who were you to him in your previous birth?

The individual under the influence of time and death meets by chance and departs from one another similar to the sands that accumulate at one corner of the river and flow away in course of its flow. One creature born of the other, similar to one seed which comes from the other simply to die away by god's illusionary power. That illusion also is due to ignorance on the part of an individual. But when he is in deep sleep, he will have no egoism to procreate the diversity of worldly things. So to a realised soul, there is no such thing as a different world."

"We as well as you and all the living creatures shall also meet the same fate so long as we are in illusion, and consequently birth and death shall occur according to the fixed law or order. So one shall certainly be killed by another individual if is so destined. Unborn perpetual God seems to create all the creatures and again to destroy them without any attachment to them like child's play. The soul which is always separate and immortal appears to be a bodily being as long as it is in the body which is material and perishable. The relation of the soul and the body is that of the wood with the fire which is immanent in the wood inactively.

"The soul is always the same and unchangeable, conscious spirit but it is supposed to be identified with worldly shapes, objects and actions. So death, birth, decay, growth, activity and inactivity are noticed similar to the fire which appears to have different in shape and dimensions according to the size and quantity of the wood that burns."

"If you think deeply you will know the soul to be only real and eternal and the body to be unreal, perishable and temporary. The individual who has realized his egoistic nature does not worry for mundane objects. He perpetually feels peace in life as he finds rest in his sound sleep. Give up all false worldly desires, restrain from your mental internal and external activities and twin yourself only towards Lord Rāma who is supreme and omnipotent in every creatures' heart." "Attachment to parents, sons, wives and near and dear ones, is due to temporal desires only. One does not allow any such attachment to rise if one fully knows ones' own soul. In fact, all these woman, wealth, prosperity, attendants, power, kingdoms, earth and other material objects seem to be perpetual and everlasting solely due to nescience."

"Get up and rule over your kingdom so long as your providence shall had you, always keeping Rāma in mind. Do not mind the past and the future but adjust yourself with the present always acting with justice and piety. You shall then never feel the hard pressure from the world."

"Lord Rāma has ordered you to perform necessary

funeral rites of your dead brother. Wise friend, console yourself as well as those ladies, send them back to the palace and see that there shall be no delay and hesitation."

Vibhīshaṇa got perfect consolation from Laxmaṇa's spiritual advice and went to see Rāma. He humbly and wisely asked Rāma whether it was proper for him to perform the funeral rites of his merciless and sinful brother Rāvaṇa.

Rāma replied.

"Brother, there is no enemity now with the dead body. So it should be properly treated by you as a younger brother."

Vibhīshaṇa performed very willingly the funeral rites of Rāvaṇa according to the religious rites in the midst of all other relatives, chiefs, ministers and retinues. The dutiful queen Mandodarī was duly consoled by Vibhīshaṇa and he sent all the queens to the palace. He went to pay respects to Rāma who was happy as Indra had been on killing his dreadful enemy Birtrasura. Mātali also returned to the heaven after paying due respects to Rāma and receiving consent and blessings from Rāma.

Then Rāma said to Laxmaṇa.

"Go to Laṅkā along with Vibhīshaṇa and install him formally on the throne with religious ceremonies."

Laxmaṇa went with Vibhīshaṇa and other monkeys and Brahmins who performed the coronation ceremony in great pomp and elate.

Vibhīshaṇa went to Rāma and with numerous articles for presentation paid his respectful homage. Rāma was very happy to see his promise all fulfilled as Vibhīshaṇa was declared the king of Laṅkā.

Rāma then embraced Sugrīva very happily and thanked him for his help which he had rendered for killing mighty Rāvaṇa. Rāma told Hanumān to go to Sītā and tell her all the news and return with message to him.

Intellectual Hanumān respected by the demons entered Laṅkā and met lean and thin but highly pious Sītā who, surrounded by demons was praying to Rāma. Hanumān respectfully bowed to her and delivered Rāma's message saying "Goddess, Rāma is quite well and happy in company of Vibhīshaṇa and all other monkeys, Sugrīva, Aṅgad and other leaders. He has killed Rāvaṇa with all his sons and relatives and he has bestowed the throne upon Vibhīshaṇa. He has sent me to convey this happy message and has also affectionately enquired about your health and condition."

Sītā was much delighted to see once more Hanumān whom she had seen earlier as Rāma's faithful messenger. She replied, "Brother! what can I give you for your goodness? I do not value all the riches of the three worlds more than these sweet words that you have brought from Rāma."

Hanumān replied.

"Mother! It is greater and more valuable than the riches and the kingdom of the heaven even for me, because I am getting the grace of victorious Rāma who is doing well to me and to whom I pay my respects daily."

Sītā said, "You have certainly been blessed with all the ideal merits and virtues. I desire to see Rāma. Try to take me to him as early as possible.

Hanumān took leave of Sītā and with her message went back to Rāma to whom he faithfully communicated everything and made his personal request too.

"Lord, please see Sītā for whose sake all our troublesome efforts have been finally crowned with success. She is very much anxious to see your esteemed self."

At this Rāma asked Vibhīshaṇa to go to Laṅkā and bring Sītā well adorned with jewels and dressed. Lord Rāma thought of quitting the artificial Sītā and bringing that real Sītā that had been entrusted to the God of fire.

Vibhīshaṇa too brought Sītā dressed finely by demons in a ground palanquin. All the monkeys rushed forward towards the palanquin to see her. The attendants and the bearers of the palanquin were surrounded by all the sides by the monkeys and there was huge rush. The attendants with canes beat and disposed the monkeys to make their way clear, but Rāma prohibited them with these words "Let Sītā come on foot so that all the monkeys may see their mother comfortably."

Sītā got down from the palanquin and got to the august presence of Rāma affectionately.

But Rāma pretended to take an indifferent attitude and said in very unpleasant and harsh words. Sītā too at such acute words of Rāma said to Laxmaṇa.

"Please blaze the fire in which I shall enter so that Rāma as well as all the people of the world may know that I am chaste and holy."

Laxmaṇa with Rāma's consent, collected a huge pile of wood sticks and set fire to it. Sītā took a round in great reverence of Rāma and said with her hands duly folded.

"May God of fire save me if I am holy and chaste and incessantly devoted to Rāma only."

She then took a round of the blazing fire to enter into it. In a soothing and fearless mood she entered into the burning fire and disappeared. At this deeply painful sight, all the dieties, sages, saints, and the monkeys were dismayed and they could not understand why Rāma had allowed Sītā enter into the fire. They began to talk among themselves as to why Rāma the highly learned Lord should get rid of Sītā, the incarnation of goddess Laxmī for whom he had suffered and endeavoured so in her absence.

Chapter XIII

AGNI AND INDRA PRAY RĀMA

Indra, Yama, Varuṇa, Kubera, Shiva, Brahmā, saints, sages, Gandharvas, fairies and all other dieties approached Rāma's camp and paid their homage in reverence and applauded him.

"Oh Rāma, you are the creator of the entire universe, and exist alone as the witness of all the creatures. You are indeed holy self and enlightened supreme soul. You are the Chief Basu, Lord Shiva and the Creator Brahmā. Your smelling energy is Ashwini Kumar, and the sun and the moon are your eyes. You are the prime source of birth of the worlds as well as their ending resort. You are the eternal, immortal, independent, unique and supreme soul. Those ignorant of your illusion take you to be a man only while who are enlightened ones, realize you to be no other but supreme God. Rāvaṇa had usurped our kingdoms by force and today we have regained them by your good grace."

Brahmā, the creator, invoked Rāma thus: "Oh Rāma, benign Lord, I bow to you the true incarnation of Supreme Lord Vishṇu. You are the omnificience of the universe and life, the chief goal of meditation for saints and sages. You are free from attachment, hatred, and love as you are imfathomable being Omnipresent, Omnipotent and Omniscient. You are a single existence and above the nature though you appear to be Omniform. I respectfully pay my respects to you. Rāma, the sages observe austerity, practise Samādhi (worship), hold communion with your real and pure self. Now you are the husband of Sītā, the incarnation of Goddess Laxmī, the real energy of life, the foundation of the Universe, and the prevailing entity.

"Rāma, you are Oṁkār, the Chief divine word, the teacher of Yoga, happiness of all the creatures, beyond the extent of birth and death, revered by the greatest Yogi, Lord Shiva, perpetual, holy, infinite, the destroyer of cruel demons and wicked beings. Lord, you are my respected Master, fulfiller of my demands, Nārāyaṇa beyond time and space, far from palpable inference and roof, the sustainer of the world, knowable by merely sincerity, faith, devotion and love, the remover of the shackles of worldiness and joy of Yogi's mind."

"Lord, you create and annihilate the Universe as you are the greatest of all the Gods, unapproachable through material objects and reasons. Lord, you reveal yourself only to your beloved aspirants. Your appearance is as handsome as a blue lotus; I bow to you again and again. Oh Lord of Laxmi, you are never known to those that are irreligious and always attached to mundane affairs. Lord, you had once changed from Rāma's to Krishna's one in Bridavan as per the aspirations of your devotees and sages when they prayed. There is no difference between Rāma and the Lord of Mathura, Lord Krishna as you are one and the same. You are as bright as blue emerald. Oh excessively handsome, eternally happy and self enlightened soul you have only incarnated yourself for no other purpose than accomplishing my mission and promoting the welfare of the world."

In the mid of cheers, appalause and prayers, Agni, the God of fire appeared gloriously from the radiant fire Sītā gorgeously and divinely dressed and he began to pray humbly.

"Lord, please accept Sītā whom you had entrusted to me at Tapovan in Daṇḍak forests. Lord Hari, you had created an illusionary Sītā with you for some purpose. Now you have fully succeeded in killing Rāvaṇa and all his prosterities and you have thus freed the earth from the clutches of cruel demons.

Rāma very happily received Sītā, worshipped the God of fire in necessary way. When Agni the Fire-God was fully satisfied with his duty he went away with the permission of Rāma. Then Indra very joyfully and honestly prayed to Rāma and Sītā together.

"Lord, I pray to Lord Rāma who has radiant blue appearance, like the lotus, whose mere name burns away the bushes of worldliness, whose blissful image is always fresh in the memory of Goddess Pārvatī, who is the destroyer of the cycle of transmigration altogether and who is the refuge of all the dieties including Lord Vishṇu. I am devoted to highly revered Lord Rāma who relieves all the gods off their miseries and hardships. He is the only saviour of gods and is now in the human incarnation. Though in reality he has no such forms I repeatedly bow to you who keeps his aspirants happy in every way and his name is perpetually chanted by the saints and sages for removal of their ignorance and misery. The sages cannot easily know him in spite their yoga and penance."

"I always lay myself at the feet of Rāma who is blissful, enlightened, the most faithful friend to Sugrīva and other monkeys, most affectionate to Sītā and who always keeps himself far away from the worldly people, but is very near and easily obtainable to holy aspirants of pure hearts and acts. Lord, you appear as a man and play the human part only through your own inscrutable power known as illusion or Māyā. The hearer of your life story and who takes interest in, shall certainly attain salvation. Lord, I was always in high spirit by drinking luxurious celestial wine and took pride in sovereignty, but now all the pride and vanity have vanished by your favour. I again pray you with brilliant and littering garlands and amulets studded with precious jewels. You are as radiant as the burning fire and have destroyed all the demons. Divine Lord, your face is as handsome as the moon of the Autumn, and your eyes are very pleasing and gleaming like lotuses. Though you have neither beginning nor end nor form your physique in this incarnation is all illustrious as blue emeralds. You have killed Rāvaṇa, Birādh and all other terrific demons and have thus established peace in the earth. You look really glorious and charming in the gorgeous and elegant dresses, crowns and ornaments and are the Lord of the dynasty of the Raghu being the most valuable cordial treasuer of Lord Shiva."

I offer humble prayer to blissful and active Rāma with Sītā in his laps, looking very glorious and glittering like shining gold and is like lightening in the clouds."

Lord Shiva too seated with Pārvatī in the air chariot in the sky, made a happy suggestion to Rāma.

"Raghunandan, I shall meet you at Ayodhyā at your coronation ceremony. Please see now your departed father.'

Then Rāma could see the departed soul of his father king Dasharatha and he together with Sītā and Laxmaṇa paid their respects.

King Dasharatha embracing Rāma said, "Son, you have emancipated me from the ocean of worldly miseries."

Rāma ordered Indra to revive all the dead monkeys lying on the battlefield by sprinkling nectar upon them. All the monkeys then got up cheerfully by the effect of nectar and paid to their homage to Rāma. But the demons whose souls had been amalgamated with Rāma's self could not come back to life though nectar had fallen upon them too. This shows that Rāma's acts and powers were far above the effects of nectar too.

Vibhīshaṇa humbly entreated Rāma to condescend to take the bath and change the garb of the hermit, as fourteen years were over by them.

Rāma replied.

"My affectionate brother Bharaṭa must be anxiously waiting for me in the garb of a hermit at Nandigrām. How can I alone change my dress? You, therefore entertain Sugrīva and all other monkeys; I shall be equally entertained if you do so."

Vibhīshaṇa distributed innumerable costly articles, jewelleries and garments to the monkeys. Rāma asked all the monkeys to go back to their homes. He took Sītā in his arms along with Laxmaṇa and got up in the Puṣpaka air chariot presented by Vibhīshaṇa.

Rāma told Sugrīva and all other chiefs.

"Please go back to Kishkindhā with the forces of the monkeys just now."

He said to Vibhīshaṇa.

"You shall rule over Laṅkā and remember me all the time. Even Indra and all the gods of the heaven shall not be able to do you harm in any way. I am going back to Ayodhyā."

All of them with folded hands prayed to Rāma thus.

"Lord, all of us desire to come to Ayodhyā along with you against self for attending the coronation ceremony and adoring mother Kaushalyā."

Rāma consented to their request and permitted them to board the grand Vimāna.

Sugrīva, Vibhīshaṇa, Hanumān together with other mighty monkey chiefs took their seats merrily on Puṣpaka which took its flight in the air.

Chapter XIV

RĀMA REACHES AYODHYĀ

Then Rāma flew in Puṣpaka showing Sītā all the places of the battlefield where he had killed Rāvaṇa, Kumbhakarṇa and several other warriors. He proceeded further and showed to her the grand bridge, the temple of Rāmeshwaram where he had adored Shiva, the city of Kishkindhā and Rishyamūk hills. Sītā, with the permission of Rāma could take Tārā and other women too from Kishkindhā and they took a lift in Puṣpaka. Rāma flew over the Daṇḍaka forest where he had met sage Agatsya, Sutīkṣṇa and others. He reached the vicinity of Ayodhyā via Chitrakūṭa and the hermitage of Sage Bhāradwāj who offered him for stay for a night there.

Rāma paid his regards to the sage and enquired him.

"My holy Lord! Have you heard anything about Bharata? Are my mothers well? Is Ayodhyā prosperous?"

Bhāradwāj replied.

"Everything is fine. Bharata, in the garb of hermit, is living in Nandigrām and simultaneously is ruling over the kingdom of Ayodhyā anxiously waiting for your return. He has placed your sandals on the throne and has thus passed fourteen years simply on fruits and roots."

"Rāma, I know all that you did in Ḍaṇḍaka forest. I also know how Rāvaṇa stole Sītā and how you could kill him, Kumbhakarṇa and others, and how Laṅkā has been in consequence brought into your full sway."

"You are Supreme Brahma and free from the bond of birth and death. You are also the creator of all the creatures of the Universe and you remain lying upon the surface of water of the vast ocean which you had yourself created in the beginning of the creation. Oh the soul of the Universe, Rāma, you are Nārāyaṇa, the universal dweller in the heart of every creature. Even the grand-father, the Creator Brahmā has got his birth from your navel and you are the highly esteemed master of the whole Universe. You are indeed Vishṇu and Sītā is Laxmī, your illusionary power called Māyā and Laxmaṇa is Seshanāg, the God of serpants. You create the Universe through the Prime Active power inherent within you and nothing is beyond you. You have in fact no attachment to any of your creatures and stand simply as the witness though everything is to be created from your own energy. Lord, you dwell outside and inside all the creatures and constantly pervade everywhere. Ignorant persons take you for only a limited human being. You are the Universe itself as well as its prime cause. You are the sustainer, fosterer, the enjoyer as well as the object of enjoyment. There is no other object but yourself because whatever is seen, felt, heard and known is none but your manifestation. Rāma, your illusive primary power procreates the Universe and you have no form, you are also called "Birāt" grand-bodied self because of your Omniscience, Omnipresence and Omnipotence. You are known as "Hiraṇyagarbha" on account of the subtle body and subtratum owing to original and conscious energy capable of giving life and birth to all the creations.

So innumerable creatures originate from your unfathomable body and they ultimately merge into you when the purpose is over."

Oh Rāma, persons who hear and read your life story fervently shall certainly attain salvation. Brahmā, the creator had performed great austerities for pleasing you so that you might relieve the earth from the heavy burden imposed on her from the sinful and cruel beings. You, therefore, incarnated yourself in the dynasty of Raghu and have accomplished the difficult task for the welfare of the world. Now you shall be renowned in all the three worlds and live in the earth for thousand of years and perform many other benevolent deeds to leave behind the ideal example to be properly and happily followed by the human beings as well as the godly souls."

"Lord, I request you for stay today at my hermitage and it will be sanctified by your kind benign halt, and you will reach Ayodhyā tomorrow."

Rāma sojourned there for the night with pleasure. The sage entertained Rāma, Sītā, Laxmaṇa, Sugrīva including the rest of his company.

Rāma then ordered Hanumān to go to Ayodhyā and Shringaberpur to inform the people of his arrival and to meet Bharata and Guhā with his mission. He should return immediately to him. Hanumān flew like the winds in the disguise of a man. He informed Guhā about Rāma's safe arrival and thereafter to Bharata at Nandhigrām. He found Bharata lean and thin in a hermitage as a recluse clad in barks and deer's skin and smearing the body with ashes, living upon fruits and roots and chanting the name of Rāma incessantly. He reigned over the state after placing Rāma's sandles on the throne.

Hanumān respectfully said to Bharata.

"Lord, Rāma for whom you are so very anxious day and night is coming safely together with Sītā and Laxmaṇa. He has asked me to convey your Lordship the message of his advent."

Most illustrious Bharata fell unconscious for a while having been overwhelmed with joy. When he came to his senses, he embraced Hanumān excitedly with his eyes shedding affectionate tears. He sighed.

"Brother, who are you some diety or a man? You have been so kind to me by telling the happy news. I must give you one lakh cows, one hundred villages and sixteen beautiful damsels grandly decorated with ornaments in reward.

He again said.

"Many years have elapsed since Rāma left me. It is

truly said that an individual certainly obtains prosperity and happiness if he can wait and live for more than a century even though he has to pass his life through the terrific visscitudes of life.

Please let me know the whole gamut of events and occurrences which took place when Rāma was in forests."

Hanumān then related to Bharata all the events right from the kidnapping of Sītā to the killing of Rāvaṇa. Bharata heard all the events anxiously from Hanumān. He then said to Śatrughna.

"Raghunandan, order all the learned pandits to worship the gods in all the temples of Ayodhyā with great ritualism and devotion. All the dancers, musicians, bards, female dancers and flute-players forming three different groups should start in a grand procession from the city to receive Rāma. All the citizens, queen-mothers, the other members of the royal family, ministers, fuedatory chiefs, and the army as well as the civil officers, should be present at the occasion."

Śatrughna got every thing ready as instructed by Bharata. The city was also elegantly decorated with flags and banners; all the gates were fantastically adorned by skillful artisans. All the galleries and pillars of the gates and palaces were ornamented with precious and shining jewels, flags and banners of different designs and hues were hunged throughout the roads. The citizens began to rush out of the city at a very early time in the morning. To entrance the grandeur of the occasion there were such things as one lac well-saddled horses, ten thousand well-decorated elephants and ten thousand chariots which were drawn by beautifully briddled horses. The citizens too fetched with them several articles for presentation.

The members of the royal family and queens in beautiful palanquins followed the grand procession. The dutiful Bharata placing sandles upon his head with

Śatrughna and other attendants walked on foot to receive Rāma.

They saw the Puṣpaka plane shining in the sky and descending towards the ground. Hanumān said to all the people.

"Look at the plane wherein Rāma, Sītā and Laxmaṇa along with monkeys are seated."

All the people cried in cheering joys.

"Oh our beloved Rāma is coming! Then jealous cries resounded the whole atmosphere.

Rāma looked like the effulgent moon in the heaven inside the divine plane when he got down on the earth.

Bharata very humbly paid his respects and Rāma asked him and Śatrughna the well being of queen-mothers, ordered the plane to alight for going to Nandigrām.

Bharata again fell and offered his obeisance by the side of the plane. He very appropriately paid his respects. He also embraced Sugrīva, Jāmbavāna, Yuvarāj Aṅgad, Mainda, Dwivida, Nīla, Nala, Rishav, Sushen, Gorakshya, Gandhmadan, Sarava and Panash one by one. He said to Sugrīva.

"Rāma has conquered Laṅkā and killed Rāvaṇa by your kind help and you are indeed my fifth brother.

Śatrughna also very respectfully paid his homage to Rāma, Sītā and Laxmaṇa. Rāma bowed before his mother Kaushalyā who had become very lean and thin on account of anxieties. He also paid his respects to Kaikeyī and Sumitrā.

Bharata offered the sandles to Rāma in great reverence and made this solemn entreaty.

"Lord, I am today handing over to you the whole charge of the kingdom entrusted to me.I find you in Ayodhyā to my entire satisfaction and I feel that my mission in life has been successfully fulfilled. Lord of the universe, I have increased stocks of grains, the treasuries and the number of the army by ten-fold. Now I hope yourself will reign in this vast country of yours."

Monkeys praised Bharata in great joy and enthusiasm. Meanwhile Rāma reached Nandigrām and got down at the hermitage of Bharata with great pleasure.

Rāma sent back with thanks the air chariot Puṣpaka to Kuber for his service as it belonged to him. Then Rāma bowed to Sage Vashiṣṭha whom he offered the highest seat and he himself sat below his preceptor.

Chapter XV

RĀMA'S CORONATION AS KING OF AYODHYĀ

On the sincere and earnest request of Bharat, Rāma accepted the throne of Ayodhyā. Necessary preparations for his coronation were made. But in fact the sovereignty of the whole earth was even a trivial thing for Rāma who was Supreme God beyond the sphere of worldly pleasures and pains. Even a twinkling of his eyelid can destroy the whole Universe. His favour grants prosperity to Lord Indra and his illusionary power can create the whole universe with the twinkling of an eye.

His human acts are intended merely for teaching a good lesson to humanity.

Rāma as well as all the brothers took holy bath and changed their dresses.

Rāma put on very gorgeous and elegant dresses of silk and precious ornaments, necklaces and amulets. Laxmaṇa, Bharata and Śatrughna themselves decorated Rāma very handsomely. Royal maids did so for Sītā and Queen Kaushalyā decorated monkey's wives.

Śatrughna ordered Sumantra to bring the chariot glowing like the rising sun for Rāma and certain other chariots for Sugrīva, Vibhīshaṇa and Aṅgad.

Horses, elephants and palanquins were all provided for other monkeys and their wives.

Rāma proceeded towards the city on the chariot and he looked as if Indra were going on his chariot drawn by green horses.

Illustrious Bharata drove the chariot. Śatrughna held the royal ensign, Laxmaṇa waved the royal fans and Vibhīshaṇa took the shining Chamar (a kind of fan made of Yaktesils). They walked beside Rāma who was seated alone on the chariot which moved slowly amidst the cheers, prayers, music and dancing which reverberated the atmosphere.

All the citizens flocked on the sides of the road to have a holy glance of Rāma whose face was like "the dūrbāgrass" and who was adored with ornaments, necklace, armlets, and the most brilliant crown on his head. His royal robes were golden and he looked elegant and cheerful when he looked at the people with his beautiful and pink eyes like the buds of lotuses. He had also worn a garland of divine flowers which shone like the moon.

He had his face finely decorated with divine paints prepared with saffron and scent and he looked as if the sun were appearing at the eastern horizon.

Every body was exceedingly happy when Rāma entered the city in the grand and majestic procession. All the city women rushed in their windows to peep at Rāma. They showered flowers upon him and they were so charmed with Rāma as if they in their hearts.

Rāma in the meanwhile entered into this father's palace which looked like that of Indra. He met all the people who had devotedly and affectionately assembled there for greeting him.

Rāma once more paid his homage to his mother to Kaushalyā and other queens with great respects and love.

Rāma soon ordered Bharat to arrange lodging for Sugrīva and their monkeys in his own grandly equipped palace.

Bharata asked Sugrīva to send swift monkeys to fetch water from the sea for the coronation of Rāma and also arranged everything for the preparation of the ceremony.

Hanumān, Aṅgad and other leaders at once flew in the air and brought the water in gold formal pots.

Sage Vashiṣṭha, the head of the sages, Bāmdeva, Jāvāli, Vishwāmitra, Gautam, and many other saints, eminent and learned pandits duly assembled there.

Rāma and Sītā on the grand throne were ritually sprinkled with holy water and Tulsi flowers in the midst of chanting of the Veda mantras. All the dieties also offered "Tilak (scented paste) to Rāma. Rāma's coronation ceremony was grand as that of Indra whom the Basus had coronated on the divine throne.

Śatrughna held a very beautiful white ensign over Rāma's head and Vibhīshaṇa waived the white chamars and fans from both sides.

The God of winds presented a celestic gold necklace, Indra offered a very costly garland studded with brilliant precious stones and pearls to Rāma on the occasion of the function.

The dieties and gandharvas sang excellent songs and fairies danced, flowers were showered upon Rāma from all sides on the heaven, and divine musical instruments were appropriately sounded.

Lord Shiva also attended the ceremony and he as well as other gods, gandharvas and sages invoked Rāma in great joy and reverence.

Rāma with Sītā seated on the royal throne looked exceedingly grand and illustrious like the Sun and their robes, crowns and ornaments excelled those of even God Cupid.

Lord Shiva prayed to Rāma.

"I respectfully bow to you, Lord Rāma gorgeously seated on the royal throne with Sītā. Lord! you have no beginning and end, neither birth nor death since you are the eternal reality of the Supreme Soul. You create and sustain the whole Universe with all the creatures of both locomotion and non-locomotion and also destroy them in due course of time. You are without modifications and self-content and you have no attachment for anything.

"You play human parts on earth in various incarnations and set examples for the many sided welfare of humanity. You support the earth by becoming Seshanāg from below and grant life and energy to all the creatures by becoming the sun and the moon with lighting medicines and the rains from above. The energy which digests the food and sustains the life of the creature is no other than yourself."

"Lord, philosophers and learned people see many gods as Indra, Vishṇu, Shiva, Sun and the Moon, the God of death, the God of Wealth and others, but in fact all these forms of gods are from you alone as you are the Supreme Soul. You are material as well as spiritual, illusionary and real.

The incarnations, such as of fish, tortoise, lion and bear and other beings are your own plausible forms. The Vedas have definitely described that incarnations are possible from you alone as you are the Supreme Soul. These incarnations are meant to serve definite motives to be fulfilled in every case. So it is clear that every thing that exists is your own manifestation from your own energy, since these are contained in you only."

"You are above nature and outside the matter. Every person, Oh Rāma, cannot know you because he or she is deluded by your illusion, and those whose minds and hearts have been holy by your grace can see you and they know what you really are. Even gods including Brahmā seem to have not known you fully what to talk of other beings."

"The only easiest way to understand you and get salvation is to love and be devoted to your human form of Rāma with Sītā.

Oh Lord, that is why I am always happy and content with chanting and singing your name "Rāma." I live with Pārvatī in Kāshi (Vārāṇasī) and grant your name to the dying persons for their redemptions."

"I again pray you. Kindly grant a boon that those who earnestly hear, learn and recite this invocation, may attain salvation, knowledge, and prosperity as well."

Indra prayed to Rāma.

"Rāma, Rāvaṇa had forcibly taken my kingdom and confiscated my properties and now I have regained them by your favour.

All the dieties prayed.

"Oh Lord Vishṇu, the killer of Moor the demon, we shall henceforth receive proper shares of offerings which Rāvaṇa had deprived of us since long."

The departed souls (spirits) said "Oh Lord, we will now enjoy "Piṇdas" offered by our relatives in Gāyā which Rāvaṇa used to devour."

Yakṣhya said.

"Oh Raghunandan, Rāvaṇa used to force us to work hard and we had to carry his palanquins and heavy loads without any remunerations. Now we are relieved of such hardships by your grace."

Gandharvas said.

"Lord, we used to take pleasure in singing your names and songs, but Rāvaṇa had compelled us to sing his name and his praises only."

All other beings as serpant God, sages, cows, lower spirits, birds, Prajāpati Brahmā's sons and the fairies paid their homage and prayed to Rāma in their proper manners. All of them including Lord Shiva, Brahmā and Indra were very respectfully entertained by Rāma and they very happily returned to their respective homes after visiting Rāma.

Lord Rāma with Sītā and his brothers Vibhīshaṇa and Sugrīva was seen shining like thousand suns when coronation was held.

Chapter XVI

RĀMA'S FAREWELL TO HIS MONKEY FRIENDS

When Rāma who gives prosperity to all the peoples of the world, ascended on the throne, the kingdom naturally was filled with wealth, prosperity and food. All the trees were laden with fruits. Fields since then never failed giving rich harvests and even the scentless flowers happened to be fragrant with beautiful flowers and soothing secrets.

Rāma with great pleasure gave away lacs of milky cows, thirty crores of gold coins, hundreds of bullocks and innumerable valuable ornaments and costly dresses to Bhrahmins.

He presented a very costly diamond necklace as brilliant as the sun to Sugrīva, two marvellous divine armlets to Aṅgad and a diamond necklace of extraordinary value to Sītā who gave it to Hanumān.

Rāma pleased with Hanumān told him.

"Hanumān, I am very much satisfied with you. You may ask any boon you wish from me. I am ready to grant any such thing which even the gods of three worlds cannot get."

Hanumān humbly requested.

"Lord, I am satisfied with chanting your names only. Let me live in this earth as long as your name will be remembered.

Rāma said.

"Let it to be so. You shall live in the earth happily and independently till the delusion of the Universe when you shall be amalgamated with my own self."

Sītā said to Hanumān.

"Hanumān, all sorts of food, and prosperity shall follow you till you live."

Hanumān paid his utmost regard to Rāma and Sītā and reluctantly left them for going to the Himālayas.

Rāma said to Guhā.

"Friend, you will enjoy all sorts of pleasure and prosperity during your life and shall attain to my form after death."

He presented to Guhā many jewelleries and riches. Guhā also happily returned to his home.

Rāma gave valuable things and costly ornaments to all the monkeys who had gone to Ayodhyā. Vibhīshaṇa and all the monkeys including Sugrīva went back to their respective homes.

Rāma said to Jāmbavāna.

"Jāmbavān, you live in the earth till Dwāpara Yuga when I shall meet in form of Krishna and I shall have to fight with you for a certain cause."

Rāma ruled over the country very happily. He made Laxmaṇa his heir apparent Yuvarāj, though Laxmaṇa was reluctant to accept the post.

Laxmaṇa always attended Rāma and Sītā and served them very carefully.

Supreme Lord Rāma performed many sacrifices and yajñas donating large amount of wealth to Brahmins as daksiṇā.

There prevailed peace, happiness and prosperity in every family throughout the country. No woman was a widow, and the young never died prior to the old age and the people always worshipped and loved Rāma.

Even the rains were punctual and every business of people went on harmoniously. There were honest dealings everywhere. Everybody followed religious rules and observed fasts willingly.

Rāma also treated his subjects as if they were his own sons and daughters.

In this way he ruled for eleven thousand years and

established fame, religion, discipline and morality all over the earth.

One attains prosperity, longevity, health, bliss and welfare if one listens to or reads the Adhyātma Rāmāyaṇa which Lord Shiva had found to be the only truth and essence of religion and had condescended to reveal to his consort Pārvatī.

PART VII

UTTARA KĀṆḌA

Chapter I

AGATSYA NARRATES DEMONS, HISTORY

Victory to Lotus-eyed Rāma, the cynosure of Raghu dynasty, the joy of Kaushalyā's heart and the pride of Dasharatha in the form of a son."

Pārvatī said to Lord Shiva, "What did Ram do after killing mighty demon Rāvaṇa and others? How many years had the all abiding God lived in form of human incarnation after his enthronement in the kingdom of Ayodhyā with Sītā and how did he leave the mortal earth in the end?"

"Lord, my desire of knowing very wistfully the nectar-like story of Rāma is all the more increasing. Please tell his story in detail.

Lord Shiva replied.

"When Rāma had returned to his kingdom after killing the evil demons all the sages went to Ayodhyā for congratulating him. Vishwāmitra, Asit, Durbāsā, Bhrigu, Angirā, Kashyap, Vāmdeva, Atri, seven holy and divine sages, called Saptarshi, and Agatsya, the great sage, together with him many desciples reached the gate of Rāma's palace and said to the guard.

"Inform Rāma of our arrival. We wish to congratulate him and offer our blessings."

The gaurd promptly went to Rāma and with folded hands uttered.

"Lord, Agatsya with all other sages has arrived at the gate to see your Lordship. They are all standing at the gate."

Rāma ordered.

"Let them come in as comfortably as it can be."

Rāma entertained the sages very reverently and prayed to them with folded hands. He offered them many such divine seats as they deserved and also various articles of food. He presented a number of cows to the various guests. The sages very much pleased at the cordial reception and enquired after their health.

They also replied with respect that they were all keeping well and also enquired after his health and the well being of this country and said.

"We are fortunate to see you. Oh Lord, you have very much fittingly destroyed all the cruel and mighty demons such as Rāvaṇa and Kumbhakarṇa and others. It was possible for your Supreme self to kill them and all other mighty demons as you can wipe out the three worlds in a trice when you firmly hold your great bow but it was almost impossible to kill Indrajit, the son of Rāvaṇa. You have very easily killed them by your powerful shafts and have thus given us shelter with all the dangers and fear completely removed from us. You now happily live with all your mission properly fulfilled."

Rāma was astonished when he heard the puzzling works of the sages. So he with folded hands said.

"Lord, why do you speak so highly of Rāma's son though I had killed Rāvaṇa and Kumbhakarṇa and all other mighty demons who had conquered all the three worlds."

Most illustrious sage Agatsya then happily replied.

Please listen to the story of their births, deeds and the boons they had obtained. All I am telling you in brief."

"In Satayuga, learned and wise son of Brahmā the creator, had gone to practise penances by the side of the mountain Meru. He lived there in the hermitage of Tribindu and performed severe penances and he was always occupied with studies and adoration.

All the maidens of gandharvas, gods, and kinnaras used to come there and molest the sage by talking, laughing and singing. One day the sage became angry with them and uttered curses saying that whoever appears before him, shall be pregnant. All the girls then went away for fear of the curse, but the daughter of Tribindu, the royal sage, fearlessely walked in front of the sage as she was not aware of the curse. Consequently she conceived and soon symptoms of pregnancy developed. She went to her father Tribindu who knew everything by his divine sight. He offered this daughter to Pulatsya. The sage too, being pleased with her at her behaviour and services said.

"I shall give you a son who shall prolong our dynasty." She gave birth to a very promising son named Vishravā who later on became very learned and famous all over the world. Sage Bhāradwāj gave his daughter to Vishravā who begot a very illustrious son like himself. He also performed hard penances and obtained boons of boundless wealth from Brahmā. He was called the God of Wealth, Kubera. He asked his father Vishravā to kindly tell him a suitable and peaceful place where no cruelty might be seen, so that he might be able to protect all the wealth with continued prosperity. Vishravā advised him to occupy the city of Laṅkā which was built by Vishwakarmā for the residence of demons as they were compelled to go to the nether world for fear of Lord Vishṇu.

The city was situated on an island and it was well surrounded by the sea and could not therefore be attacked even by powerful enemies.

The God of wealth lived there merrily for a long time.

Once Sumālī, a demon with his beautiful daughter who looked like a goddess, went to the earth and he saw Kubera, the God of wealth living in Laṅkā. He said to his daughter, "Dear, you have been quite young and you should marry the sage born in Brahmin's family and you shall then bear children like Kubera, the God of Wealth, the son of Vishravā.

"She approached to Vishravā with the hope of being his wife, and stood at the door of the hermitage. The sage meditating for a while knew her desire and said to her "Pretty damsel, who are you and what brings you here?" She replied.

"Lord, you can know everything. You are Omniscient." The sage replied "Really you desire sons. You shall give birth to dreadful and ferocious demons because you have arrived here at the inauspicious moment."

She humbly requested, "Lord does it look well if I get such furious sons from such a holy person as you?"

The sage replied "All right, you shall have another son who shall be very pious, intellectual and be a sincere devotee to Rāma."

"So Kekasī, the maiden, Sumāli's daughter produced Rāvaṇa with two heads and twenty arms. The earth shook at the moment of his birth and many evil omens were noticed everywhere which indicated grave danger to the people of the earth. She next gave birth to Kumbhakarṇa who was as big as a hill. Then Suparṇakhā was born to her. She was also as terrible as her brothers. Last time she gave birth to Vibhīshaṇa who was very handsome and gentle. He was very fond of learning when he grew up, and became a sincere devotee to Rāma."

"Cruel Kumbhakarṇa roamed throughout the earth and devoured Brahmins, sages as well as other human beings mercilessly. Mighty Rāvaṇa terrified all the three worlds by his inhumanity and cruelty and his atrocities reached far and wide like an epidemic disease."

Agatsya continued to say.

"Rāma, you are immanent in the hearts of every

creature and see every action because you are the holy and Omniscient, and Omnipotent Supreme God. You act on the earth as a mortal being only by your illusionary power but you are never attached to the human plausible activities. You have thus asked me about the history of the demon simply because you pretend to know nothing; but in fact you know everything."

"I fully know that you are the one Absolute truth. You are indeed limited unimmagingly powerful, imperishable, unborn, essence and the ultimate source of happiness. I always take shelter in you and live happily by your grace only."

Rāma happily replied to the sage.

"The whole universe appears to be illusionary. It is not wholly separate from me. Chantings of my name and prayers are certain means for the atonement of all sins."

Chaper II

RĀVAṆA'S PENANCES FOR BRAVERY

Agatsya further said to Rāma.

"Once Kubera, the God of wealth visited his father Vishravā. Kekasī saw him and said to her son Rāvaṇa.

"Son, Look at Kubera so illustrious and enlightened! You also shall try yourself to be like him."

Rāvaṇa angrily replied to his mother.

"I pledge myself to you that I shall be even greater and even more powerful and more prosperous than Kubera. Please do not worry."

He and his brothers Kumbhakarṇa and Vibhīshaṇa immediately started for the purpose with full determination and sincerity. Their hard austerities seemed to have burnt all the three worlds.

Kumbhakarṇa passed ten thousand years in severe austerity, Vibhīshaṇa stood by one foot for five thousand years during the panances, and Rāvaṇa spent one thousand divine years without food and water and then sacrificed one of his heads at he expiry of every one thousand years.

Brahmā, the creator, appeared before him and said.

"Son, Rāvaṇa, I am satisfied with you by your penances, and shall grant you boons as desired by you."

Rāvaṇa supplicated.

"Please grant me such power as may perpetually spare me from Gods, Garuda, serpants, Kinnaras, Yakshas, and Gandharvas. I need not care for men who are nothing to me." Brahmā replied "You shall regain your heads you had sacrificed and they will not be destroyed in the future."

"Brahmā, then said to Kumbhakarṇa "Son, what do you wish for?"

Kumbhakarṇa said.

"Lord, I want that I may sleep for six months and be appeased with the food to be taken only once in six months."

Brahmā then went to Vibhīshaṇa and asked him what he had desired. Then Vibhīshaṇa said in the humble supplication.

"Lord, I want that I should always pass my life peacefully and piously and I may never think of cruel and sinful deads."

Brahmā was pleased with him and said.

"You shall be very religious and pious. In addition to this boon, I grant immortality to you, though you have not asked foɪ it."

Harsh minded Kumbhakarṇa repented afterwards that he had asked such foolish boons.

Sumāli knowing that his grandsons had obtained boons, he came from the underworld. Prahastu and many other demons also followed Sumāli and they congratulated Rāvaṇa. Sumāli boldly said to Rāvaṇa.

"Son, by our good luck, you have secured the desired boons. Now we are free from all dangers. We should return to Laṅkā and live there in prosperity, because Laṅkā was built for our residence by Vishwakarmā. But we had to go to the netherland only for fear of Vishṇu. You shall take possession of Laṅkā from Kubera either by force or by persuasion." Rāvaṇa replied sharply.

"It does not behave you to give such wrong advice."

But Prahastu interfered and persuaded Rāvaṇa saying.

"Dear Rāvaṇa! You have not learnt politics, so you have said merely from the point of view of your kindred relation to Kuber. There can be no such relation to be considered by the mighty person like you. The sons of Kashyap were both gods and demons but they forgot brother-hood and struggled hard with one another for the supermacy of power. The enmity between the gods and us existed from ancient times, even."

Rāvaṇa grew fully impressed by Prahastu's speech; and soon he sent Prahastu as his messenger to Kuber and could consequently drive away Kubera from Laṅkā to take possession solely of the kingdom.

Pious and gently Kubera went to the Himālayas and performed penances to please Lord Shiva who advised him to live in Alkāpurī built by Vishwakarmā for his residence.

Rāvaṇa became the King of Laṅkā and began to reign and also terrorise the people of all the three worlds. He gave his sister Suparṇakhā to Brihat Jiva, the son of Kalkanja and himself married Mandodari, the most beautiful of all the girls in the three worlds. Diti's son, the great and skillful engineer, called the Maya was her father and he had also presented an informidable weapon or shaft to Rāvaṇa. Kumbhakarṇa was married to Bairochan's daughter Brihatjwālā, and Bibhīshaṇa to Surabha, the daughter of sage Saibush. Meghanāth was born to Mandodarī. He roared at his birth so loudly as if the thunder-clouds were roaring, and so he was called the roar of clouds, Meghanād.

Kumbhakarṇa slept in a solitary deep cave, and Rāvaṇa was always occupied in harassing Brahmins, sages, serpants, Gandharvas, and all other beings in the three worlds. He forcibly looted god's property and damaged their palaces.

Kubera sent a message to Rāvaṇa prohibiting him from such evil deeds, but he became angry and defeated Kubera even and took his airchariot Puṣpaka forcibly.

Rāvaṇa went to fight against Indra but was defeated and captured. Meghanāth went to the heaven to defeat Indra whom he captured and brought to Laṅkā. Most valiant Meghanāth could release his father also and he got many divine boons from Brahmā, the creator who in turn persuaded him to set Indra free. Rāvaṇa subdued all the inhabitants and the Kings of the heaven, the earth, and the nether-world and he became the Supreme sovereign who ruled over the even gods.

He once went to the Kailāsh mountain which he tried to move. But he was cursed by Nandy—the attendant of Shiva that Rāvaṇa would one day be killed by men and monkeys.

Rāvaṇa went to Sahastrārjuna with whom he fought, but he was made captive by Sahastrārjuna and shut up in the horse-stable. Pulatsya released him there. Once Bāli also pressed Rāvaṇa under his arms and threw him away into the sea hundreds of miles far away. Consequently Rāvaṇa made friendship with him.

When Rāvaṇa became the master of all the three worlds, conquering gods and men by virtue of the boons he had obtained from Brahmā, religious rites, Yajñas, worshipping to Lord Vishṇu, Shiva and other gods were forgotten and prohibited and there were tyranny, autrocities, high handedness and misery every where."

Agatsya further said to Rāma.

"Lord, virtually you and Laxmaṇa have killed all these demons who were so terrible and mighty. You are in fact Supreme god Nārāyaṇa, the creator of the Universe. In fact you are Omnipresent.

All the animate and inanimate objects are but your forms. Brahmā, the creator has come into existence from your naval. The Gods of fire and the speech have come out of your mouth. The guards (pillars) of all the worlds are your mighty arms, the sun and the moon are your eyes. All directions and inter-directions are extended from eạrs; and Ashwini Kumars from your nostrils. The lokas (worlds) such as Bhu, Bhuva, Swa, etc. are manifested from your thighs, knees, buttock, legs etc. Lord Hari, the vast oceans have been formed from your belly. Indra, and the god of winds are born from chest, Bāli and other sages are produced from your semen. Yama from your lower part of the body, the God of death from plevis, three eyed Lord Rudra from wrath, mountains from your bones, rains from your hair, herbs from your tiny hairs of the body, insects and animals from your nails. We can, therefore say that the complete Universe containing living creatures and life as objects are only your manifestations. So, everything is one without the second. All the objects in diverse forms are only seen by your illusive power. Even nectar produced in Yajña (sacrifices) is available to gods through your energy and they are always looked after by you."

"Oh Rāma, you are immanent in all the created objects of the Universe similar to the butter in the milk. The sun and the moon shine through you but they cannot enlighten you. You, are omnipresent, eternal and absolute and known by those only who have divine insight, but ignorant persons cannot fully know you like the blind who can not see the sun. Sages study philosophy and ethics and seek after you in themselves and they pray to you day and night, but they ultimately find you by love or devotion only and that is the only way to please you."

Sage Agatsya further prayed to Rāma with great dedication knowing him to be Supreme God.

Chapter III

BIRTHS OF BĀLI AND SUGRĪVA

Rāma said to Agatsya.

"Kindly tell me the story connected with the births of Bāli and Sugrīva, who were the son of Indra and the Sun God, respectively."

Agastya said.

"Brahmā, the creator was once staying at the top of the mountain Meru which was very lofty with the golden peak glittering like gems. He was sitting on the grand hall of hundred miles long, in deep contemplation when he shed tears in divine bliss. He took some of the drops of the tears in his hand and enchanting them, softly dropped them upon the ground. A great monkey appeared out of it and Brahmā blessed him and advised him to live there happily. The monkey was named Riksharāj who was very intellectual also."

"One day he saw a very beautiful divine lake. He saw his own reflection upon the water and jumped into it thinking that another monkey was attacking him. He was turned into a very beautiful damsel when came out of the lake. Indra and the sun-god who were going to worship Brahmā, the creator saw her and they had sexual contact with him. Consequently Bāli was born from Indra and Sugrīva from the Sun God. Riskharāja in the form of girl had two sons in such a miraculous manner. She took rest in the night as a woman, but he got up in his own monkey form, next morning, and he went to Brahmā with his two sons." "Brahmā was happy to see the two brave and handsome monkey lads. He then sent Riksharāj and his sons with a messenger to Kishkindhā which was very beautiful city built by Vishwakarmā. Bāli was made the king of all the countries which were inhabited by monkeys and Kishkindhā became its capital town."

Sage Agastya further said to Rāma, "Rāma, you are the lord of all the beings and have now relieved the earth of its burden of sins by incarnating yourself as a human individual on the solemn solicitation of Brahmā. As a matter of real truth, it is not a great deed in your case, you reside in the hearts of all the creatures, you are sole energy of life, you assumed innumerable forms, but are only one infinite Energy."

Saints and supplicants praise your human deeds which sanctify the sinners and make the living beings happy.

Those that will read and recite the divine story of Bāli and Sugrīva births, shall certainly be blessed and pious".

Rāma, I shall now tell you why Rāvaṇa had kidnapped Sītā. Once Rāvaṇa respectfully made a request to Sage Sanat Kumar thus.

"Who is Supreme God to whom all other dieties pray and by whom they are blessed with marvelous energy to conquer their enemies and whom the saints and sages worship? "Lord, you know every thing and can exactly tell the truth."

Sanat Kumar replied.

"Son, Hari Nārāyaṇa is lord of the Universe, he is infinite, unborn and eternal. He is the foremost cause of all the living beings, and is worshipped by all the dieties day and night. Even Brahmā, the creator has been born from his naval. He is Almighty God, none else but he has created all the worlds and the Universe, saints, deities, and people pray to him and gain great energy. He has no form though he occasionally assumes it. He is immanent in lakes, rivers, and in all animate and inanimate objects. He is "Omkar" the Supreme Logus-Speech, and is the eternal truth. He is Sāvitri, the Goddess, the support of the Universe and the earth called Śesh. All the deities, oceans, Yama, the sun, the moon, the death, the sunrise, day and night, the winds, fire, Indra, clouds, rains, Basus, the creator Brahmā, Rudra, and all the creatures, and the Universe itself, are all his forms only.

"He is the Supreme God though he is without attributes and activities and unchangeable. He acts and plays in various ways. He shines in the form of lightening, burns in the form of fire, protects all the creatures as Viṣṇu destroys everything as Rudra, and in fact all the Universe is contained within him only."

"In his incarnated form, he looks like the blue lotus, is dressed yellow Satin Pitāmbar, and is always accompanied by Shakti, His consort who sits on his lap embracing him in great affection. He is inseparably allocated with Laxmi—his constant companion who looks as effulgent as gold."

"Nobody, neither gods nor serpants, giants, nor men can know him, but only those whom he favours, can see and meet him. Even sacrifices yajña, penances (tapa), charity, mortification, and learning, cannot help one in finding him.

"Only those who take refuge in him can hold communion with him. Thus, by virtue of this unflinching association and by the knowledge in philosophy, they have become sinless and can realise Vishṇu in their own hearts."

"If you also desire to see him, he will take incarnation in the form of Rāma in Tretā Yuya. Rāma will be born as the son of King Dasharatha of Ayodhyā, he will marry Sītā and go to forest in exile by his father's orders."

"Oh Rāvaṇa, I have told you every thing clearly, which you desired to know from me. It is upto you to see and please him when he descends in the earth from the heaven for the prosperity and welfare of the people."

Agatsya further said to Rāma.

"Rāma, Rāvaṇa, and the king of demons had determined to be your rival in order to have contact with you. He roamed all over the three worlds with desire of fighting against the mighty people living there. He had also kidnapped Sītā only with the intention of being killed by you, because he had no expectation that he would be ever able to please you."

Agastya said that if the people with high and earnest regard are interested in hearing the story, they would attain longevity, wealth, infinite happiness, and shall get their desired objects and all kinds of prosperity.

Chapter IV

SENDING OF SĪTĀ TO FOREST

Agatsya further said.

"Once Rāvaṇa came across Nārada and respectfully asked him. Lord, where do the mighty people live? I shall conquer them if you please let me know where I can find such mightiest people".

Nārada replied.

"There is a beautiful continent called "Śwetadvīpa". There dwell the people who happened to have met with death from the hands of Lord Vishṇu and many others who are his sincere aspirants and sole devotees. There they remain with unswerving courage and invincible powers." Rāvaṇa immediately flew to the continent of Puṣpaka which could not land there due to the powerful and glaring light of the ground. He, therefore left his air-chariot somewhere and reached the land on foot."

"Even the woman of the continent were so big and strong that they caught hold of the neck of Rāvaṇa, lifted him as if he were a tiny doll. He with great difficulty managed to free himself from their clutches. They asked him as to his whereabouts and then flung him into the air. Rāvaṇa had, therefore, determined to fight against Lord Vishṇu with desire that he would be happy and mighty if he was killed by Lord Viṣṇu Himself. He had therefore, taken away Sītā stealthily, but had respected, as her mother. Reality he had already known that you were Vishṇu.

Agatsya further said to Rāma.

"You are Omnipresent Lord and know that the past, present and future. You are simply a witness of all the actions of the individuals, as you have no attachment to and concern with them. You merely set examples of human works and highest kinds of rightousness to be followed by the people for the real achievements in life. You are at present only listening to my speech as if you were a human being."

Finally Sage Agatsya took leave of Rāma whom he thus pleased by adorations and prayers.

Then Rāma spent happily with Sītā and ruled over the country for many years. Hanumān, Sugrīva and other monkeys used to come to him frequently in tokens of the implicit regards for him. Once Kubera sent Puṣpaka the air-chariot to Rāma for keeping it with Rāma as long as he would live in Ayodhyā but Rāma sent it back with thanks and expressed at the same time his opinion that he might occasionally use it when it should be necessary.

The earth became very rich and prosperous during his reign and he also devoted himself very earnestly to doing public welfare.

All the people were religious and pious and no body in his region died immature death, no body would ever see the death of his son or younger one than he.

He would frequently tour all over his country on Puṣpaka and personally knew the condition of his subjects.

Once a Brahmin brought his son to Rāma and requested him to revive the boy who had died prematurely. It was an extraordinary event as no body else had died in young age and the Brahmā reproached Rāma for this sort of unnatural event. Rāma, therefore revived the boy. He knew that Sūdra's penances were the cause of the premature death of the Brahmin and he, therefore gave Sūdra the residence in heaven, for his sincerity by killing him for the revival of the boy.

Rāma installed crores of Shiva's idols and temples in different places for the well-being and instructions of the mankind.

He proved himself to be the most righteous and glorious king that had ever existed in the earth. He ruled for eleven thousand years.

Sītā also was the most dutiful queen and pleased Rāma every way. She was indeed endowed with all the noble virtues of a chaste woman.

One day Rāma was sitting with Sītā in his room very happily when she duly made this request.

"Lord, all the gods have requested me to suggest your supreme self that we should now ascend to our Esylium because they desire to serve you there as you have nothing left to do in the earth. They suggested me that if I would go to the heaven, you would naturally follow me. It is out of your sweet will for you to do as you like."

Rāma replied.

"I am also thinking of going to the paradise. It is true my mission in the earth is now completed. I shall send you to forests as if it were a banishment for you, because I hear that the public are against me for they have thought that I have done wrong in keeping you with me even after you had been taken by Rāvaṇa by force into Laṅkā, and you had lived alone at another house. You will give birth to two sons as you are pregnant, and you should live with Sage Vālmīki.

After some years, I shall bring you back and you shall then enter into the earth when I shall ask you to prove yourself to be chaste. I shall then ascend to the heaven after your departure."

Next day Rāma called a meeting and asked one of his detectives named Vijay.

"Vijay! tell me honestly, what is the public opinion about me.

Vijaya humbly reported to Rāma the public opinion together with his view.

"Lord! people of the city say that Rāma has not done right by keeping Sītā with him because she had been kidnapped by Rāvaṇa. It is true that the subjects shall follow the examples of the ruler. We shall also have to bring back our wives who have been abducted by others; and if we do so righteouness will no longer be maintained in our families."

Rāma next day ordered Laxmaṇa to take Sītā from the city and leave her in the forests near Vālmīki's hermitage.

Laxmaṇa had to do the same very reluctantly as Rāma had told him not to speak out any word on that decision.

Chapter V

LAXMAṆA PRAYS TO RĀMA

Laxmaṇa said.

Attached to you with intense devotion as bees to the lotuses, Lord, I recommend myself wholly to your feet which are sought for by the saints and sages by their meditation and which only can break the shackles of worldly bondages.

Please award me such spiritual knowledge as may help me easily to cross the ocean of worldly ignorance."

Exalted monarch Rāma, the grandeur of kings, the shelter of the devotees, heard all the words of Laxmaṇa and he in a very happy mood began to explain the scripture's knowledge capable of rooting out ignorance.

"Laxmaṇa, in the beginning, an individual should discharge with a pure mind all the household and religious duties according to the decrees enjoined by the Vedas to one's case in all different stages of like, i.e. Brhamacharya— continence or students' life, Grihastha— household life, reclusion, Vanaprasth life.

"When one's mind is settled and satisfied owing to performance of religious deeds, one should control one's external and internal sense organs by rigid practice of yama, niyama, dhyāna, Dhāraṇā and Samādhi and should realize one's soul on honest pursuit of the teachings of the "Śatguru", the spiritual preceptor who has already realized God.

"Actions always allure persons towards pleasures and in consequence results are endless circles of rebirths. A person, is entangled with shackles of births and deaths which are the consequences of deeds of his previous births. So long there is continuity of actions, there are rotations of births and deaths because the seed of life grown from his actions which in fact have originated from ignorance.

Attainment of knowledge only can remove such ignorance but not the actions of any kind."

"Ignorance and actions are not opposed to each other; because the former is the cause of the latter and every actions leads to another, the consequence of which is nothing but rebirths."

"Some people argue that just as knowledge is necessary for accomplishment of actions, so religious actions are also accessories to the acquisition of knowledge. Even the vedas sponsor relative action to be the means for salvation similar to those articles which are required for performing (Yajña) sacrifices. They also say that it is wrong for the aspirants to ignore actions ordained as essential duties by the Vedas for absolution to be finally achieved. But in fast, the argument is fallacious because actions and knowledge are contradictory to each other and the former is the result of egoistic activities which the latter completely eliminates and denies. In fact, knowledge is the ultimate way to realise the pure soul."

"A person attains supreme knowledge when the waves of thought of his called "Vṛttis" are totally immersed in the consciousness of his soul. All actions rise for egoistic notions and mental activities which are totally annihilated by knowledge. A person, therefore, should negate actions because there is no agreement and compromise between actions and knowledge i.e. (Karma and Yajña). This knowledge i.e. realisation of one's soul or God, is known as pure and effulgent because it is the outcome of the properly sanctified self. So a person should properly know his soul by restraining all his sense organs and their activities.

"It is necessary for him to perform actions by right methods as long as he has not transcended or removed his egoism which is the main source of all attachment to the body. By absolutely discarding every object and clearly knowing it to be unreal, he should realise the reality which is the supreme soul, Paramātmā. When a person does not feel difference between his soul and God by his enlightenment of inner consciousness all sorts of nescience or ignorance vanish away."

"If a person removes his ignorance by the application of logical argument based on scriptures, it (ignorance) cannot have any further hold and he becomes one with God. But if he is elightened by knowing the pure absolute fully at one time how can ignorance, egoism, worldliness, etc. crop up? For they have been already eradicated."

"By the above mentioned reasons, it is quite clear that knowledge, or Vidyā is independent and does not require any other kind of accessory objects for its attainment."

"The Upanishads, and avabadi branch of Brihadāraṇyak Upanishad also clearly mention that one should renounce worldly actions for the attainment of Vidyā which does not require any other for its attainment. No right example is given by the holders of the oppossite view in the cases of Karma and Jñāna, because Karma or sacrifices cannot be performed without help of others, such as priests and other articles and accessories of worship, whereas jñāna is attained by itself, with no need of other articles, and assistance. So, the goals to be achieved in these two cases are diagonally oppossed. Wisemen, therefore should know that there is no impiety even though they renounce "Karma" or actions, because only ignorant persons think they will commit sins or be impious if they forsake any religious "Karma". It is necessary therefore for the wise to abandon gradually all the sorts of religious rights and duties when their minds have been really settled by self-realisation. So a person when favoured and instructed by his preceptor should understand the purport or essence of the statement of the Vedas such as 'Tattwamasi' which means that you are He, the Supreme God.

Then the servant will be happy and content and his

mind will be settled similar to mountain Sumeru; because he will know that his soul and God are the same with this much of difference only that God is almighty soul and he is only a limited individual soul. If the differential attributes or capacities which are finite in the individual but infinite and omnipotent in God are duly rejected, the pure common consciousness or the soul of an individual and of God is logically to have the same proved. To accomplish this one should first know the word meaning in the high oppossite sentence. "He is thou". Then repudiate the unnecessary epithets in "He" and "thou" to find out the pure and abiding point in them and bring the subject "He" and the complement "Thou" and the eternal predicate "is" for noting true symbol of unity of "He is thou" or thou art he. "When the essence of inseparably inherent in "He is thou" is realised with the reasonable processes of what should be discarded and what should be retained then He and thou will be fully and justly identical.

"The material body is the gross formation in an individual being. It grows, lives, and decays and is simply the result of his deeds of previous births which fetch him pleasure, prosperity, misery and pain and adversity too. It is the composition of natural and manifested elements such as earth, water, fire, air, ether etc. which are called five gross phenomena, Pañchatattwa or five natural elements. The individuals' soul is known to have another sublte body called "Sūkshma Śarīra" which is, composed of the mind with thinking, feeling and willing with the determinative faculty. "Five Prāṇas" life elements, five external and internal senses and with five undeveloped natural elements or essence of air, earth, fire and water called Apañchīkṛt Mahābhūt, and it (the subtle body resides in the material body with feeling and experience of all sorts of happiness, misery or pleasure and pain. The soul has also the casual body called "Kāraṇa Saīra" (the cause or the foundation of the two bodies) which has its existence mainly on God's illusion which is "Anirbachanīya" that is neither real nor unreal."

"The formless, infinite and perpetual soul has got these three bodies and is supposed to be mixed with them. In order to distinguish the soul one should know with proper care and reason these bodily impositions; as the essential soul is different from these colourable bodies, similar to a pure crystal which looks different when it comes into the contact with different colours. In the same way the soul reflected in the five cavities, called "Pancha Kosha" is supposed to have their characteristics but in face of it, the soul is quite apart and free from them. "When the waves of thoughts, called "Vṛttis" of mind rise or move with organs, Prāṇas, or life elements in three stages of wakefulness, dreaming and sound sleep, the soul too seems to have become active in the body. But in fact the waves of thought are mere productions of illusion and are unduly attributed to pure absolute spirit called Absolute Soul, Shiva. So the life with births and deaths continue so long as mind prevails with the wave of thoughts in this perishable corporal frame which is composed of apparently diverse elements."

"A person should know his own soul and immerse his mind in its sweetness, rejecting all material objects and negating decrees similar to one who extracts the juice of coconut and throws the outer useless cover away.

"The soul is unborn, immortal, indestructible, eternal, attributeless, unstained, pure and perpetually blissful, self enligtened, omniscient, omnipresent, and unique, so there is no reason for its being miserable and ignorant, and in fact it is the only real cause of misery in an individual and spiritual knowledge is eternal bliss. He by misconception thinks worldliness to be reality similar to a person who by mistaking one thing for another, thinks a rope to be a snake, and he in the same way thinks his material body as real. Similarly God is mistaken for the world, because worldliness is attributed to God by ignorant people.

"Egosim is conceived by ignorance and misconception upon Brahmā. Thus stainless Supreme reality which has no illusion, modification, and it is above all the individual souls. Desires, jealousy, greed, happiness and misery are at the root of perturbation and discontentment which certainly cause endless births and death for an individual otherwise he is always blissful, peaceful and divine. For he himself is continually realising his blissful and blessed soul when he is in deep sleep in the absence of mind's vibrations or activities."

"The spirit or Jiva of a man is light which is brought about in his mind or intellect owing to illusionary sources the way of reflections of his soul or Brāhmā which is in truth beyond the sphere of intellect or the determinative faculty of mind. The so-called Jiva is therefore, not other than the reflection of eternal conscious spirit when there will be no ignorance, the entity and Jiva will not remain. His soul stands as the mere witness of all his activities. Though it is granting life, it is so limited in the mind or intellect. This conscious soul is mistaken for the body and the body for the soul because they appear to mix with the mind the heated iron which looks like fire and similar to the fire which looks like around iron-ball. So it is ignorance alone by which spirit reflected on the matter and the matter on spirit seem to be reality."

"By preceptors (Śatgurū's) contact and by the study of Vedas, one should understand the difference between the soul and the matter and should then reject all gross things which are believed to be real or spiritual."

Rāma further said to Laxmaṇa.

"I am the eternal reality and self enlightened so I am unborn, infinite, effulgent, all the time, excessively pure and holy, resplendant, perfect, constant, blissful, free, beyond imagination, imperceivable, vast without any limitation, and supreme. Still I am constantly visible to scholars in their purified hearts because they know the ultimate purport as on which they deeply meditate."

Such highly consecrated thoughts which by the spiritual knowledge shall certainly eradicate all branches and accessories of ignorance similar to the medicines that cure a malady."

"An aspirant can see by his inner sight, the soul residing in his self, if he purifies his mind and contemplates in a lonely and peaceful place with all his deluding activities of the mind and sense organs fully controlled. He will remain perfect, conscious, pure, self content, and blissful if he sees God outside and inside and in the whole Universe. In fact God is the only cause of all the worldly objects and phenomena. Through practices, he can realise that one eternal God within himself too."

"Before absorbing himself "into Samādhi" the stage of holding identified communion with the pure self, he should know that the world is nothing but the word "Om" consisting of three letters, A.U.M. A, indicates the Purusha or the gross cover on the soul, U, indicates the subtle body with the soul and M, indicates the causal side with the soul. But these processes are merely preludial, not final. So savants follow so long as Samādhi is not accomplished but never after Samādhi is achieved. So the aspirant should first absolve his gross body called "Bishva" into the subtle body" Taizas" which should also be merged into third body called Prajñā the causal body. Thus the process should go on "A into U, and U and into M and in the end, the compound word Oam, should be absolved into the soul, the basic cause of all the causes and energy. Thus he realises that he himself is nothing but Supreme Soul Brahmā and finds himself emancipated from all the worldly bondages and to be the pure and holy asylum of eternal light or knowledge. He thus possessing the divine conception lives blessed and self content. He forgets every external thing of the world and is also happy, settled, and free as the undisturbed and peaceful ocean.

"If a person practices Yoga and attains Samādhi by restraining all activities of his organs he suppresses all evil notions with his full control over his six-fold hostile attitudes (i.e. lust, greed, anger, attachment, egoism, jealousy, and finally finds himself to be one with Me i.e. God."

"Thus the sage who meditates upon his soul day and night is emancipated from all worldly bondages. If he passes his life and lives simply upon what he gets by his providence will all his egoistic waves be fully subsided, he will certainly immerse himself into Myself. Knowing that the worldly life is miserable from the beginning to the end, he should only meditate upon his soul which forms the part and parcel of the Universal Soul and reject all those vedic retuals that encourage the side of actions only. When he becomes habituated to feel everything to be the same with his soul, he naturally sees no difference between his soul and mind too. For there is no difference between the drop of water of the ocean and the other mass of water of the same ocean. In the same way milk in milk, space in space and wind in wind, shall be virtually to be the same.

"If the sage decides the world to be false as the two moons to be seen in the sky by defective sight, he will be fully aware of what is the meaning of all common vedic rituals and "Karma" which shall lead the doer towards worldiness for some purpose or other. So long as an aspirant does not see the whole world to be nothing but my own form of god, he should fervently continue his spiritual practices and adoration with love and faith day and night, and such a sincere devotee shall always find me present in his heart."

Rāma further says to Laxmaṇa, "Dear brother, I have extracted the essence of all the vedas which I shall realise to be fully true and helpful. And I have explained to you in brief. Aspirant who will fully follow them shall at once be absolved of even heaps of sins. Brother, discard the world which is only illusory, it should not have any hold in your mind. If such a worldly vision ever arises in you, you should negate it with firm resolve and find your heart thoroughly with my immanent presence to make yourself eternal, blessed and completely free from all sorts of causes and anxieties."

Any aspirant who meditates upon my formless supreme existence or may even happen sometimes to adore my incarnated and universal form is identical with my own self. He is regarded pure and holy and even the dusts of his feet illumine and sanctify the three worlds similar to the rays of the sun."

"I have explained to you, Oh Laxmaṇa, the main purport of the sacred thing secretly hidden in scriptures. You know the scriptures are my experienced and cherished songs of the spiritual side of Vedas. Any person who understands through the help of this preceptor and follow them with sincere conviction shall not fail to find himself one with Me."

Chapter VI

KILLING OF LAVAṆA BY ŚATRUGHNA AND BIRTH OF LAVA AND KUSHA

Once at the head of countless sages who were in great fear from the terrible demon Lavaṇa living on the banks of the Yamunā, the foremost sage Chyavana, along with all sages went to see Rāma and he was very much pleased to receive them. He told them that he would render all services to them as he was always the servant of saintly Brahmins.

Then Chyavana said to Rāma.

"There was a pious demon named Madhu in Satya Yuga. Shiva was pleased with him to his devotional services and he had given Madhu a three-piked trident which whenever used could burn any creature to ashes. It was heard before that his wife was Rāvaṇa's younger sister named Kumbhanasa. Most dreadful and cruel demon Lavaṇa was born to Madhu. He is now oppressing and killing all the sages and we, therefore seek your shelter."

Rāma replied.

"I shall certainly kill him. Please go back to your hermitages safely."

Rāma asked his brothers as to who would go to kill Lavaṇa.

Bharata politely said to Rāma.

"Lord, permit me so that I may go to do this work."

Śatrughna interfered.

"Brother, Bharata has done his arduous duty by living in Nandigrām and Laxmaṇa too has achieved great success in battles by going to forests with your divine self. It is now my duty of killing Lavaṇa."

Rāma was very much pleased with Śatrughna who said in that way. Rāma, then immediately ordered him to go to Mathurā and also made him the king of Mathurā with the materials arranged at once by Laxmaṇa for the coronation of Śatrughna.

Rāma said to Śatrughna.

"Brother! Go and stand at the gate of the city of Mathurā early in the morning when Lavaṇa goes to forests on hunting for his food. Then kill him easily when he returns. Lavaṇa at that time goes out without taking his trident which he worships and leaves at home in the morning. After he is killed, you enter into the city and live there. I shall send thirty thousand soldiers and one thousand elephants and horses after your departure for your help.

Rāma blessed and bade farewell to him.

Śatrughna very easily killed Lavaṇa and ruled over the kingdom of Mathurā as he was instructed by Rāma. He pleased the public of Mathurā by his benign rule and made the country prosperous.

There in the hermitage of sage Vālmiki, Sītā delivered birth to a son. The sage named the elder son Kush and the younger one Lava. The boys were very handsome and intelligent.

Sage Vālmiki undertook the investure ceremony for them (including the sacred thread ceremony). He taught them Vedic principles and all sorts of skill of archery and fighting. He also taught them in the epic form, the Rāmāyaṇa which he had elaborately composed in true conformity to the facts God Shiva had already related to Goddess Pārvatī.

Lava and Kusha used to sing very sweetly the hymns from the extract of the Rāmāyaṇa in the vicinity of the hermitage. In this way, they lived with Vālmīki and were highly extolled by wisemen and saintly groups that they had not heard such songs on earth and other heavenly words even.

Righteous and illustrious Rāma once decided to perform Ashwamedh Yajña ceremony by keeping gold statue of Sītā by his side as the substitute of Sītā living in exile, since the ceremony could not have been completed without the married wife by his side. He invited all the eminent sages, learned people and Brahmins whom he offered huge amount of gold as Dakṣhiṇā. "Vālmīki also was respected as the greatest sage who had gone to see the ceremony with Lava and Kush. They desired to request Vālmiki in calm and quiet mood to explain spiritualism to him. So he said to Vālmiki.

"Lord, how is the individual soul attached to the worldly affairs? How can his bondage be removed so that his salvation is attained? Please explain to me clearly and briefly as you are really Omniscient".

Vālmiki replied.

"Beloved Kusha, I shall tell you in brief what are called bondage and absolution and also tell you the proper method by which you will thoroughly understand them and will be realised soul."

"The soul has no form, but when it prevails in the material body, egosim of the individual, like the minister of a monarch, is the main agent which acts in the body. As the soul seems to be mixed with its ego, it seems as if it were the soul which acts. In fact the ego alone with mind and intellect is attached to family groups and worldly acts with notions, motives, desires etc. and begins to do accordingly all sorts of things. Such predetermination, attachments or thoughts which the individual has in his mind are called "Sankalpa" and they are the causes of activities which result in pleasure, pain, prosperity and adversity together with all sorts of worldiness. These Saṅkalpa or thought are of three kinds i.e. saintly, materialistic and predatory. Insects, beasts and other animals are born through predatory kinds or Tāmasik Sankalpa. Ordinary men who have family life are guided through Rājarish or material thoughts and saints and peaceful persons are guided through saintly or sāttwik thoughts."

An aspirant, therefore, should give up all such thoughts and be self content only immersing his mind into soul's consciousness. An individual can never attain salvation and peace unless he controls his mind and discards his desires and thoughts even though he may continue his hard penances for years. There is no other way for the attainment of salvation for him without restraining himself from the external and internal thoughts and activities of mind called "Saṅkalpa which will mean" I shall do this and that etc."

Sage Vālmīki finally instructed Kusha by saying thus.

"You must abandon all your desires for actions as well as your thoughts which compel you to act. With great perseverence and strong efforts, because all actions are linked together with the thoughts and desires it must be eliminated from your mind. You should simply be content in passing your life in performing your duties and deeds as your providence leads you; and you shall be detached from all actions and desires which tempt you towards worldly desires, prosperity, jealousy, anger, lust and greed etc. So you should completely merge your mind into pure consciousness of your soul.

"Thus with spiritual knowledge you must renounce all illusive mazes for the attainment of the highest beatitude of perfection and eternity.

Chapter VII
RĀMA RETAINS LAVA AND KUSHA

Kusha could banish all misconception in his mind by the instructions of Vālmīki and he was outwardly doing his duties without attachment.

Once Vālmiki advised Kusha and Lava to go the city of Ayodhyā and sing the hymns of the Rāmāyaṇa and he also told they could go and sing if king Rāma liked to hear but they should not accept any reward.

Rāma was also interested in hearing the songs from them when he came to know that they were singing the extracts from the Rāmāyaṇa fully saturated with his own biography and they were continually heard by the sages and all the people in rapt attention everywhere and in the city also.

Rāma sent for the boys for singing during the recreation time of the great sacrificial rites, when all the public, fuedal chiefs, philosophers politicians had assembled. They were surprised to find the two lads exactly looked like Rāma. Every body was charmed by their wonderfully sweet melody. Rāma ordered Bharata to give thirty thousands gold coins which they refused to accept and then they returned away.

Afterwards everybody came to know that they were Sītā's sons. Rāma then ordered Śatrughna, Hanumān, Vibhīshaṇa, Aṇgada, Bharata and Laxmaṇa to bring Sītā for taking an oath in the presence of all the people to prove her chastity. They soon went to Vālmiki's hermitage and delivered to the sage what Rāma had said. The sage Vālmiki promised that Sīta would take the oath on the next day in the presence of all because Rāma was the only Lord for Sītā and she must carry out his intended orders.

There was a mass gathering of the citizens and

officers of all the ranks for attending the oath-ceremony on the appointed day. They all greeted Sītā and sage Vālmiki with great applauses full of enthusiasm and respect when they arrived in the manner as needed for them at the occasion. Sage Vālmīki spoke aloud.

"Oh Rāma, Sītā has been living in my hermitage since you deserted her. But I swear before you that I very well know that she is a chaste woman always faithful to you and these two boys are your own twins. I shall lose all my piety which I have gained by my penances if I have told any falsehood. Besides I am tenth son of Prajāpati Prachetā and as such I can never tell lie and unjust".

Rāma replied.

"I am very sorry as I had to leave Sītā whom I too very well know to be faithful to me when she had entered into the blazing fire for proving her chastity. It was when I had brought her from Rāvaṇa's Ashoka garden in Laṅkā. I fully believe in your words. Please forgive me because I had to banish Sītā for so many years as the people had defamed me for keeping her with me. I also know fully well that Kusha and Lava are my own sons. May my perpetual love be centered in Sītā! Even gods including Brahmā, Shiva and Indra were present among the huge bodied monkeys and the people gathered there when Sītā was prepared for taking the oath.

Sītā spoke humbly and sincerely by addressing Goddess Earth.

"Respected mother earth, please grant me shelter in your bossom if I am faithful to none but Rāma."

Instantly a gold resplendant throne appeared out of the earth and goddess earth with great respect held Sītā and placed her on the throne and disappeared. Flowers were showered from the heaven, continuously and hailings of words and cheers began to be heard from all sides of the earth and heaven. Everyone was greatly surprised at the sight. Some people looked towards Rāma and some at the scene while others remained quiet in surprise. The scene lasted only for to the great wonder of the spectators.

Rāma also looked very sad and wept like an ordinary man at Sītā's mysterious disappearance although he fully knew what would follow and he was pacified by sages and wise Brahmins. He however completed the yajña ceremony with due rites giving innumerable jewels, gold, money to Brahmins and other priests. He took both his sons into his own care and began to pass his life as a Yogi, saintly, recluse from that time onwards.

Once Kaushalyā said to Rāma, "Oh Rāma, you are in fact Supreme God, Absolute Being, Paramatmā, immanent spirit in every creature. You are also the master of the Universe though you are born as my son. It is the result of my past pious deeds that you incarnated yourself as my son. I am in my last stage of this human life so kindly advise me the real knowledge in brief so that I may attain salvation."

Rāma replied.

"There are three ways of attaining the cherished knowledge, abstinence and love with devotion to God by selfless actions. Bhakti yoga, jñāna yoga and karma yoga are thus the three ways for the attainment of salvation."

"Bhakti yoga is of three kinds, Tamas, Rajas and Sāttwik, and Parā Bhaktī is the Supreme love of God above all of them.

A devotee who is worldly and sees difference between himself and other fellow beings and who simply tries to please God for fulfilling his worldly desires even at the cost of other's interest is Tāmasic (low Bhakti).

He who wants to please God to gain wealth, prosperity and name but has no ill-will towards other people is Rājasic. He who worships God thinking it to be his duty is Sāttwic (high class devotion). An aspirant who joins his purified mind to myself with incessant love similar to a river which has the only aim at being mixed with the ocean, is the greatest of all three for he has nothing to do other than to love me. He has already discarded all worldly frivolities, so he is fully contented as he is only in search of me. In this way, his aim is only the attainment in absortion in myself."

"Either he is united with my soul or he may be allowed to live by my side or he may obtain my own form or live with me in my elusion abode or he may gain divine power to become Omnipresent, Omniscient and Omnipotent or live in eternal presence as my beloved devotee.

Of the four kinds of realised or absolved souls, the greatest devoted soul never aspires after any other thing than my own love as he is always satisfied at only seeing and worshipping me."

"Such a profound and holy aspiration, combined with unswerving love can be obtained by doing his duties with no desire of any result, by being non-violent and peaceful, by feeling or seeing God in every creature, by worshipping me in any image, by way of singing prayers earnestly with pure mind, by discarding all his vice-falsehood, and dishonesty and by eliminating all his egoistic impressions by virtue of his practices of true Yogi. A Yogi's mind is infact unmixed with worldiness similar to the scent which leaving it temporary sources of flower, mixes with its true form of the smelling sense organ. Any worship of idols is due to ignorance so long a person does not realize that I am immanent in every creature. This sort of worship in images is meant for the beginners and an aspirant who is advanced, sees me everywhere and does not require to fix his mind to the idol only."

"Mother, either by Bhakti yoga or jñāna yoga, you shall be happy and emancipated from the shackles of worldliness provided that you shall see me everywhere immanent, you love me as a your son, this too will lead you to the attainment of salvation.

Thus, queen Kaushalyā could transcend all the three stages of life to achieve the highest goal by perpetually meditating on Rāma, and his nectar like words. All of them Kaikeyī, Kaushalyā and Sumitrā ascended to heaven after their death and joined their husband King Dasharath there.

Chapter VIII

LAXMAṆA TAKES SAMĀDHI

Mighty Bharat went to Yuddhajit's home and defeated three crores of Gandharwas and founded two cities, Puskar and Taxilā. He returned to Ayodhyā to see Rāma handing over the conquered countries to his two sons.

Rāma ordered Laxmaṇa to conquer the tyrant kings that lived in the Western part of India and to give the conquered countries to his sons, Aṅgad and Chitraketu. Laxmaṇa conquered all the Bhīlls and established two kingdoms for Aṅgad and Chitraketu and returned Ayodhyā.

The god of Death Yama, disguised as a sage reached Ayodhyā and wanted an interview with Rāma who received him with due respects.

On request of Rāma, the sage said, "Lord! I have very secret message to tell you and I can tell you only if you promise to kill any person if he hears our conversation or even sees us talking together.

Rāma promised to do so and ordered Laxmaṇa to stand outside the door and not to allow any body inside.

The sage said.

"Brahmā has sent me to inform you that the time for your going to the heaven has come and gods are very eagerly waiting for your arrival."

Brahmā further said. "I am the master of creation and your eldest sons because I had come into existence when you had created the universe by your illusion, you had first created me and then Seshnāg, the God of serpants named Ananta who lives in the ocean since the beginning of creation of inanimate and animate objects. You had killed too great giants, Madhu and Kaitabh and earth was composed for their flesh and bones. You had named me Prajāpati, Brahmā and entrusted to me the duty of creation. You always therefore protect my creations from destructions and evils whenever necessary. Now you have accomplished your mission of destroying the cruel demons including Rāvaṇa. I had fixed the period of eleven thousand years for your residence in the earth. Now it is my wish whether you should prolong your stay or return to the paradise."

Rāma replied to the sage for conveying the message to Brahmā.

"I have completed my mission of incarnation. Now I also wish to return to heaven and see you and all other gods very soon."

Sage Durbāsā reached the door when Rāma and god of death were conversing alone and asked Laxmaṇa to go to Rāma to inform his arrival.

Laxmaṇa hesitatingly requested "Lord, Rāma is busy in very private business, I myself shall comply with your orders.

"Durbāsā very angrily retorted. "You must instantly go to tell Rāma what I wish otherwise I shall turn all of you and even your progenies into ashes in no time.

At this Laxmaṇa instantly went to Rāma as he was afraid lest the suge would certainly destroy all of them and it was better for him to be killed himself by saving all others. He requested Rāma.

"Lord, Durbāsā sage is waiting at the door."

Rāma dismissed the god of death and allowed Sage Durbāsā and interviewed.

Rāma was deeply aggrieved to notice that he had to kill Laxmaṇa to keep his promise but could not say anything to Laxmaṇa.

Sage Durbāsā requested Rāma to offer pure Siddha food to break his fast which he had been observing for twelve years.

Rāma satisfied the sage by offering the desired food and bade farewell to him.

Laxmaṇa requested Rāma.

"Lord, you must kill me to keep your words. It is better to carry out your promise than to let me live, because you shall lose your piety if you fail to keep your words and your uprighteousness shall cause destruction of the whole universe itself."

Rāma called on a meeting and consulted with his people and ministers as well as Vāshiṣṭha, his preceptor who also advised Rāma to keep his promise.

Rāma said to Laxmaṇa.

"Brother, now leave Ayodhyā and go wherever you like. Banishment is equal to death punishment."

Laxmaṇa very sorrowfully left Ayodhyā and left his mortal frame at the banks of the river Ganges by performing Samādhi.

In fact, Brahmā had taken Laxmaṇa to the heaven alive, but people could not know it.

Chapter IX

RĀMA'S DEPARTURE TO HEAVEN

Rāma expressed his desire to ascend to the paradise handing over the kingdom of Ayodhyā to Bharat. But Bharat fell down to hear that he was not allowed by Rāma to go to the heaven with him.

So he requested Rāma.

"Lord, I cannot stay even for a moment in your absence in this earth. Kindly grant the kingdom to Kusha and Lava and take me with you."

Messengers were sent to Śatrughna and all the people of Ayodhyā wanted to follow Rāma whom they never desired to leave. Rāma, therefore, allowed all the people as well as his brothers to ascend to the heaven with him.

Śatrughna soon reached Ayodhyā. He gave his kingdom to his sons and was prepared to go to the heaven with Rāma.

The day of departure from Ayodhyā or the paradise was fixed. All the monkeys, bears, demons, with Vibhīshaṇa, Sugrīva and Aṅgad reached Ayodhyā in due time, and they requested Rāma for the permission to follow him.

Rāma ordered Vibhīshaṇa and Aṅgad to stay in the earth and to rule over their respective kingdoms, and he said to Jāmbavān to wait till Dwāpara Yuga when he would reincarnate in form of Krishṇa and would have to fight with him (Jambavān) for a certain cause.

Rāma said to Hanumān to live in the earth forever so long as his name shall be remembered. He then allowed all the people to go with him.

Every one was very happy and was completely detached from worldliness and had forgotten his earthly pleasure and wealth when he or she followed Rāma. The city of Ayodhyā was completely vacant. Not even an insect was there and all the people and creatures reached at the banks of the river Sarayū in preparation of ascending to the heaven.

In the meantime Brahmā, Shiva and other gods, sage, seers, appeared over in the sky which was filled with their air chariots of various sizes and designs.

The very atmosphere became fragrant with the flowers that were showered over Rāma. All the Gandharvas, fairies and deities began to play music and sing hymns and divine songs in various melodies.

Brahmā with folded hands prayed to Rāma.

"You are supreme God Vishṇu, Master of the Universe, Omniscient, Omnipresent, Omnipotent and perpetual. You have accomplished your mission on earth, and have fulfilled the wishes of all your aspirants and devotees as well as your objects. I am but your humble servant and always devoted to your lotus feet. You are really very kind to your devotees whom you look after with every care. Kindly now ascend to your heavenly abode, the paradise and thus make us happy and prosperous. My Lord, "Rāma transformed himself in form of Lord Vishṇu. Lạxmaṇa became Seshnāg, Bharata and Śatrughna turned themselves into Vishnu's couch-shell and mace respectively and Sītā appeared as Goddess Laxmī. Brahmā the creator, Indra deities and all Gandharvas, Kinnaras and fairies danced and sang in joy and prayed to Lord Vishṇu surrounding Him on all sides.

Rāma said to Brahmā.

"Please create a separate Loka or abode in the heaven for the residency of all my aspirants, the people and animals and insects even who are following me to go to the heaven."

Brahmā instantly created a Loka (heavenly abode) named "Santanik". All the devotees of Rāma shall also find their place in this heaven in the future after their death similar to those who had ascended with Rāma.

Sugrīva was united with the sun and all others went to Santanik which was like Rāma's paradise after Rāma directly had left the earth for the eternal abode, the paradise called Vishṇu Loka.

God Shiva thus has revealed the history of Rāma of his later period of life in Uttara Kāṇḍa" which is consecrated as holy and its every hymn has the power to sanctify at once all the sins.

Those who will recite and hear Rāma's history, will be absolbed of all their sins and find their place in the heaven after their death, and gain prosperity with longevity during their life time here.